Good Faith in International Arbitration

ASA Special Series

VOLUME 49

Introduction

The Swiss Arbitration Association (ASA, Association suisse de l'arbitrage) is Switzerland's leading arbitration organization. With more than a thousand members, it brings together the world's most eminent arbitration practitioners from six continents and 50 + jurisdictions.

Since its foundation in 1974, ASA helps shape the development of international arbitration for the benefit of users worldwide. Its signature Annual Conferences in Zurich and Geneva explore topical issues with high-calibre experts from all over the world. The papers and materials are subsequently published in the ASA Special Series.

Editors

Each volume of the ASA Special Series is edited by different editors from among the ASA members and who have been the (co-)organizers of the pertinent ASA Annual Conference or are specialists in a particular topical issue to which a volume is dedicated.

Objective

The ASA Special Series are published to foster innovation in and to promote international arbitration globally.

They contain the full edited versions of the papers of the ASA Annual Conferences as well as ad hoc arbitration brochures published by ASA.

Frequency

One to two volumes per year, with one volume typically published following the ASA Annual Conference.

The titles published in this series are listed at the end of this volume.

Good Faith in International Arbitration

Myth, Reality, Label ... or All of the Above?

Edited by

Elliott E. Geisinger

Christoph Müller

Andrea Menaker

Sabrina Pearson-Wenger

Wolters Kluwer

Published by:
Kluwer Law International B.V.
PO Box 316
2400 AH Alphen aan den Rijn
The Netherlands
E-mail: lrs-sales@wolterskluwer.com
Website: www.wolterskluwer.com/en/solutions/kluwerlawinternational

Sold and distributed by:
Wolters Kluwer Legal & Regulatory U.S.
920 Links Avenue
Landisville, PA 17538
United States of America
E-mail: customer.service@wolterskluwer.com

ISBN 978-94-035-4267-6

e-Book: ISBN 978-94-035-4277-5
web-PDF: ISBN 978-94-035-4287-4

Editors

Elliott Geisinger is a partner at Schellenberg Wittmer in Geneva. Elliott Geisinger heads Schellenberg Wittmer's International Arbitration Group. Since 1995, his practice has focused on international commercial and investor-State arbitration. Elliott has acted as counsel and arbitrator in complex commercial disputes involving international construction contracts, consortia and joint venture agreements, sponsorship contracts and sales and distribution contracts, among others. He has also acted as lead counsel in several of the most high-profile investor-State cases of the last decade. Elliott regularly represents clients in arbitration-related court proceedings, and several of his cases have been reported on in the official collection of leading Swiss Supreme Court cases and in arbitration journals.

Andrea Menaker is a Partner in the London Office of White & Case. Andrea Menaker is Head of the Firm's Public International Law Group and specializes in investment arbitration, where she has represented respondent States and claimant investors in equal measure in some of the most ground-breaking investment arbitration cases. Andrea also has an active practice in relation to the enforcement of arbitral awards and has coordinated such actions worldwide for clients, in addition to serving as arbitrator and expert witness on investor-State issues. Andrea is an Executive Committee member of the Swedish Arbitration Association, a Council Member of the Hong Kong International Arbitration Centre (HKIAC) and an elected member of the American Law Institute. She is a former Board Member of the Arbitration Institute of the Stockholm Chamber of Commerce and the Association Suisse de l'Arbitrage, a former member of the Executive Council of the American Law and served as Chair of the Programme Committee for ICCA's 2016 Congress in Mauritius. She has been appointed to the ICDR Panel of Arbitrators and the P.R.I.M.E. Finance Panel of Experts. Andrea has served as an adjunct professor at Georgetown University Law Centre, where she taught international commercial arbitration for several years, and has lectured at several other universities.

Christoph Müller is a professor at the University of Neuchâtel (Switzerland) teaching contract law, tort law, comparative private law and contract drafting. He is also a life member of Clare Hall College (Cambridge, UK). Over the last twenty-five years, Christoph has acted as (presiding, sole and co-) arbitrator, legal expert and counsel in more than 200 international commercial and sports arbitrations. He is familiar with various substantive laws (in particular Swiss, English, US, German and French) and both institutional (ICC, Swiss Rules, LCIA, DIS, WIPO, TAS) and ad hoc arbitration. His main fields of arbitral practice are distribution, corporate law, finance and banking, JV, consortia and shareholder agreements and sale and purchase agreements. Christoph is ASA Vice-President and a CIArb fellow. He is also a former member of the Court of the Swiss Arbitration Centre (including its special committee). He is a head lecturer of the Swiss Arbitration Academy and the CAS in arbitration at the Universities of Neuchâtel and Lucerne. He also is an arbitrator on the general list of the Court of Arbitration for Sport (CAS). Christoph is the author of numerous books and articles in the fields of international arbitration, contract law, tort law and comparative private law. His last book, *Swiss Contract Law in International Commercial Arbitration*, was published by Cambridge University Press.

Sabrina Pearson-Wenger is the co-founder of Arbius AG, a firm specializing in international arbitration and IT legal services, as well as a collaboratrice scientifique at the University of Neuchâtel. Prior to founding Arbius AG, Sabrina was a PhD candidate and Teaching Assistant to Professor Christoph Müller at the University of Neuchâtel. She also previously worked as an associate in the international arbitration departments of two leading law firms in Paris and Geneva. Sabrina graduated with a double Masters' in Law from the Université de Paris 2 Panthéon-Assas and the University of Cambridge in 2007 and also holds an LLM in International Legal Studies from New York University (2008). In 2023, she was awarded the ICC Institute Prize for her PhD thesis entitled Good Faith in International Commercial Arbitration: its Application of Good Faith by Arbitrators to the Parties' Contract and the Arbitration Agreement.

Contributors

Mohamed S. Abdel Wahab is Professor of International Arbitration, Private International Law and English Contract Law at Cairo University. He is also Founding Partner and Head of International Arbitration, Construction and Energy Groups at Zulficar & Partners Law Firm (Egypt). Among the positions held by Professor Abdel Wahab are: Member of the Governing Board, ICCA; Dean of the Africa Arbitration Academy; Vice Chair of the ICC Governing Body for Dispute Resolution Services; Deputy President (2024) and President-elect of the CIArb (2025), CIArbVice-Chair of the Advisory Committee of the CRCICA; Member of the Advisory Board of the MIAC; Member of the LACIAC Court of Arbitration; Member of the Board of Trustees of the CIArb; Member of the ITA Academic Council; Member of the Advisory Board, Indonesian Arbitration Centre; and Member of the Court, PCA. He regularly serves as arbitrator and counsel in commercial and investment treaty arbitrations and has featured in no less than 260 arbitration cases involving parties from Africa, Asia, Europe, the Middle East, North America and South America.

Adetola Adebesin is an international arbitration attorney at Sidley Austin LLP – London, United Kingdom. He has over seven years of experience representing corporates, multinationals and governments in several high-profile commercial and investment disputes. He regularly acts as counsel under most of the institutional arbitration rules, including the ICC, LCIA, SIAC, Swiss Rules, UNCITRAL and ICSID. He holds a Master's from the prestigious Geneva LLM in International Dispute Settlement (MIDS), a diploma in international arbitration from the Africa Arbitration Academy and is currently one of the LCIA – YIAG regional representatives for Africa. Adetola is admitted to practice in Nigeria.

Neil Andrews is Barrister and Bencher of the Middle Temple, Fellow and former Director of Studies in Law at Clare College, as well as Professor of Law at the University of Cambridge, United Kingdom. He is the author of works on English contract law and dispute resolution, including Neil Andrews, Contract Law in Practice (Oxford University Press, 2021) and Andrews on Civil Processes 2nd Edn Intersentia, Cambridge (2019).

Andrea Bianchi has been Full Professor of International Law at the Graduate Institute of International and Development Studies, Geneva, since 2002 and was previously Full Professor at the Catholic University in Milan, Associate Professor at the University of Parma, and Professorial Lecturer at the Johns Hopkins SAIS Bologna Centre. Andrea Bianchi has been a Visiting Professor at King's College London; Hebrew University, Jerusalem; the University of Vienna Faculty of Law; the Catholic University in Milan and the University of Paris 1 (Panthéon-Sorbonne). He has consulted for international organizations on matters related to security and human rights, for multinational corporations on business and human rights issues, and for States and private parties in international investment arbitration.

Anya George is a Partner in Schellenberg Wittmer's Dispute Resolution Group in Zurich. As a trilingual and dual-qualified lawyer, she represents clients in complex international commercial and investment arbitration matters, as well as in enforcement and setting-aside proceedings before the Swiss Supreme Court. Her main areas of expertise are energy infrastructure, natural resources, insurance and reinsurance contracts and manufacturing and sales agreements. Anya is considered an 'incredibly bright advocate' and 'one of the best of her generation worldwide' (Who's Who Legal) and is praised by clients for her 'excellent responsiveness' and 'complete control of her practice' (Legal500).

Céline Greenberg is a partner of the firm Mayer Greenberg, founded in 2021 with Professor Pierre Mayer. She acts as counsel or arbitrator in domestic or international arbitration proceedings and before French courts in proceedings related to arbitration (recognition or enforcement of an arbitral award, annulment proceedings, etc.).

Duarte Henriques is a lawyer and arbitrator based in Lisbon – Portugal. He is ranked as Global Leader in Arbitration by Who's Who Legal and recommended by 'WWL' Arbitration 2019 as a 'go-to lawyer in Portugal, standing out for his extensive knowledge of commercial and investment treaty disputes' and in 'WWL Arbitration 2020' as 'an outstanding practitioner, who is well versed as both counsel and arbitrator in investment, banking, finance and construction disputes'. Since 1990, he has acted as both counsel and arbitrator in a number of litigation and arbitration cases related to investment disputes, banking & finance, corporate, commercial, distribution and construction disputes. Duarte Henriques has strong experience in advising and securing 'third-party funding' for clients.

Flavio Peter is a partner at Peter & Kim in Zurich, specializing in domestic and international arbitration and related litigation proceedings, including enforcement and attachment proceedings before local courts and setting aside proceedings before the Swiss Federal Supreme Court. Flavio primarily acts as party representative in disputes arising under construction contracts, international sales contracts and disputes concerning not only long-term gas supply contracts but also agency and distribution agreements, joint venture contracts, and post-M&A disputes. Flavio regularly also sits as chairman, sole arbitrator or co-arbitrator and has gained vast experience as administrative secretary to arbitral tribunals in several international and domestic arbitration proceedings (conducted in accordance with the ICC Arbitration and ADR Rules, Swiss Rules, UNCITRAL Arbitration Rules, VIAC Rules, DIS Rules as well as in ad hoc proceedings). He is a member of the Swiss Arbitration Marketing Committee, former co-chair of ASA below 40, holds a teaching assignment with the University of Zurich (for international arbitration and CISG) and is a Fellow of the CIArb. Flavio has been continuously ranked as Global Leader in Arbitration by Who's Who Legal.

Philippe Pinsolle is a partner of Quinn Emanuel Urquhart & Sullivan LLP, and he is head of the international arbitration group for continental Europe. He is based in the firm's Geneva Office. Philippe Pinsolle has over twenty-five years of experience as counsel, expert and arbitrator in international arbitration. He has acted as counsel in more than 300 international arbitrations, with a particular focus on investor-State arbitrations and commercial disputes involving the energy, power, oil & gas, construction and defence industries. He has been involved in arbitrations under the auspices of virtually all major arbitration institutions, including the ICC, the LCIA, the ICSID, the SCC, the AAA, the ICDR, the Swiss Chambers of Commerce, the AFA, the ADCCAC, as well as in ad hoc cases under the UNCITRAL rules or otherwise. Philippe Pinsolle has also served as an arbitrator in more than sixty cases, as well as an expert witness on arbitration and French law issues.

Natalie L. Reid is a partner in the International Dispute Resolution Group and co-chair of the Public International Law and Caribbean practices at Debevoise & Plimpton in New York. She focuses on international arbitration, public international law, and complex commercial litigation matters. Ms Reid advises on a broad range of international matters, with particular experience advising on ESG issues, including business and human rights considerations. She has deep sector experience with clients in energy (including renewables), natural resources, mining, and oil and gas. A Jamaican national, she advises and represents multinational corporations, sovereign States, international organizations, and non-governmental organizations in proceedings in international courts and tribunals and in US courts. Ms Reid acts as counsel in commercial, investment treaty, and public international law arbitrations and sits as an arbitrator in a wide range of commercial cases.

Emily Sipiorski is an Assistant Professor of International and Comparative Law at the Department of Public Law and Governance, Tilburg Law School. She completed her doctoral project at Martin Luther University, Halle-Wittenberg, in the area of international investment law, publishing Good Faith in International Investment Arbitration with Oxford University Press. She has also worked on issues of sustainability, environmental issues in economic law, energy law, and global constitutionalism.

Philippe Stoffel-Munck is a Professor of Law at the Université de Paris I: Panthéon Sorbonne, specializing in the French law of obligations. He is the author of various works on French contract law, including: Les obligations (with Ph. Malaurie and L. Aynès, coll. Droit civil, 12th edn LGDJ 2022); Droit de la responsabilité et des contrats (directed by. Ph. le Tourneau, Dalloz Action, 2008) and L'abus dans le contrat, essai d'une théorie (LGDJ 2000). He writes the quarterly 'Torts and contractual Liability' column in La Semaine Juridique and the 'Contract Law' column in Revue des contrats. In parallel to his academic position, Philippe Stoffel-Munck is registered at the Paris Bar and has eighteen years of experience as an arbitrator as well as substantial experience as a consultant and legal expert in French law, acting before state Courts as well as before arbitral tribunals. Upon Ministerial appointment, he constituted and presided the Law Commission tasked with the draft reform of the French law of Contrats spéciaux (Sale, Lease, Loan, Licence, Deposit, Manufacture, Construction, Agency). The draft bill was completed and officially presented to the Minister of Justice in April 2023.

Summary of Contents

Table of Contents

CHAPTER 1

Good Faith in Civil Law

Philippe Stoffel-Munck

Good faith is the very type of concept civil lawyers are all familiar with but can hardly define. To this extent, it reminds us of the paradox of time as explained by Saint Augustine: 'What is time then? If nobody asks me, I know; but if I am asked to explain it, I do not know.'[1] Hopefully, the riddle seems less difficult to elucidate in respect of good faith. However, it is true that we often approach good faith in a rather intuitive way, which tends to give credence to the blame common lawyers often put on this 'hazy' concept, as they say.

Nonetheless, it is indeed a key civil law concept; a typical concept of civil law, one might even say. It may look somewhat 'hazy' at first sight, given the variety of its applications and the apparent paradoxes they give rise to. However, it is merely a behavioural standard, which does not equate with a licence-to-kill legal reasoning. And the duty to act in good faith is a standard worth digging into, given the solid legal effects it bears in civil law. Let's see these points in turn.

§1.01 A KEY CONCEPT IN CIVIL LAW

The meaning of good faith is twofold. First, it refers to a psychological reality: an ignorance of the defects of one thing, be it a good or a legal title, or of the defects of one's own conduct. That is, for example, *guter Glaube* referred to by Article 3 of the Swiss Civil Code[2] or the *bonne foi* mentioned in Article 2274 of the French Civil Code.[3]

1. 'Quid est ergo tempus? Si nemo ex me quaerat, scio; si quaerenti explicare velim, nescio' (Confessiones, XI, 14).
2. Swiss Civil Code, Art. 3 : '(1) Where the law makes a legal effect conditional on the good faith of a person, there shall be a presumption of good faith. (2) No person may invoke the presumption of good faith if he or she has failed exercise the diligence required by the circumstances.'
3. French Civil Code, Art. 2274: 'Good faith is always presumed, and it is on the person who alleges bad faith to prove it.'

This concept is mainly used in law of goods, in particular, to decide whether possession is sufficient to found ownership and in liability law to designate one's certain state of innocence of the wrongfulness of one's own doing. This meaning of good faith is not the one we are interested in here.

Second, good faith is a duty incumbent on a person negotiating an agreement or performing it. It is likely that all civil law legal systems provide for a duty to conclude and to perform a contract in good faith. In 1992, the 'Association Henri Capitant' organized in Louisiana its annual international symposium. Its topic was 'Good faith', especially in the formation and the performance of contracts. It was premised on a survey of French law-inspired legal systems throughout the world in that respect. Unsurprisingly, all these countries adopted, in one way or another, the principle that was at the time enshrined in Article 1134 §3 of the Napoleonic Code: 'They [the agreements] must be performed in good faith.' Following the 2016 reform of French Contract Law, the rule is now set out in Article 1104 of the French Civil Code.

French Civil Code, Article 1104: 'Contracts must be negotiated, formed and performed in good faith.'

German law, the other seminal legal system for civil laws, converges with French law in that respect. The general rules set out in sections 157 and 242 of the BGB emphasize the role of good faith as follows:

> BGB §157: 'Contracts are to be interpreted as required by good faith, taking customary practice into consideration.'
>
> BGB, §242: 'An obligor has a duty to perform according to the requirements of good faith, taking customary practice into consideration.'

It is, therefore, understandable that the laws that took inspiration from both French and German laws, like Japanese law or Swiss law, have adopted that principle in the most general form. The former in its Article 1, the latter in its Article 2:

> Japanese Civil Code, Art. 1 §2: 'The exercise of rights and performance of duties must be done in good faith.'
>
> Swiss Civil Code, Art. 2 §1: 'In exercising his rights and in performing his duties everyone has to act in accordance with good faith.'

Wherever they took their inspiration from, it seems that contract laws from all civil law countries adopt these principles.

In continental Europe, Article 288 of the Greek Civil Code is a copy-paste from the wording of section 242 of the BGB. The Belgian or Luxembourgian Code reproduces Article 1134 §3 of the Napoleonic Code.[4] Article 1375 of the Italian Code is alike,[5] and

4. The Belgian reform of contract law has been adopted on 21 April 2022. The principle regarding the duty to perform in good faith is now expressed in Art. 5.73 of the Belgian Civil Code. It reads as follows: 'The contract must be performed in good faith. According to para. 1: 1° each of the parties must, in the performance of the contract, behave as a prudent and reasonable person in the same circumstances would do; 2° no one may abuse the rights which he derives from the contract.'
5. Italian Civil Code, Art. 1375: 'The contract must be performed in good faith' ('*Il contratto deve esserer eseguito secondo buona fede*').

one could also cite to laws of the Netherlands, Austria, Poland, Romania, Portugal, Spain, etc.[6] to illustrate this observation.

In North America, the Civil Code of Quebec repeats that, generally speaking, 'Every person is obliged to exercise his or her civil rights according to the requirements of good faith' (Article 6). In the field of contract law, it then adds that 'The parties shall conduct themselves in good faith both at the time the obligation arises and at the time it is performed or extinguished' (Article 1375). Throughout Central and South America, that rule is also acknowledged. For example, Brazilian law has particularly developed the duty to perform in good faith,[7] but you find it also in Argentina, Columbia, Chile, etc.

In Africa and the Middle East, the situation is the same. That is clear in the former French, Belgian or Portuguese colonies, and the 2004 draft OHADA (Organisation pour l'harmonisation en Afrique du droit des affaires) act on contract law, prepared by Professor Marcel Fontaine, envisions its uniform enshrinement.[8] That is also true for countries that remained outside of that colonial scope. In particular, given the influence of Egyptian law on the civil laws of Middle East countries, it is worth noting that the Egyptian Civil Code recognizes that duty:

- Egyptian Civil Code, Article 148: 'A contract must be performed in accordance with its contents and in compliance with the requirements of good faith.'

  In Asia, the principle was sometimes inherited from former colonial powers, be they French or Portuguese. However, it is also acknowledged in countries that were never colonized. Japan was already mentioned above, but Thailand may be added to the list, and the recent Chinese Civil Code is on the same line.
- Thai Civil and Commercial Code, section 368: 'Contracts shall be interpreted according to the requirements of good faith, ordinary usage being taken into consideration.'
- Chinese Civil Code, Article 7: 'When conducting a civil activity, a person of the civil law shall, in compliance with the principle of good faith, uphold honesty and honour commitments.'

That principle is so widespread that it may well look like a core principle of Lex Mercatoria to the extent it is inspired by civil law. It is therefore not surprising that the Principles on International Commercial Contracts prepared by Unidroit reserve a particular section for 'Good Faith and Fair Dealings'.

6. *See* the various national reports in *La bonne foi*, Travaux de l'Association Henri Capitant, Journées internationales de Louisiane (Litec ed., 1992), and the general report by Prof. Claude Masse on the duty to perform the contract in good faith (pp. 217 et seq.).
7. A. Wald, Rapport brésilien, in *La bonne foi*, Travaux de l'Association Henri Capitant, Journées internationales de Louisiane, pp. 251-263 (Litec ed., 1992).
8. Article 1.6 of the Draft Act reads: 'The parties have to comply with the demands of good faith. (2) They may not depart from that obligation or limit its scope.'

UNIDROIT Principles, Article 1.7:

(1) Each party must act in accordance with good faith and fair dealing in international trade.
(2) The parties may not exclude or limit this duty.

But that just means that the UNIDROIT Principles have their roots in a civil law legal culture because they form a list of general principles, while Common Law is somewhat allergic to such a broad and vague way to articulate law. That allergy might be the key to the common lawyers' reluctance to good faith. In their authoritative textbook on 'Good Faith in European Contract Law', Professors Zimmermann and Whittaker note that, in spite of some debates, '*English law does not recognize a general duty to negotiate nor to perform contracts in good faith.*'[9] Among numerous references, they cite the 1987 case *Interfoto Picture Library Ltd v. Stiletto Visual Programmes Ltd*, where Lord Justice Bingham noted that 'English law has, characteristically, committed itself to no such an overriding principle', but immediately added that it rather 'has developed piecemeal solutions in response to demonstrated problems of unfairness'.[10] It is indeed true that modern English law invented particular doctrines to defeat certain claims that a civil lawyer would have dismissed for breach of the duty to conclude or perform the contract in good faith. For example, when Lord Denning presented the foundations of what would become the doctrine of promissory estoppel,[11] a civil lawyer would have put that proposition under the umbrella of the principle of good faith.

In a nutshell, the contrast between the common and civil law systems may be more a result of the way to answer the questions than a difference in the substance of the answers. Common lawyers find and refine their legal propositions on a case-by-case basis that may eventually give rise to a more general doctrine. By contrast, when approaching a case, civil lawyers start reasoning on the basis of general concepts and descend to the solution by way of successive deductions. Good faith is one of those very general concepts and is, therefore, typically a civil law tool: a fluid concept prone to generate particular solutions, slowly crystallizing in specific legal institutions once crafted by case law and being sometimes eventually fixed in statutory rules.

However, in spite of its undisputable flexibility, good faith does not give credence to whatever more or less equity-inspired proposition. Its content and its effects follow rationality, albeit a complex one.

§1.02 THE CONTENT OF THE GOOD FAITH PRINCIPLE

Good faith might be described as a fluid behavioural norm, but its sources are well-identified and quite instructive.

9. Reinhard Zimmermann & Simon Whittaker, *Good Faith in European Contract Law: Surveying the Legal Landscape*, in Zimmermann and Whittaker (eds), Good Faith in European Contract Law, p. 39 (Cambridge University Press, 2000, p. 6).
10. *Interfoto Picture Library Ltd v. Stiletto Visual Programmes Ltd*, [1987] EWCA Civ 6, (12 November 1987), [1989] QB 433.
11. *Central London Property Trust Ltd v. High Trees House Ltd* [1947] KB 130.

[A] The Common Roots of the Duty of Good Faith

History confirms that good faith does have an 'air de famille' with equity. That comes from Roman Law, where '*bonae fidei*' contracts were opposed to contracts governed by strict civil law (*stricti juris*) and let the judge a broad discretion to consider all the circumstances of the case and to adjudicate it in light of the requirements of good faith. Such judgments (*bonae fidei judicia*) were allowed by the Praetor in the context of the formulary procedure. While fides commanded the judge to assess whether the parties strictly stuck to the binding words that formed the *stipulatio*, bona fides were required to also take into account the honesty of the parties' conduct and their respective interests.[12] The contracts that were under this aegis were *tutela, fiducia, mandatum* and *societas*. They implied a certain duty of care analogous to the one between a Roman patron and its clients. It might be that, under certain circumstances, sales, lease and services agreements could be added to the list.[13] With respect to those *bonae fidei contractus*, 'the *bonae fidei iudicia* were intended to provide the opportunity to weigh up both parties' interests in assessing an enforceable claim'.[14] On that basis, good faith became 'the yardstick of praetorian actions', to use Professor Schermaier's words, inducing the judge (i) to assess the parties' conduct further to the standard used in fiduciary relationships (*bene agere*), (ii) to bind a party even to an informal promise, and (iii) to balance both parties' interests.[15]

That method allowed for a touch of *aequitas* in the legal reasoning. Hence, the middle-age lawyers, blending Roman law and Christian doctrine, subsequently tended to conflate good faith and equity, as Professor Reinhard Zimmermann observed.[16] As a result, the association of those concepts became commonplace in European law of contracts, where it progressively became 'a fundamental principle of the medieval and early modern *lex mercatoria*'.[17] At the same time, however, not all contracts were concerned with that principle, for the category of contracts *stricti juris* remained alive.

It is in this context that one of the first modern civil codes, the 1804 Napoleonic Code, justified a general duty to perform in good faith by the suppression of the category of contracts *stricti juris*. Commenting on the new Code, Toullier, for example, noted that §3 of Article 1134 'does not merely mean that deceit and fraud are banned

12. M.J. Shermaier, *Bona Fides in Roman Contract Law*, in Zimmermann and Whittaker (eds), Good Faith in European Contract Law, pp. 81-82 (Cambridge University Press, 2000, p. 63).
13. *Ibid.*, pp. 80-81.
14. *Ibid.*, p. 82.
15. *Ibid.*, p. 82: 'The three central elements of the classical *bona fides*, i.e. the substantive determination of the old fiduciary relationships (*bene agere*), the binding nature of even an informal promise, and the *officium* of the judge who had to balance both parties' interests, provided, however, the pattern for the development of the *bonae fidei iudicia*.'
16. Reinhard Zimmermann & Simon Whittaker, *Good Faith in European Contract Law: Surveying the Legal Landscape*, in Zimmermann and Whittaker (eds), Good Faith in European Contract Law (Cambridge University Press, 2000, p. 6): the 'decline, and eventual abolition, of the formulary procedure had led to an absorption of the concept of bona fide into the broader notion of *aequitas* (equity). Throughout the Middle Ages, and in the early modern period, *aequitas* remained in the forefront of discussion as a counterpoise to the *ius strictum* (strict law), but it was commonly identified with *bona fides*' (p. 17).
17. *Eod. Loc.*

in performing the contract, it also means that we repel the distinction found in Roman law or in its interprets, between contracts in good faith and contracts in strict law, *contractus bonae fidei*, and *contractus stricti juris*'.[18]

That observation does not mean, however, that the leeway gained by the Roman judge under certain contracts became blindly and wildly general. That did not mean either that equity would allow courts to create excuses, obligations or rights as they saw fit despite the black letter of the contract. A mere glance at French case law is sufficient to see that, on the contrary, equity was refused an open role in assessing the performance of contract law. The famous 'Canal de Craponne' case, rejecting the 'théorie de l'imprévision' is exemplary in this respect. The French *Cour de cassation* then held that 'under no circumstances is it for the courts, however fair [equitable] their decision may appear to them, to take into account the time and the circumstances in order to substitute new terms for those which have been freely accepted by the contracting parties'.[19] What the general application of the duty of good faith meant was that the conduct of a party, either in negotiating or in performing the contract, could bear certain legal consequences, as we shall see below, if it departed from the standard applicable to that relationship.

In other words, good faith refers to a behaviour, i.e., to a way to conduct negotiations, to perform the contract or to apply its terms. The breach of that duty is supposed to positively prove a conduct in the context of the contractual relationship and to establish what is wrong with it. But what are the references appropriate to allow the assessment of the compliance or breach of the duty of good faith?

[B] The Parameters Controlling the Assessment of Good Faith

In accordance with its Roman and Canonist roots, and to schematize a bit, the duty of good faith refers to three registries and seems oriented in two directions. The three registries are honesty, reasonableness and coherence.

It is difficult to define in the abstract what honesty positively is. However, it is less difficult to see what it is not in a given set of circumstances. For example: deceit is a clear-cut dishonesty, but how transparent must one be? To what extent must one

18. C.B.M. Toullier, *Le droit civil français suivant l'ordre du Code*, vol. 6, §195 (2nd ed., Paris 1819): 'Les conventions doivent être exécutées de bonne foi (1134); ce qui ne veut pas dire seulement que le dol et la fraude doivent en être bannis, mais que nous rejetons la division des conventions que l'on trouve dans le droit romain ou dans ses interprètes, en contrats de bonne foi et contrats de droit strict, *contractus bonae fidei*, et *contractus stricti juris*.'
19. Cass. Civ., 6 March 1876, D. 1876, 1, 193, n. Antoine Giboulot ; Grands arrêts de la jurispr. civ. par F. Terré et Y. Lequette and F. Chénédé, vol. 2, 13e éd., Dalloz, 2015, No. 165: 'Vu l'art. 1134 c. civ.; – Attendu que la disposition de cet article n'étant que la reproduction des anciens principes constamment suivis en matière d'obligations conventionnelles, la circonstance que les contrats dont l'exécution donne lieu au litige sont antérieurs à la promulgation du code civil ne saurait être, dans l'espèce, un obstacle à l'application dudit article ; – Attendu que la règle qu'il consacre est générale, absolue, et régit les contrats dont l'exécution s'étend à des époques successives de même qu'à ceux de toute autre nature ; Que, dans aucun cas, il n'appartient aux tribunaux, quelque équitable que puisse leur paraître leur décision, de prendre en considération les temps et les circonstances pour modifier les conventions des parties et substituer des clauses nouvelles à celles qui ont été librement acceptées par les contractants.'

share information that may be relevant to the other party? As will be explained further, it depends on the nature of the contract and of the relationship.

Reasonableness is also difficult to account for in the abstract, but that standard is certainly not one that should frighten an experienced lawyer. Common law uses it thoroughly. From a civil lawyer's perspective, it invites to assess the rationality of one's decision-making process and calls for a duty of moderation on the parties. For instance, when a delay, a default or any form of disappointment occurs, it advises not to react in a disproportionate manner. Proportionality is an important facet of the standard of reasonableness and, in turn, of good faith.

Lastly, coherence in conduct is factored in the assessment of one's good faith.[20] To begin with, that means coherence with the agreed purpose of the contract: good faith in performance requires that parties refrain from hindering the performance of the contract and act so as to favour its completion. It also means coherence not only with one's words but also with one's non-verbal language: one ought to respond to the legitimate expectations one caused. We are not that far away from the concept of promissory estoppel.

Those references do not aim at turning a contracting party into a saint. Their orientation makes them more pragmatic than that and less demanding. To synthetize the way that duty seems handled in case law, it seems oriented in two directions.

First and foremost, the duty of good faith is performance oriented. It commands to behave as required to fulfil the promise. As was abruptly recalled at the end of the 19th century by an author commenting on the duty to perform in good faith laid out in the Napoleonic Code, 'the relaxations required by Equity should not be exaggerated (…) [for] what Equity requires above all when the obligation is established, is the payment from the debtor'.[21] Thus, good faith first binds the parties to do their best to deliver what they promised as it was promised, i.e., to perform the contract in application of its black letter, along the lines of its provisions and, if necessary, beyond the black letter of its provisions so to complete the economic operation the contract was supposed to achieve. The objective is to act so that the contract may deliver its economic utility. In that sense, the duty is certainly not opposed to *pacta sunt servanda*. On the contrary, it bolsters the legal force of the agreement.[22]

However, there are contractual stages where there is nothing yet - or nothing left - to perform. That points to the negotiation phase or the termination. In those instances, it becomes obvious that the duty of good faith can have a second, and quite different, orientation.

The duty of good faith may also be oriented towards the respect, if not the protection, of the other party's interest. That orientation was already present in Roman law, and it remains quite lively in modern law. That is perhaps the most controversial aspect of the duty, but it is illustrated in the law, though. To take a basic example, one can cite the duty to give sufficient prior notice before termination. This obligation

20. *See*, for example, R. Jabbour, *La bonne foi dans l'exécution du contrat*, §§ 331-336 (LGDJ ed., 2016).
21. Theophile Huc, *Commentaire théorique et pratique du Code civil*, vol. 7, § 90 (Paris 1894).
22. *See*, for a recent demonstration to that effect, R. Jabbour, *supra*, *passim*.

originates in the duty to perform in good faith, and purports to let the other party have time to reorganize and mitigate the adverse consequences of the termination. It is founded on the idea that respect – at least some respect – is due to the preservation of the other party's interests.

In many circumstances, good faith may also imply refraining from acting without reason in a way that harms the other party. However, if the duty of good faith often implies giving some thought to the other party's interests, it does not direct promoting them. But it sometimes does. Think of the fiduciary relationships, and it occurs in other contexts too.[23]

This shows, and it is the last factor to bear in mind, that good faith, especially this last facet of the duty, is imposed on the parties to a varying degree.

[C] The Varying Intensity of the Duty of Good Faith

A frequent misunderstanding with regard to the duty of good faith is due to the impression that its various illustrations may apply in every context and for every type of contract. That is not correct. It must be emphasized that its intensity, i.e., the force of its demands, is not the same from one relationship to another and is highly fact-sensitive.

At first, its intensity depends on the expectations that have been created. The confidence that one party could legitimately put in the other is crucial in that respect.

Second, it depends on the type of contract in issue. Contracts are more or less antagonistic. The less they are, the more intense the duty of good faith becomes. The evolution of French case law over the last forty years is quite instructive in this respect. Until the 1980s, the duty of good faith set out in Article 1134 §3 of the Napoleonic Code did not give rise to many disputes, either in courts or in the legal literature. In Belgium, its potentialities were more discussed, and in 1983, the Belgian *Cour de cassation* connected it with the abuse of right doctrine, allowing for its expansion. The Court held the following:

> Whereas the principle of the performance of agreements in good faith, enshrined in Article 1134 of the Civil Code, prohibits a party to a contract from abusing the rights conferred on him by the contract, such abuse requires a party to use, in his sole interest, a right deriving from the agreement, and to derive from such use a benefit which is disproportionate to the correlative burden on the other party.[24]

23. For instance, a contract for heating maintenance entails the obligation for the maintenance company to inform the client about a cheaper system (French Cass. civ. 1, 11 June 1996, No. 94-18250; Bull. civ. I, No. 245). Similarly, in the context of a distribution agreement, good faith entails the duty for a party to put the other party in a competitive situation. Hence, an oil company breaches this duty by setting prices which make it impossible for its distributors to be competitive (French Cass. com., 3 November 1992, No. 90-18547; Bull. civ. IV, n° 338).
24. Belgian Cass. civ. 3rd, 19 March 1983, RCJB 1986, 282, n. J. L. Fagnart: 'Attendu que si le principe de l'exécution de bonne foi des conventions, consacré par l'article 1134 du Code civil interdit à une partie au contrat d'abuser des droits que lui confère celui-ci, pareil abus suppose que lorsque cette partie use, dans son seul intérêt, d'un droit qu'elle puise dans la convention, elle en retire un avantage disproportionné à la charge corrélative de l'autre partie.'

In spite of its very general wording, the principle was applied in the context of a distribution agreement where a car dealer had passed on to its commercial agents the limitations that had been imposed on him by the main supplier. Did this circumstance have bearing on the ambit of the solution? It was not apparent at the time, but French case law has progressively manifested that the nature of the relationship plays a role with regard to the requirements of the duty to perform in good faith.

Indeed, the French *Cour de cassation* followed the same stance as its Belgian peer a few years later. The most remarkable cases also dealt with distribution agreements, but that was not considered, at the beginning, as a significant factor. In 1992, the French *Cour de cassation* held that a gas supplier had breached its duty to perform the contract in good faith in selling gas to its retailer for a higher price than it was selling the same to end customers, depriving thereby the retailer of the possibility to practice competitive prices.[25] This solution was subsequently confirmed, once again, in the context of a distribution agreement, which became the main field for the expansion of the duty to perform in good faith. In 2001, the *Cour de cassation*, for example, held that the head of a distribution network breached that duty in passing on to its retailers the complete burden of the financial efforts required to face the crisis in the sector, so as to keep its profits at the same level as before.[26] At the same time, the French legal doctrine had started to identify the specificity of distribution agreements as being part of a category that some called 'contrats-organisation' while echoing the category of 'relational contracts' conceived by some American authors.[27] It slowly crystallized in the category of 'contrats-coopération', which formed only a part of the wider class of agreements that one author convincingly called 'contrats-alliance.'[28] This category, the archetype of which is the antique *societas*, goes from the various forms of joint ventures to collective contracts such as intercreditor agreements, or distribution agreements, viewed as an elementary part of a distribution network. The performance of such a contract generally calls for a mutual investment and the completion of a mutually beneficial scheme. For instance, publishing contracts are cooperation contracts: an author transfers to a publisher the right to exploit a work, and the proceeds received by the author are proportional to the revenue generated by the exploitation. Good faith requires that each party prioritises the interest of the common project. Moreover, the long-term perspective of many of these contracts requires some flexibility, which in turn calls for a decision-making process for various rights to unilaterally modify or supplement some aspects of the initially agreed scheme, etc. Thereby, a party is

25. French Cass. com., 3 November 1992, No. 90-18547; Bull. civ. IV, No. 338.
26. French Cass. com., 15 January 2002, No. 99-21172.
27. *See*, in particular, I Mac Neil, *Contracts: Adjustment of Long-Term Economic Relations under Classical, Neoclassical, and Relational Contract Law*, 72 Nw. U. L. Rev. 854 (1977-1978). I. Mac Neil, *Relational Contract: What We Do and Do Not Know*, 1985 Wis. L. Rev. 483 (1985). J.M. Feinman, *Relational Contract Theory in Context*, 94 Nw. U. L. Rev. 737 (1999-2000).
28. *See* Suzanne Lequette, *Le contrat-coopération: contribution à la théorie générale du contrat* (Economica ed., 2012) and Jean-François Hamelin, *Le contrat-alliance* (Economica ed., 2012). The category of 'contrat-alliance' had been first characterized by Professor Alain Seriaux in *Le droit: une introduction*, § 125 (Ellipses, 1997).

generally in a leading and dominant position. All that invites a reinforced duty of good faith, which includes considering how to preserve the interests of the other party.

Fiduciary relationships form another category of contracts where the duty to perform in good faith proved to be reinforced. For example, in a 1996 French case, the director of a company had accepted to acquire another shareholder's stake without informing the latter that he was about to sell his own stake for a much higher price to a third party. The French *Cour de cassation* held that he had thus breached the duty to act in good faith 'incumbent on a director of a company with respect to the other shareholders'.[29] A few years later, the *Cour de cassation* distinguished this case from the situation where the shares are purchased by a shareholder who does not hold the position of director of the company. In that context, it was held that 'the purchaser is not obliged to inform the seller either of negotiations aimed at the acquisition by a third party of other shares of the same company or of those which he himself conducts with that third party with a view to transferring to him or contributing to him the shares which are the subject of the sale'.[30] Thus, it was made clear that the enhanced duty of good faith fell only on the director in his specific capacity.

To sum up, antagonistic contracts where the parties merely intend to exchange one thing for another are not looked at, under the lens of good faith, as those agreements instating a fruitful relationship thriving from the combination of the reciprocal skills and assets of the parties. 'Alliance-contracts' and fiduciary relationships bring, therefore, the duty to perform in good faith to its highest degree. The effects of that duty reach, in these cases, their broadest and strongest effects.

§1.03 THE LEGAL EFFECTS OF THE DUTY OF GOOD FAITH

To continue the metaphor presenting good faith as a fluid norm, that duty seems to irrigate many areas of civil contract law. It thus underpins a wide range of legal mechanisms and sometimes has self-standing effects.

[A] An Ingredient of Various Legal Mechanisms

The good or bad faith behaviour of a party is considered in many legal mechanisms. One can only give some examples to manifest it.

The operation of a condition, either precedent or resolutory, is one of them. Reiterating the rule that was set forth in Article 1178 of the Napoleonic Code, the current Article 1304-3 of the French Civil Code sets out that 'a suspensive condition is deemed to have been fulfilled if the party who is interested in its failing has obstructed its fulfilment' and adds that 'A resolutory condition is deemed to have failed if its fulfilment has been caused by the party who had an interest in this occurring.' In either case, the conduct of the party invoking the condition has been inconsistent with the requirement of good faith and is sanctioned by a loss of the benefit of the condition.

29. French Cass. com., 27 February 1996, No. 94-11241; Bull. civ. IV, No. 65.
30. French Cass. com., 12 May 2004, No. 00-15618; Bull. civ. IV No. 94.

Article 156 of the Swiss Code of Obligations has the same rule and expressly grounds it on the requirements of good faith. It reads as follows: 'The condition is deemed to have been fulfilled when one of the parties has prevented it in disregard of the rules of good faith.'[31]

Interpretation is also a major area wherein good faith plays a role. Section 157 of the German BGB was already quoted above in that respect, but other laws expressly mention its role. For example, Article 961 of the Argentina Civil Code sets out that 'Contracts must be made, interpreted and performed in good faith.'[32] The French law basic rule on the interpretation of contracts, i.e., the current Article 1188 of the French Civil Code, does not refer to good faith as such but to the understanding of a reasonable person, which is quite similar.[33] And from an objective interpretation to the 'gap filling' of the contract, there is just one step to go.

Gap-filling of the contract is also one mechanism that coincides with the demands of good faith. Section 242 of the German BGB has been thus interpreted as allowing courts to supplement the contract with additional duties deriving from the general duty to perform in good faith. French law has devoted a specific article to the completive function. It does not refer to good faith but to equity. It was Article 1135 of the Napoleonic Code, which has become the current Article 1194 of the Civil Code. It reads as follows: 'Contracts create obligations not merely in relation to what they expressly provide, but also to all the consequences which are given to them by equity, usage or legislation.'

Those rules show the overlap between good faith and equity, which is in line with the Roman law origin of our continental law systems. In a famous definition, Papinian thus described the '*jus praetorium*' as being what the '*praetores*' would introduce to 'supplement the law'.[34] This definition also referred to the correction of the law, which is a function sometimes connected to good faith.

Correction of the contract may also have some connection with the requirement to act in good faith. However, this is not always the case, and when it occurs, good faith is only an ingredient of a specific norm. In German law, the control of unfair standard terms was initially based on section 242 of the BGB until the 1976 AGB Act provided a specific statutory basis to that effect.[35] However, the test of unfairness still referred to the requirements of good faith. At present, the first paragraph of section 307 of the

31. Swiss CO, Art. 156.
32. Argentina Civil Code, Art. 961 (original spanish full text): 'Los contratos deben celebrarse, interpretarse y ejecutarse de buena fe. Obligan no sólo a lo que está formalmente expresado, sino a todas las consecuencias que puedan considerarse comprendidas en ellos, con los alcances en que razonablemente se habría obligado un contratante cuidadoso y previsor.'
33. French Civil Code, Art. 1188: '(1) A contract is to be interpreted according to the common intention of the parties rather than stopping at the literal meaning of its terms. (2) Where this intention cannot be discerned, a contract is to be interpreted in the sense which a reasonable person placed in the same situation would give to it.'
34. Pap. D. 1, 1, 7, 1 (2 def.) 'Ius praetorium est, quod praetores introduxerunt adiuvandi vel supplendi vel corrigendi iuris civilis gratia propter utilitatem publicam.'
35. *See* Xavier Favre-Bulle, *Le rôle du principe de la bonne foi et de l'abus de droit dans le domaine des clauses abusives*, in Pierre Widmer & Bertil Cottier (eds), Abus de droit et bonne foi, pp. 139 ff., spéc. pp. 157-159 (Editions universitaires de Fribourg, 1994).

German BGB provides that 'Provisions in standard business terms are ineffective if, contrary to the requirement of good faith, they unreasonably disadvantage the other party to the contract with the user.' Nevertheless, the similar mechanisms known in France do not refer to this assessment of good faith. Article 1171 of the French Civil Code thus reads as follows: 'Any non-negotiable and unilaterally predetermined term of a standard form contract which creates a significant imbalance in the rights and obligations of the parties to the contract is deemed not written.'

The same observation can be made with respect to the rules accounting for hardship. In German law, the *Wegfall der Geschäftsgrundlage* is seen as a development of the duty to perform in good faith set out by section 242 of the BGB, although it has progressively become an autonomous doctrine.[36] In France, Article 1195 of the Civil Code now provides for a possible judicial revision of the contract in case of hardship, but the rule does not mention the duty to perform in good faith, although a duty to renegotiate has long been discussed as a possible implication of that duty.

Thus, good faith has played the role of a seminal concept for many sophisticated legal tools contributing to improve fair dealings. It sometimes remains an ingredient of those rules, sometimes not. In any event, those mechanisms do not appear as part of the specific legal effects of the duty to act in good faith, which will now be presented to conclude.

[B] The Self-Standing Effects of the Duty of Good Faith

The core effects of the duty to perform in good faith are threefold. First, the breach of that duty allows for the neutralization of the exercise of a right, thus overlapping with the doctrine of abuse of right. Second, a breach of the duty to perform in good faith is a stand-alone cause for termination. Third, the breach of the duty of good faith, either in the context of negotiating or performing the contract, is a cause for liability.

The first point is sometimes termed the limitative effect of the duty to perform in good faith. It is acknowledged under either German, French or Swiss law. It differs from the control of unfair terms insofar as it does not strike out the disputed clause from the contract but merely neutralizes its implementation if and when it appears to be invoked in breach of the duty to perform in good faith. It also differs from the classical approach of abuse of rights insofar as its specific remedy is rather preventive than curative. It consists of depriving the exercise of the right of its purported legal effect, although damages might also be awarded if harm was caused by that exercise.[37]

Under French law, the commonplace example of such a control is the implementation in bad faith of a resolutory clause. If the termination right set forth by that clause is exercised by the creditor on the basis of a breach that is attributable to the conduct of that same creditor, the clause will simply not operate. Typically, the *Cour de*

36. Reinhard Zimmermann & Simon Whittaker, *Good faith in European contract law: surveying the legal landscape*, in Zimmermann and Whittaker (ed.), Good Faith in European Contract Law, p. 26 (Cambridge University Press, 2000, p. 6).
37. For a French law approach, *see* Ph. Stoffel-Munck, *L'abus dans le contrat*, §§ 789-802 (LGDJ ed., 2000).

cassation held that a landlord abuses his/her contractual right to terminate the contract when he/she serves the tenant with a summons while knowing that he/she is away on holiday. It does not mean that the clause will never be effective in the future, assuming the contract is continued. It just means that this implementation of the clause is not. In other terms, the right is not and may not be deleted from the contract because its holder behaved in breach of the duty to perform in good faith when invoking it.

As a result, under French law, a debt may not be cancelled because of the bad faith of the creditor claiming for payment. There are specific statutory mechanisms, such as the judicial granting of a period of grace, to deal with the concerns a claim for immediate payment may give rise to. But if the right is lawfully established, it is valid and enforceable.

This is what the French *Cour de cassation* held in the famous 'Les Maréchaux' case, handed down in 2007. In that landmark case, the Court ruled as follows:

> If the rule according to which contracts must be performed in good faith allows the judge to censure the disloyal exercise of a contractual prerogative, it does not allow him to violate the substance of the rights and obligations lawfully agreed by the parties.[38]

Another self-standing remedy against a breach of the duty to perform in good faith is unilateral or judicial termination. That remedy is generally the consequence of a failure to complete adequately a specific act of performance. However, there is no impediment to the operation of that remedy where the breach relates to a general duty, provided it bears serious consequences. Under French case law, it is thus admitted that a party's material breach of its duty to perform in good faith may warrant a rightful termination, even though that party diligently discharged its other obligations under the contract. A typical illustration in that respect comes from a French case that dealt with the termination of a commercial agency contract. The facts were the following.

A company had hired a commercial agent for a couple of years. The successful development of this arrangement led the agent to hire a set of sub-agents. However, the relationship deteriorated, and the principal then tried to convince the sub-agents to become directly its agents instead. As a result, the agent claimed for judicial termination of the contract with damages. The principal contended that it could not be considered as having committed a material breach of its undertaking since it was not in default of its financial obligations and since its attempts to divert the sub-agents had been unsuccessful. The French *Cour de cassation* found that the facts characterized 'a breach of the duty to perform the contract in good faith' that legally justified a judicial termination of the contract.[39]

In that decision, the Court also awarded damages, which illustrates the third remedy that is available for such breach.

38. French Cass. com., 10 January 2007, No. 06-14768; PBRI; Bull. civ. IV, n° 188; Grands arrêts de la jurisprudence civile, par Terré, Lequette et Chénédé, t. 2, 13e éd., Dalloz 2015, n° 164, Annual Report of the Cour de cassation for 2007, p. 436.
39. French Cass. com., 10 January 1979, No. 77-12320, Bull. Civ. IV No. 17.

That last stand-alone remedy is commonplace, irrespective of whether the breach occurred in the context of negotiating the contract or in its performance. However, the compensable damage will differ. Under German, French or Swiss law, compensation will be limited to the reliance interest in the first case.[40] By contrast, positive interest may be compensated if the breach of good faith occurred in the performance of the agreement, especially where it caused the termination of the contract.

To sum up, the duty of good faith in civil law is neither a wild norm nor a wizard's wand lost in contract law. Good faith is flexible; good faith is a range, but there is a framework guiding its application. On the one hand, it certainly is an inspirational concept for some other rules. As such, it did fuel evolution in the law and remains available to that aim. In that perspective, it is correct to see it as a last resort argument, i.e., an argument apt to make the law change when reason and fairness incline to adopt a certain solution while the straightforward application of the existing legal tools cannot warrant that conclusion. On the other hand, it is a sensible standard of conduct, bearing some specific and identified effects. One of those general tools civil law cannot and should not do without.

40. *See*, for a comparative approach of French, German, Chilean and English laws, Isabel Zuloaga, *Reliance in the Breaking-Off of Contractual Negotiations: Trust and Expectation in a Comparative Perspective* (Intersentia ed., 2019).

CHAPTER 2

Good Faith in English Contract Law

Neil Andrews

§2.01 INTRODUCTION

It is a pleasure to present this chapter, which is a fuller account of the points which were orally summarized at the ASA Conference held in Geneva in February 2022.

The topic, even from a Common law perspective, has generated a vast literature.[1] However, (a) English law has refused to imply a general duty to negotiate a contract in

1. Neil Andrews, *Contract Law in Practice* (Oxford University Press 2021), paras 2.69 to 2.72, and Chapter 19 (hereinafter, 'Andrews: Contract Law in Practice (2021)'); *Chitty on Contracts* (H.G. Beale, gen. ed., Sweet and Maxwell 34th ed. 2021), paras 2-024 to 2-093 (hereinafter, 'Chitty (2021)'). *See also*: Michael G. Bridge, *An English Lawyer Looks at American Contract Law*, in F.H. Buckley (ed.), *The American Illness: Essays on the Rule of Law* (Yale University Press 2013), 291-311; Roger Brownsword, *Contract Law: Themes for the Twenty-First Century* (Oxford University Press 2d ed. 2006), Chapter 6 (also in Roger Brownsword, in Michael Furmston (gen. ed.), *The Law of Contract* (LexisNexis, 6d ed., 2017), Chapter 1, section E); Hugh Collins, *Implied Terms: the Foundation in Good Faith and Fair Dealing* [2014] C.L.P. 297; Edward Granger, *Sweating Over an Implied Duty of Good Faith* [2013] L.M.C.L.Q. 418; Sir George Leggatt, *Contractual Duties of Good Faith*, The Commercial Bar Association Lecture (18 October 2016) (http://www.combar.com/public/cms/260/604/384/2566/Mr%20Justice%20Leggatt%20 lecture%2018.10.16.pdf?realName=qxp9PW.pdf&v=); Ewan McKendrick, *Contract Law: Text, Cases and Materials* (Oxford University Press, 10d ed., 2022), Chapter 15; Ewan McKendrick, *Good Faith in the Performance of a Contract in English Law*, in Larry DiMatteo and Martin Hogg (eds), *Comparative Contract Law: British and American Perspectives* (Oxford University Press 2015), Chapter 10; Hector MacQueen, *Good Faith*, in Hector MacQueen and Reinhard Zimmermann (eds), *European Contract Law: Scots and South African Perspectives* (Edinburgh University Press 2006), Chapter 2; Gerard McMeel, *The Construction of Contracts: Interpretation, Implication and Rectification* (Oxford University Press 3d ed., 2017), paras 11.01 to 11.11; Gerard McMeel, *Foucault's Pendulum: Text, Context and Good Faith in Contract Law* [2017] C.L.P. 365, 385 ff.; David R. Percy, *The Emergence of Good Faith as a Principle of Contract Performance*, in Simone Degeling, James Edelman, James Goudkamp (eds), *Contract in Commercial Law* (Thomson Reuters 2016), Chapter 11; Severine Saintier, *The Elusive Notion of Good Faith in the Performance of a Contract: Why Still a 'Bête Noire' for the Civil and the Common Law?* [2017] J.B.L. 441; Lord Steyn, *Contract Law: Fulfilling the Reasonable Expectations of Honest Men* (1997) 113 L.Q.R. 433;

good faith or (b) to perform a contract in good faith. As for (a), even a promise to negotiate reasonably or in good faith is void for uncertainty. The House of Lords in *Walford v. Miles* (1992)[2] decided that the nub of the problem is that the courts should not become embroiled in the dispute whether one party was bargaining unreasonably. No workable criteria can be applied. *Walford v. Miles* remains the fundamental authority on this point.[3] As for (b), the fear is that a dynamic concept of implied good faith in performance might unduly unsettle the law (*see* the quotations presented in §2.03 below).

The notion of 'good faith' or 'fair dealing' can be used as an organizing general rubric or pervasive principle, which (whether articulated or not) underpins many contractual doctrines. As the author has explained elsewhere,[4] there is a wide range of contexts in which English courts have implicitly acted on a principle of good faith or fair dealing, not as the source of an implied duty to act in good faith, giving rise to a cause of action upon breach, but instead as an overarching characteristic of various contractual doctrines.

§2.02 THE IMPLICIT PRINCIPLE OF GOOD FAITH

The following is a list of the many contexts in which English courts have acted implicitly on a principle of good faith or fair dealing (even though there is no articulated general principle of good faith in English contract law, in this absence, *see* §2.03

Sir Johan Steyn, *The Role of Good Faith and Fair Dealing in Contract: A Hair-Shirt Philosophy?* [1991] Denning L.J. 131; Gunther Teubner, *Legal Irritants: Good Faith in British Law or How Unifying Law Ends Up in New Divergences* (1998) 61 M.L.R. 11; Stephen Waddams, *Good Faith, Good Conscience, and the Taking of Unfair Advantage*, in Andrew Dyson, James Goudkamp, Frederick Wilmot-Smith (eds), *Defences in Contract* (Hart Publishing 2017), Chapter 4; Reinhard Zimmermann and Simon Whittaker (eds), *Good Faith in European Contract Law* (Cambridge University Press 2000); for the position in Canada: a duty not to engage in deliberate untruthfulness was recognised by the Supreme Court in *Bhasin v. Hrynew* (2014) SCC 71; [2014] 3 S.C.R. 494, [73] to [92] and [93] (3)); for the position in Singapore, *Ng Giap Hon v. Westcomb Securities Pte Ltd* [2009] SGCA; [2009] 3 S.L.R. (R.) 518: *Cheah Peng Hock v. Luzhou Bio-Chem Technology Ltd* [2013] 2 S.L.R. 577 at [40] to [60]. Andrew Phang, *The Challenge of Principled Gap-Filling: A Study of Implied Terms in a Comparative Context* [2014] J.B.L. 263, 298-307 (a rich comparative resource); for the position in Australia: Marilyn Warren, *Good Faith: Where Are We At?* (2010) 34 Melbourne L. Rev. 344.

2. [1992] 2 AC 128 (H.L.).
3. *Barbudev v. Eurocom Cable Management Bulgaria Eood* [2012] EWCA Civ 548, [2012] 2 All E.R. (Comm) 963, at [46]; *BJ Aviation Ltd v. Pool Aviation Ltd* [2002] EWCA Civ 163, [2002] 2 P. & C.R. 25, at [27], [29], [32]; *Shaker v. Vistajet* [2012] EWHC 1329 (Comm), [2012] 2 All E.R. (Comm) 1010 [8] to [18] (Teare J); *Rosalina Investments Ltd v. New Balance Athletic Shoes (UK) Ltd* [2018] EWHC 1014 (QB), at [48] to [52] (May J); *BBC Worldwide Ltd v. Bee Load Ltd* [2007] EWHC 134 (Comm) (Toulson LJ); *Dhanani v. Crasnianski* [2011] EWHC 926 (Comm), [2011] 2 All E.R. (Comm) 799 (Teare J) (notably at [95], [104], [105]; in effect an agreement to agree; many points yet to be settled).
4. Andrews: Contract Law in Practice (2021), paras 2.69 to 2.72; 19.27 to 19.38; Neil Andrews, *Good Faith Beneath the Surface: the Ethical Sensitivity of English Contract Law*, in the Michael Joachim Bonell festschrift, *The Age of Uniform Law: Essays in Honour of Michael Joachim Bonell* (UNIDROIT, Rome and Oxford, 2016), 953-997; these discussions include substantial bibliographical references.

below). This list shows that English contract law intervenes in numerous respects to ensure a minimal level of fair dealing between the parties:

(1) protection where, prior to the formation of the contract, one party has unconscionably acquiesced in the other's mistake;[5]
(2) rectification, notably based on unilateral mistake unconscionably acquiesced in by a bad faith party;[6]
(3) specific duties to disclose;[7]
(4) refusal of specific performance where the claimant has employed the element of surprise in circumstances not consistent with 'good faith';[8]
(5) the doctrines of promissory and proprietary estoppel in Equity, waiver, estoppel by representation, and estoppel by convention;[9]
(6) fiduciary duties: the duties of fair dealing imposed on agents and other fiduciaries[10] when they contract with their principals, beneficiaries, or other protected persons;[11]
(7) equitable relief against forfeiture of proprietary or possessory interests;[12]
(8) the general principle that equitable relief will be withheld if the applicant has behaved shabbily and so lacks 'clean hands'; that is, discretionary refusal of specific performance and injunctions;[13]
(9) rescission for misrepresentation;[14]
(10) rescission for undue influence;[15]
(11) rescission for unconscionability;[16]
(12) duress;[17]

5. Chitty (2021), paras 5-022 ff.; Andrews, Contract Law in Practice (2021), paras 3-187 to 3-198.
6. *Hodge on Rectification* (Sweet and Maxwell 2d ed. 2016), Chapter 5; Chitty (2021), para. 5-070; Andrews, Contract Law in Practice (2021), paras 21-35 to 21.49.
7. John Cartwright, *Misrepresentation, Mistake and Non-disclosure* (Sweet and Maxwell 5th ed. 2019), Chapters 16 and 17; Chitty (2021), paras 9-167 ff.; Andrews, Contract Law in Practice (2021), paras 11-174 to 11-192.
8. For example, Lord Campbell LC said in *Walters v. Morgan* (1861) 3 718, 724; 45 E.R. 1056, 1059, that there was a lack of 'good faith' in the procuring of a long extension of a lease by the tenant.
9. Chitty (2021), paras 6-093 to 6-193; 25-042 to 25-049; Andrews, Contract Law in Practice (2021), paras 2-51 to 2-68.
10. James Edelman, 'When Do Fiduciary Duties Arise?' 126 L.Q.R. 302 (2010).
11. *Bowstead and Reynolds on Agency* (F.M.B. Reynolds and P. Watts, eds) (21st edn, Sweet and Maxwell 2018); *Snell's Equity* (John McGhee and Steven Elliott, eds) (34th edn, Sweet and Maxwell, London, 2019); Chitty (2021), paras 21-129 ff.
12. Chitty (2021), paras 29-266 to 29-272; Andrews, Contract Law in Practice (2021), paras 24-115 to 24-119.
13. Chitty (2021), para. 30-054.
14. John Cartwright, *Misrepresentation, Mistake and Non-disclosure* (5th edn, Sweet and Maxwell 2019), Part I; Chitty (2021), Chapter 9; Andrews, Contract Law in Practice (2021), Chapter 11.
15. Nelson Enonchong, Duress, Undue Influence and Unconscionable Dealing (3rd edn, Sweet and Maxwell 2019) (hereinafter 'Enonchong'), Chapters 6 to 14; Chitty (2021), paras 10-072 ff.; Andrews, Contract Law in Practice (2021), Chapter 14.
16. Enonchong, Chapters 15 to 20; Chitty (2021), 10-0161 ff.; Andrews, Contract Law in Practice (2021), Chapter 15.
17. Enonchong, Chapters 2 to 5; Chitty (2021), paras 10-003 to 10-071.

(13) decisions denying that a party has a right to terminate a contract where this would be a wholly disproportionate response to the relevant breach;[18]
(14) the penalty rule;[19]
(15) 'corrective construction' (judicial re-arrangement of manifestly imperfect contractual wording) when interpreting written contracts;[20]
(16) the ascription of duties not to prevent the other's performance, based on the implied term of (a) cooperation[21] or (b) avoidance of stultifying conduct.[22]

§2.03 JUDICIAL RECOGNITION THAT THERE IS NO GENERAL DUTY TO PERFORM IN GOOD FAITH

English judges have observed on many occasions that there is no general duty to perform in good faith.[23] For example, in *Pakistan International Airline Corporation v. Times Travel (UK) Ltd* (2021),[24] Lord Burrows said:

> [95] … I do not think that this is an appropriate case in which to rely on a general principle of good faith dealing in so far as that would require a court to try to apply a standard of what is commercially unacceptable or unreasonable behaviour. That would be a radical move forward for the English law of contract and the uncertainty caused by it seems unlikely to be a price worth paying.

Earlier, in *MSC Mediterranean Shipping Co SA v. Cottonex Anstalt* (2016), Moore-Bick LJ declared that there is no 'general duty of good faith' in English contract law:[25]

---

18. Andrews, Contract Law in Practice (2021), paras 24-100 to 24-189.
19. Roger Halson, *Liquidated Damages and Penalty Clauses* (Oxford University Press 2018); Chitty (2021), paras 29-203 ff.; Andrews, Contract Law in Practice (2021), paras 27-69 ff.
20. Kim Lewison, *The Interpretation of Contracts* (7th edn, Sweet and Maxwell 2021), Chapter 9; Andrews, Contract Law in Practice (2021), paras 20-083 to 20-114.
21. Co-operation: *see* Lord Blackburn in *Mackay v. Dick* (1881) 6 App. Cas. 251, 263 (H.L.); Kim Lewison, *The Interpretation of Contracts* (7th edn, Sweet and Maxwell 2021), para. 6.15; Chitty (2021), para. 16-026; Gerard McMeel, *The Construction of Contracts: Interpretation, Implication and Rectification* (3d ed. Oxford University Press 2017), para. 9.56; Angela Swan, Jakub Adamski, 'The Development of an Obligation to Perform in Good Faith', in Paul Daly (ed.), *Apex Courts and the Common Law* (University of Toronto Press, 2019), 303, at 330, footnote 78; the Canadian Supreme Court in *Bhasin v. Hrynew* (2014) SCC 71; [2014] 3 S.C.R. 494, at [47] to [51]; in *Sanderson Ltd v. Simtom Food Projects Ltd* [2019] EWHC 442 (TCC); [2019] B.L.R. 260, at [25], Judge Halliwell recognized that a duty of cooperation will be recognized where this is necessary to carry out an interactive contract.
22. Avoidance of stultification, that is, prevention of performance: the case law lineage of this species of implied term is set out in *Ali v. Petroleum Co of Trinidad and Tobago* [2017] UKPC 2; [2017] I.C.R. 531, at [8]. This category of implied term is considered in Kim Lewison, *The Interpretation of Contracts* (7th edn, Sweet and Maxwell 2021), para. 6.14 and Chitty (2021), para. 14-027, and Gerard McMeel, *The Construction of Contracts: Interpretation, Implication and Rectification* (3rd edn, Oxford University Press 2017), para. 9.57.
23. Chitty (2021), paras 2-036 to 2-042.
24. [2021] UKSC 40, [2021] 3 W.L.R. 727, [2021] 3 W.L.R. 727, at [95].
25. [2016] EWCA Civ 789; [2017] 1 All E.R. (Comm) 483, at [45].

> The recognition of a general duty of good faith would be a significant step in the development of our law of contract with potentially far-reaching consequences and I do not think it is necessary or desirable to resort to it in order to decide the outcome of the present case ... In my view the better course is for the law to develop along established lines rather than to encourage judges to look for what the judge in this case called some 'general organising principle' drawn from cases of disparate kinds.

Also, in *MSC Mediterranean Shipping* (2016), Moore-Bick LJ commented on the dangerous link between the principle of good faith and the process of contractual interpretation:[26]

> There is ... a real danger that if a general principle of good faith were established it would be invoked as often to undermine as to support the terms in which the parties have reached agreement.

§2.04 GOOD FAITH IN 'RELATIONAL CONTRACTS'

The courts have developed the notion of especially close contracts (so-called relational contracts), which import a commercial expectation of cooperation and fair dealing. This has been described as an 'implied term of good faith'. Its content is subject to judicial definition.

The modern impetus for this analysis is *Yam Seng Pte Ltd v. International Trade Corp Ltd* (2013),[27] in which Leggatt J (now Lord Leggatt, who sits in the Supreme Court of the United Kingdom) found an implied term within an exclusive distributorship. The term imposed an obligation that the wholesale supplier would not consciously mislead the other party concerning the pricing of the relevant product(s) in competing markets. Inaccurate information had been supplied by that wholesale supplier. This proved to be disastrous for the claimant's airport duty-free distributorship because (unknown to the claimant) the products were being sold more cheaply in the ordinary shops beyond the airport. The case contains an enthusiastic recognition of a context-specific implied duty of good faith.

In greater detail, in this case, (1) there had been an initial misrepresentation concerning the grantor's rights; and (2) after formation, International Trade Corp falsely indicated that non-airport prices had risen to a specified level (in fact, there had been no such an increase in the non-airport market prices).[28] This placed Yam Seng at an obvious disadvantage when selling these products at duty-free prices in the relevant airports. Yam Seng terminated the contract and sought damages (with respect to its wasted business expenses): (1) under section 2(1) of the Misrepresentation Act 1967 and (2) for breach of contract. Both claims (1) and (2) succeeded.[29]

---

26. *Ibid.*; for comment on the *MSC* case, Michael G. Bridge, *The Exercise of Contractual Discretion*, 135 L.Q.R. 227, 245-246 (2019).
27. [2013] EWHC 111 (QB), [2013] 1 All E.R. (Comm) 1321, [2013] 1 Lloyd's Rep. 526 (Leggatt J).
28. *Ibid.*, at [171].
29. *Ibid*, at [230].

Leggatt J said:[30]

> [131] Under English law a duty of good faith is implied by law as an incident of certain categories of contract, for example contracts of employment and contracts between partners or others whose relationship is characterised as a fiduciary one. I doubt that English law has reached the stage, however, where it is ready to recognise a requirement of good faith as a duty implied by law, even as a default rule, into all commercial contracts. Nevertheless, there seems to me to be no difficulty, following the established methodology of English law for the implication of terms in fact, in implying such a duty in any ordinary commercial contract based on the presumed intention of the parties.

On the special position of so-called relational contracts, Leggatt J said:

> [142] ... 'relational' contracts, as they are sometimes called, may require a high degree of communication, cooperation and predictable performance based on mutual trust and confidence and involve expectations of loyalty which are not legislated for in the express terms of the contract but are implicit in the parties' understanding and necessary to give business efficacy to the arrangements. Examples of such relational contracts might include some joint venture agreements,[31] franchise agreements and long-term distributorship agreements.

Leggatt J suggested that the content of the implied duty of good faith might encompass the following four aspects:

(1) *honesty:* '[135] an expectation of honesty', indeed '[137] ... it is hard to envisage any contract which would not reasonably be understood as requiring honesty in its performance';
(2) *avoidance of commercially unacceptable conduct:* '[138] ... conduct [which is] "improper", "commercially unacceptable" or "unconscionable";
(3) *promotion of the contract's values:* '[139] ... good faith [extends to] ... fidelity to the parties' bargain [namely the fact that] contracts can never be complete in the sense of expressly providing for every event that may happen ... [and so] the language must accordingly be given a reasonable construction which promotes the values and purposes expressed or implicit in the contract ...';
(4) *calculated silence or evasive answers:* '[141]...[Where initially accurate statements become falsified] it may be dishonest for A to keep silent and not to disclose the true position to B [or it may] be dishonest [to] deliberately avoid... giving an answer, or [to give] an answer which is evasive, in response to a request for information'.

§2.05 IDENTIFYING 'RELATIONAL CONTRACTS'

In *Bates v. Post Office Ltd (No 3: Common Issues)* (2019), Fraser J held that the contract between the Post Office and individual sub-postmasters is 'relational' and thus

30. *Ibid.*, at [131], [142], [143], [154], [230].
31. For example, *Al Nehayan v. Kent* [2018] EWHC (Comm) 333 (Leggatt LJ, trial judge).

involves a duty of good faith or fair dealing, on which basis a set of more specific implied terms of fact could be recognized.[32] Fraser J presented this list of *indicia*:[33]

> the following characteristics are relevant as to whether a contract is a relational one or not: 1. There must be no specific express terms in the contract that prevents a duty of good faith being implied into the contract. 2. The contract will be a long-term one, with the mutual intention of the parties being that there will be a long-term relationship. 3. The parties must intend that their respective roles be performed with integrity, and with fidelity to their bargain. 4. The parties will be committed to collaborating with one another in the performance of the contract. 5. The spirits and objectives of their venture may not be capable of being expressed exhaustively in a written contract. 6. They will each repose trust and confidence in one another, but of a different kind to that involved in fiduciary relationships. 7. The contract in question will involve a high degree of communication, co-operation and predictable performance based on mutual trust and confidence, and expectations of loyalty. 8. There may be a degree of significant investment by one party (or both) in the venture. This significant investment may be, in some cases, more accurately described as substantial financial commitment. 9. Exclusivity of the relationship may also be present.

John Kimbell QC, sitting in *Cathay Pacific Airways Ltd v. Lufthansa Technik AG* (2020),[34] provided this summary of the process of identifying relational contracts and their significance:

> [218] Whilst the law is clearly still in a state of development, I find that the present state of the law in this area can be summarised as follows:
>
> a. A term of good faith may be implied in a relational contract as a matter of law....
> b. The test for incorporation as a matter of law is whether the contract is a long-term contract which requires the parties to collaborate in future in ways that respects the spirit and the objectives of their joint venture but which the parties have not specified or have been unable to specify in detail. The contract will also involve trust and confidence that each party will act with integrity and co-operatively...
> c. A good faith term may be implied as a matter of fact in a relational contract but there is no special rule for incorporation in a relational contract. Each term must be considered against the usual test for implied terms...
> d. The main test of whether a term of good faith is to be implied in a contract is whether a reasonable reader of it would consider the term to be so obvious as to go without saying or the term is necessary for business efficacy...
> e. The overall character of the contract is an important consideration. In relation to this question the indicia in *Bates v Post Office Ltd (No 3: Common Issues)* [2019] EWHC 606 (QB), at [725] may be helpful
> f. The implication of a good faith term as a matter of fact is possible even in the case of long, complex and sophisticated contracts expressed in writing … .

32. [2019] EWHC 606 (QB) (Fraser J), citing, at [736], Hugh Collins, *Is A Relational Contract a Legal Concept?* in Simone Degeling, James Edelman, James Goudkamp (eds), *Contract in Commercial Law* (Thomson Reuters 2016), which had been earlier cited by Jackson LJ in *Amey Birmingham Highways Ltd v. Birmingham CC* [2018] EWCA Civ 264, at [92].
33. [2019] EWHC 606 (QB), at [725].
34. [2020] EWHC 1789, at [216].

§2.06 RECENT CASE LAW ON THE RELATIONAL CONTRACT: IMPLIED DUTY TO ACT IN GOOD FAITH

No breach of an implied term of good faith was found in the following case. In *Essex CC v. UBB Waste (Essex) Ltd* (2020),[35] Pepperall J held that a local authority, which was the claimant seeking a declaration, had been justified in terminating the twenty-five-year contract under which the defendant was required to provide waste disposal facilities. The defendant's facility did not meet environmental targets. The claimant authority owed a duty both under the relational contract analysis and in respect of its exercise of contractual discretion. But it had not acted wrongly in either respect. In the absence of any breach by the local authority, the only relevant constraint on the exercise of a right to terminate for breach is the ordinary law of affirmation of the contract (i.e., the innocent party's election not to terminate for serious breach), supplemented by the doctrine of estoppel.[36] This long judgment contains careful examination of implied terms in general,[37] including the exercise of options within a reasonable time,[38] *Braganza/Socimer* terms fettering exercises of contractual discretion,[39] and good faith with respect to relational contracts,[40] the law concerning declarations,[41] and the absence of a general implied term that a right of termination must be exercised promptly or in a reasonable time.[42]

No implied duty of good faith was found to be appropriate in the following case. In *Cathay Pacific Airways Ltd v. Lufthansa Technik AG* (2020),[43] the claimant airline had hired the defendant to maintain twenty-seven engines used in its fleet. The airline's claim, which was upheld by John Kimbell QC, was for monies contractually repayable following the claimant's withdrawal of certain engines from the agreement. Clause 21.2 gave the claimant the right to withdraw engines from that part of the agreement, which would generate enhanced revenue for the defendant (the 'Flight Hour Services Programme'). The claimant airline had exercised this right. The defendant unsuccessfully challenged this on the basis that this was contrary to the spirit of the agreement. It was held that: (i) clause 21.2 was clear and unfettered by any alleged mutual extrinsic understanding;[44] (ii) there was no scope to subject the option to a *Braganza/Socimer* implied term;[45] (iii) the agreement was not a relational contract, but an ordinary commercial agreement of long duration for the provision of services, and so an implied duty of good faith could not be inserted, whether by law or on the basis of fact.[46] He then summarized the law on this aspect.[47] No implied term in law or, in

35. [2020] EWHC 1581, *see* conclusion at [452].
36. *Ibid.*, at [414] to [419].
37. *Ibid.*, at [92] to [95].
38. *Ibid.*, at [337] to [343].
39. *Ibid.*, at [96] to [98].
40. *Ibid.*, at [99] to [117].
41. *Ibid.*, at [384] to [387].
42. *Ibid.*, at [400] to [413].
43. [2020] EWHC 1789.
44. *Ibid.*, at [121] to [124].
45. *Ibid.*, at [183].
46. *Ibid.*, at [241].

fact, was appropriate here.[48] Moreover, it would be 'incongruous' if the optionholder were required to consider the other side's financial position.[49]

An implied term of 'fair dealing' will apply within 'relational contracts' such as 'joint venture agreements, franchise agreements and long-term distributorship agreements'.[50] Chitty (2021) states that a 'relational contract' is a 'long-term' agreement which is 'very often cooperative' and involves 'a significant degree of flexibility'.[51] But Chitty (2021) also rightly states that a 'relational contract' is too imprecise a categorization to bear the weight of an imputation of an implied term of good faith and that the appropriate approach is to apply the ordinary criteria for the implication of a term implied in fact, based on necessity and obviousness.[52]

There might be a special need to construe a 'relational contract' so as to give effect to the intended long-term relationship, as noted by Butcher J in *Teesside Gas Transportation Ltd v. CATS North Sea Ltd* (2019),[53] citing *Globe Motors TRW Lucas Varity Electric Steering* (2016).[54] In the latter case, Beatson LJ examined case law indicating a tendency to construe such contracts so as to uphold them despite the fact that the transaction's terms might not be entirely pellucid.

When treating the terms of a relational contract, nit-picking interpretation is inappropriate because, as Jackson LJ said in *Amey Birmingham Highways Ltd v. Birmingham CC* (2018):[55]

> Any relational contract of this character is likely to be of massive length, containing many infelicities and oddities. Both parties should adopt a reasonable approach in accordance with what is obviously the long-term purpose of the contract. They should not be latching onto the infelicities and oddities, in order to disrupt the project and maximise their own gain.

§2.07 EXPRESS DUTY TO PERFORM IN GOOD FAITH

Such drafting has become quite common and has been analysed in the literature.[56]

In *Unwin v. Bond* (2020),[57] majority shareholders had committed a breach of contract by unjustifiably summarily terminating the claimant's employment and the

47. *Ibid.*, at [218].
48. *Ibid.*, at [219] to [221] (implied in law), [223] (implied in fact); and *see* the conclusion at [219].
49. *Ibid.*, at [240].
50. [2013] EWHC 111 (QB), [2013] 1 All E.R. (Comm) 1321, [2013] 1 Lloyd's Rep. 526, notably, at [141], [144], [147], and [154]; 'fair dealing' contrasted with the 'red flag' of 'good faith', at [150]; and on 'relational contracts' such as 'joint venture agreements, franchise agreements and long-term distributorship agreements', at [142].
51. Chitty (2021), para. 15-084, footnote 389; *see also* Mark Freedland (ed.), *The Contract of Employment* (Oxford University Press, 2016), Chapter 7, by Douglas Brodie, 'Relational Contracts'.
52. Chitty (2021), 2-091.
53. [2019] EWHC 1220 (Comm), at [38].
54. [2016] EWCA Civ 396, [2017] 1 All E.R. (Comm) 601, 168 Con. L.R. 59, [2016] 1 C.L.C. 712, at [64] to [68].
55. [2018] EWCA Civ 264, [2018] B.L.R. 225, at [93].
56. Chitty (2021), paras. 2-052 to 2-061.
57. [2020] EWHC 768 (Judge Klein).

associated shareholding interest which he had in the company. The claimant had then received the bare issue price of his minority shareholding interest. Expert evidence was received to calculate the probable negotiated selling price if there had not been a breach of the duty of good faith.[58] The judge said that an express duty of good faith comprised these 'minimum standards':[59]

> (i) they must act honestly; (ii) they must be faithful to the parties' agreed common purpose as derived from their agreement; (iii) they must not use their powers for an ulterior purpose; (iv) when acting they must deal fairly and openly with the claimant; (v) they can consider and take into account their own interests but they must also have regard to the claimant's interest.

Expanding on element (iv), he said:[60]

(a) 'the claimant is entitled to have fair warning of what the defendant proposes';
(b) the claimant is to be 'given an opportunity to put their case before the defendant makes the decision and the defendant is likely to be required to consider the claimant's case with an open mind';
(c) 'the fact that a defendant could have achieved the same result in a procedurally compliant way does not amount to a defence where the approach they adopt does not meet the minimum standards'.[61]

§2.08 IMPLIED TERM TO AVOID ARBITRARY EXERCISE OF CONTRACTUAL DISCRETION

This sub-topic is now a major focus of analysis in the courts.[62] The *Braganza* case (*see* below) is arguably the leading authority, but other judicial statements are important.

In *Paragon Finance plc v. Nash* (2001), the Court of Appeal found an implied term which required a lender to exercise an express power to vary the rate of interest payable by its customer without dishonesty, capriciousness or for an improper purpose.[63] This was not a requirement of simple reasonableness.[64] The court followed Mance LJ in *Gan Insurance Co Ltd v. Tai Ping Insurance Co Ltd (No 2)* (2001)[65] who, in the Court of Appeal, had implied a term that a reinsurer's discretion to approve a

58. *Ibid.*, at [312], the figure being an estimated 75% of the fair value of the shares.
59. *Ibid.*, at [230], after a review of the authorities, [215] to [229].
60. *Ibid.*, at [231].
61. *Ibid.*, at [232].
62. Chitty (2021), paras 2-066 to 2-079.
63. [2001] EWCA Civ 1466, [2002] 1 W.L.R. 685, at [36] to [42] (Dyson LJ); generally on this topic, Michael G. Bridge, *The Exercise of Contractual Discretion* 135 L.Q.R. 227 (2019); Richard Hooley, *Controlling Contractual Discretion* C.L.J. 65 (2013); Jonathan Morgan, *Resisting Judicial Review of Discretionary Contractual Powers*, L.M.C.L.Q. 484 (2015).
64. [2001] EWCA Civ 1466, [2002] 1 W.L.R. 685, at [37] to [42].
65. [2001] 2 All E.R. (Comm) 299 (CA) at [64] to [73]; noted, V. Sims and R. Goddard [2002] C.L.J. 269.

proposed settlement must not be wholly unreasonable or actuated by non-commercial considerations.

Rix LJ said in *Socimer International Bank Ltd v. Standard Bank London Ltd* (2008) that:[66]

> a decision-maker's discretion will be limited, as a matter of necessary implication, by concepts of honesty, good faith, and genuineness, and the need for the absence of arbitrariness, capriciousness, perversity and irrationality. The concern is that the discretion should not be abused ....

The Supreme Court in *Braganza v. BP Shipping Ltd* (2015) held that the exercise of a contractual discretion must be conducted genuinely and that the decision cannot be irrational.[67] Lord Hodge said:[68] 'the court is not entitled to substitute its own view of what is a reasonable decision for that of the person who is charged with making the decision; it [instead] conducts a rationality review'. In that case, Lord Hodge admitted that some decisions will defy 'intense scrutiny', where the issue is the allocation of enhanced rights without 'specific criteria' or 'established criteria'.[69] But in other contexts, objective criteria will illuminate the field of decision. Then, the court can determine whether the decision-maker referred to the right issues or to the wrong matters and whether the decision was extremely doubtful.

On the facts of the *Braganza* case, the Supreme Court held, by a 3-2 majority, that there had been a breach of the *Socimer/Braganza* implied term. Mrs Braganza claimed that her husband, while employed on the defendant's ship, had drowned in circumstances which entitled her to a death-in-service benefit. The employer's investigation led it to conclude that he had jumped from the ship. If so, suicide would not entitle her to this benefit. However, the majority (Baroness Hale and Lords Kerr and Hodge) held that the employer's decision was flawed. First, it noted that the employer bore the burden of proof because it was seeking to take advantage of an exception clause, that is, a provision which would deny the employee's widow a prima facie right to death-in-service benefits.[70] Second, the court held that the employer had not given enough weight to the inherent implausibility of suicide and that the employer had given excessive weight to factors which (in their opinion) did not constitute a strong enough basis for inferring suicide. In their dissents, Lords Neuberger and Wilson held

66. [2008] EWCA Civ 116, [2008] 1 Lloyd's Rep. 558, at [66]; on the *Socimer* case, *see* Richard Hooley, *Controlling Contractual Discretion*, C.L.J. 65, 68-69, 73, 76 (2013); *see also* Mary Arden, *Coming to Terms with Good Faith*, 30 JCL 199, 204-6 (2013); also Cooke J in *SNCB Holding v. UBS AG* [2012] EWHC 2044 (Comm), at [72] and [112] (avoidance of dishonesty).
67. [2015] UKSC 17, [2015] 1 W.L.R. 1661, [2015] ICR 449, at [18] to [32] (Baroness Hale); [52] to [60] (Lord Hodge); and [102] to [103] (Lord Neuberger); Jonathan Morgan, *Resisting Judicial Review of Discretionary Contractual Powers*, LMCLQ 484 (2015).
68. *Braganza* case, at [52].
69. *Ibid.*, at [57]; and *see* [52] to [56], citing cases concerning bonus arrangements, *Clark v. Nomura International plc* [2000] I.R.L.R. 766, at [40], an 'irrationality' test (Burton J); *Keen v Commerzbank AG* [2006] EWCA Civ 1536, [2007] I.C.R. 623, at [52], whether 'the Bank had exercised its discretion to award bonuses irrationally, arbitrarily or perversely' (Mummery LJ) and [110] (Moses LJ); noting *Horkulak v. Cantor Fitzgerald International* [2004] EWCA Civ 1287, *[2005] I.C.R. 402, at [47] (Potter LJ).*
70. [2015] UKSC 17, [2015] 1 W.L.R. 1661, [2015] ICR 449, at [14] (Baroness Hale).

that the factors indicating suicide were strong enough to justify the employer's decision.

It has become common for a party to plead both the *Braganza/Socimer* term and that the contract is 'relational' and so imports an implied duty to act in good faith. This is not surprising because there is an obvious overlap and similarity between these two implied terms. Examples of such double-barrelled pleading, but where, on the facts, neither a *Braganza/Socimer* implied term nor an implied duty of good faith was held to apply, are: *Cathay Pacific Airways Ltd v. Lufthansa Technik AG* (2020),[71] *TAQA Bratani Ltd v. Rockrose UKCS8 LLC* (2020),[72] and *Essex CC v. UBB Waste (Essex) Ltd* (2020).[73]

The Court of Appeal in *Equitas Insurance Ltd v. Municipal Mutual Insurance Ltd* (2019)[74] held that claims for reinsurance with respect to mesothelioma liability should be worked out by reference to the respective periods of exposure of employees to this hazard, having regard to the *Braganza* implied term.[75] Males LJ[76] and (inevitably) Leggatt LJ[77] perceived a link with the wider notion of 'good faith' (although Males LJ described this as merely a 'label').

The *Socimer/Braganza* term was also breached in *Watson v. Watchfinder.co.UK Ltd* (2017). Judge Waksman QC held that the grantor of an option had failed to satisfy the *Braganza* requirement and had instead made a peremptory and unacceptably unreasoned decision. This failure meant that there had been no exercise of discretion, with the result that the court would treat the option permission as having been granted.[78] Specific performance was granted with respect to the relevant private shares. The judge said:[79]

> there was hardly any real exercise of the discretion at all here but in any event in no way could it be described as in compliance with the Braganza Duty. There was no real discussion, it did not focus on the correct matters, it proceeded on a mistaken view of what it was about and it was arbitrary. I reach that conclusion taking full account of the fact that this was a decision of a private company and not a public authority.

71. [2020] EWHC 1789, at [183]; also noting at [169] to [173], that even if the *Braganza/Socimer* implied term is not applicable, a court might adopt a middle position, as in *Property Alliance Group Ltd v. Royal Bank of Scotland* [2018] EWCA Civ 355, [2018] 1 W.L.R. 3529, at [169], where a bank's right to call for a valuation, to be charged to the borrower, would need 'to be exercised in pursuit of legitimate commercial aims rather than, say, to vex PAG maliciously'.
72. [2020] EWHC 58 (Comm), [2020] 2 Lloyd's Rep. 64; 188 Con. L.R. 141, at [53] (Judge Pelling QC).
73. [2020] EWHC 1581, at [96] to [98] (Pepperall J).
74. [2019] EWCA Civ 718, [2020] Q.B. 418; Michael Bridge, *The Exercise of Contractual Discretion*, 135 L.Q.R. 227, 228 (2019).
75. *Ibid.*, at [114] (Males LJ).
76. *Ibid.*, at [116].
77. *Ibid.*, at [148] and [162].
78. *Ibid.*, at [126].
79. [2017] EWHC 1275 (Comm), [2017] Bus. Rep. 1309, at [124].

No *Braganza/Socimer* implied term was held to apply in *Cathay Pacific Airways Ltd v. Lufthansa Technik AG* (2020).[80] This case concerned an airline's decision to rely on an express term contained within a ten-year commercial aircraft maintenance contract. To save money, the airline withdrew certain engines from the agreement. It was held that this was justified. Nor did the *Braganza/Socimer* implied term apply in *TAQA Bratani Ltd v. Rockrose UKCS8 LLC* (2020).[81] This case concerned a North Sea gas operator's decision to terminate the contract. It was held that this implied term should not be imported wholesale into commercial relations.

In *Essex CC v. UBB Waste (Essex) Ltd* (2020),[82] it was held that the *Braganza/Socimer* term had not been breached. Essex had validly terminated the twenty-five-year contract for the provision by the defendant of waste disposal facilities because the defendant's facility had not met environmental targets, and the authority's decision was not flawed.

Similarly, no breach of the *Braganza/Socimer* implied term was found in *LBI EHF v. Raiffeisen Bank International AG* (2018).[83] The case concerned the process of valuation by the lender of securities provided by a borrower who had defaulted. The issue was whether the wide contractual wording permitted the lender, when conducting its valuation, to have regard to market prices, which reflected distress and financial difficulty suffered by other asset-holders. Finding in favour of the lender's construction of the document, the Court of Appeal, upholding Knowles J, held that (i) the wide wording was subject to the *Braganza/Socimer* implied term so that the lender's fixing of the price had to be conducted in a way which was rational and other than perverse; but (ii) there was no reason to import a requirement that the price-fixing should be made without regard to events which involved financial distress and difficulty, and to do so would be inconsistent with the contract's language. Flaux LJ said:

> [36] ... the starting point must be the definition [in the contract] of 'Net Value' in which the phrase 'fair market value' occurs. This clearly gives a wide discretion to the [lender to consider] 'such pricing sources and methods (which may include, without limitation, available prices for Securities with similar maturities, terms and credit characteristics as the relevant Equivalent Securities or Equivalent Margin Securities) as the non-Defaulting party considers appropriate ...' [38] In the absence of some express or implied limitation in the contract on the exercise of the discretion, as a matter of principle, the only limitation will be [the *Braganza/Socimer* implied term which requires] that the decision-maker must have acted rationally and not arbitrarily or perversely...[39] [The borrower's contention] that the assessment of 'fair market value' must be by reference to a price agreed between an unimpaired/willing buyer and an unimpaired/willing seller, neither being under any particular compulsion to trade, so that any illiquidity or distress in the market is to be left out of account, is not one which is to be found in the express terms of the [agreement]. Nor is there any basis for its implication, because it is contrary to the express language of the [agreement] and, in particular, the wide discretion conferred on the [lender].

80. [2020] EWHC 1789, at [183].
81. [2020] EWHC 58 (Comm), [2020] 2 Lloyd's Rep. 64; 188 Con LR 141, at [53] (Judge Pelling QC).
82. [2020] EWHC 1581, *ibid.*, at [96] to [98] (Pepperall J).
83. [2018] EWCA Civ 719, [2018] 2 B.C.L.C. 506.

O'Farrell J held in *Multiplex Construction Europe Ltd v. R&F One (UK) Ltd* (2019)[84] that the claimant contractor had been justified in suspending building works because of the defendant employer's breach. Under a settlement, the employer was required to provide security for GBP 15 million but had instead paid that sum into court. The judge noted that this did not swell the claimant's cash flow and that it constituted a breach by the employer. The issue was the validity of the contractor's response to that breach. It was held that the contractor's discretion whether to suspend works was subject to the *Braganza/Socimer* criteria of rationality and the absence of caprice, arbitrariness, or perversity. But those criteria had not been infringed. The contractor's decision to suspend the contract, applying those criteria, could not be characterized as irrational, capricious, or arbitrary.[85]

§2.09 CONCLUDING REMARKS

'Good faith' can be used to denote an organizing or overarching principle linking a miscellany of legal doctrines. In this sense, it is referred to as a doctrinal common thread. Or 'good faith' might refer to a generic implied duty to perform in good faith. That general duty has been denied in English law. It is considered unsafe to recognize such a general obligation. To do so would involve letting the Genie out of the bottle. There is no reason to think that the position will change and that English courts will adopt such a sweeping general requirement.

But it is in a sense uncontroversial that 'good faith' can be regarded as a doctrinal common thread, which is manifested in an array of doctrines and techniques designed to reflect objective notions of fair dealing. There is a long tradition of ethical sensitivity within the English case law. In this spirit, Sir Frederick Pollock (1881) spoke of the law of contract as the legal system's 'endeavour ... to establish a positive sanction for the expectation of good faith which has grown up in the mutual dealings of [men and women] of average right-mindedness'.[86]

It can be predicted that the *Braganza/Socimer* implied duty to exercise contract duties rationally and other than perversely will continue to become embedded as a feature of commercial adjudication. It is also likely that the category of 'relational contracts' will become better delineated, for it is here that the cutting-edge implied duty of good faith is active.

84. [2019] EWHC 3464 (TCC), notably at [28].
85. *Ibid.*, at [25] to [29].
86. Frederick Pollock, *Principles of Contract* (3rd edn, Stevens Publishing 1881), Preface at p. xx.

CHAPTER 3

Good Faith (or Violation Thereof) as a Negative Defence Against Claims or as a Positive Basis for Claims in International Arbitration

Céline Greenberg

§3.01 INTRODUCTION

The principle of good faith in the performance of a contract is embedded in many legal systems and all those belonging to the 'Civil law world'.

Its versatility, adaptability to an infinite number of circumstances and moral flavour have made it a popular fixture in both the parties' submissions to the arbitral tribunal as well as in the reasoning of international arbitral awards.

There is, however, a very unpopular aspect of the principle of good faith. Many are those who have said that reliance on the principle of good faith is a red flag of an empty case. This assumption appears even stronger among those with a Common law background.

This contribution does not purport to discuss in any detail the intricacies of the principle of good faith under various domestic laws. Instead, it presents the challenges that arise for arbitrators faced with submissions based on the good faith principle and proposes a methodology which aims to strike a balance between the various conflicting interests at play.

The first part of this contribution presents the starting point of the exercise, which is the provision of the applicable law on good faith and/or the contractual provision on good faith or the absence thereof.

The second part explores the question of whether the good faith principle may be applied in international arbitration irrespective of whether there is a good faith contractual provision or whether good faith forms part of the law applicable to the merits.

The third part deals with the pragmatic difficulties that arbitrators have to resolve when applying the principle of good faith and those that lead them to apply this principle as a fallback option when nothing else works better. The principle of good faith can indeed often present itself as a very versatile tool, such as a Swiss army knife, to cut through pragmatic challenges and reach the right outcome within a reasonable time, often through a unanimous decision.

Finally, the fourth part warns of the pitfalls to be avoided by arbitrators when relying on the principle of good faith in their reasoning.

§3.02 THE PRIME IMPORTANCE OF THE PROVISIONS OF THE CONTRACT AND OF THE APPLICABLE LAW

The availability of the principle of good faith for arbitrators should be approached first and foremost by analysing the provisions of the relevant contract and the law applicable to the merits.

Two broad scenarios should be distinguished. The first is when the contract is silent as to any obligations of good faith. The second is where the contract provides for a general duty of good faith in the performance of the contract.

[A] First Scenario: The Contract Is Silent as to Any Obligations of Good Faith

Where the contract does not require the parties to observe a general duty of good faith, the applicable law will normally determine whether a general principle of good faith applies nonetheless, as well as the extent of this duty and the consequences of any failure to comply.

In such a case, arbitrators should consider very carefully the exact content of the duty of good faith under the applicable law. Indeed, there are noticeable differences in domestic laws as to what the duty of good faith entails.

This is so even where the duty of good faith might be expressed in the same way in various domestic laws.[1] This is the case for most contract laws which derive from the

1. In Belgian law the principle of good faith is found in Arts 5.71 and 5.73 of the New Civil Code. Art. 5.73 provides as follows 'le contrat doit être executé de bonne foi' (unofficial translation: the contract must be performed in good faith). Art. 5.71 provides that 'le contrat oblige non seulement à ce qui y est convenu, mais encore à toutes les suites que la loi, la bonne foi ou les usages lui donnent d'après sa nature et sa portée' (Contracts bind not only to what is expressed in them, but also to all the consequences which equity, usage or the law give to the obligation according to its nature (unofficial translation)). This wording was identical to the French Civil Code provisions, until the reform of the French law of obligations in 2016. The new Art. 1104 of the French Civil Code provides as follows: 'Les contrats doivent être négociés, formés et executés de bonne foi'. (Contracts must be negotiated, formed and performed in good faith. This provision belongs to public policy' (unofficial translation)). In German law, the principle of good faith is contained in section 242 of the Bürgerliches Gesetzbuch (BGB), which provides that 'Der Schuldner ist

Napoleonic civil code. However, the duty of good faith has been interpreted and applied differently by the various domestic courts.

For example, the duty of good faith may or may not include the concept of changed circumstances/hardship or '*clausula rebus sic stantibus*', i.e., the obligation to renegotiate the contract when a change of circumstances renders its performance not impossible but more onerous for one party and authorizing the judge or arbitrator to modify or terminate the contract when attempts to renegotiate fail.

Whilst some domestic laws consider this principle to be an application of the general principle of good faith, others do not.

It is established in Swiss case law that when certain conditions are met, an obligation to renegotiate the contract arises from the duty of good faith.[2]

In German and French law, changed circumstances/hardships are codified in Article 313 of the German Civil Code and Article 1195 of the French Civil Code, respectively.[3]

By contrast, at the time, Belgian law did *not* accept that the general duty of good faith includes hardship.[4] Changed circumstances theory is now enshrined in the New Belgian Civil Code.[5]

Because of this diversity, applying the good faith principle should be approached very carefully, paying special attention to case law in order to understand the contours of the notion under the applicable law and refraining from assuming homogeneity in the notion, which is largely absent.

This will be especially challenging if the contract is governed by the *lex mercatoria*. Indeed, ascertaining the content of the *lex mercatoria* in any detail is

verpflichtet, die Leistung so zu bewirken, wie Treu und Glauben mit Rücksicht auf die Verkehrssitte es erfordern' (The debtor must perform in good faith, taking into account the customs of the trade (unofficial translation)).

2. Pascal Pichonnaz, *Impossibilité et Exorbitance. Étude analytique des obstacles à l'exécution des obligations en droit suisse (art. 119 CO et 79 CVIM)* (1997).
3. Article 313 of the German Civil Code provides as follows: 'Haben sich Umstände, die zur Grundlage des Vertrags geworden sind, nach Vertragsschluss schwerwiegend verändert und hätten die Parteien den Vertrag nicht oder mit anderem Inhalt geschlossen, wenn sie diese Veränderung vorausgesehen hätten, so kann Anpassung des Vertrags verlangt werden, soweit einem Teil unter Berücksichtigung aller Umstände des Einzelfalls, insbesondere der vertraglichen oder gesetzlichen Risikoverteilung, das Festhalten am unveränderten Vertrag nicht zugemutet werden kann.' (If circumstances which have become the basis of the contract have changed seriously after the conclusion of the contract and if the parties would not have concluded the contract or would have concluded it with different content if they had foreseen such change, adjustment of the contract may be demanded to the extent that one party cannot reasonably be expected to adhere to the unchanged contract, taking into account all circumstances of the individual case, in particular the contractual or statutory distribution of risk' (unofficial translation)); Art. 1195 of the French Civil Code similarly provides that: 'Si un changement de circonstances imprévisible lors de la conclusion du contrat rend l'exécution excessivement onéreuse pour une partie qui n'avait pas accepté d'en assumer le risque, celle-ci peut demander une renégociation du contrat à son cocontractant. Elle continue à exécuter ses obligations durant la renégociation.' (If a change in circumstances unforeseeable at the time of conclusion of the contract makes performance excessively onerous for a party who had not agreed to assume the risk, that party may request renegotiation of the contract from its co-contractor. It continues to perform its obligations during the renegotiation' (unofficial translation)).
4. G. Jannone, Belgian Private Law Knows No Default Hardship Provision, 2022.
5. Article 4.75 of the New Belgian Civil Code.

always tricky.[6] While there is a consensus that the *lex mercatoria* includes the general duty of good faith,[7] the diversity of understandings of the general duty of good faith in comparative law leaves an arbitral tribunal with a very large margin of appreciation as to what consequences to draw from it in a given case.

[B] Second Scenario: The Contract Contains a Good Faith Clause

In the absence of a contrary provision or relevant case law, nothing restricts the reliance on the principle of good faith as a positive and standalone basis for a claim or as a negative defence, just like any other contractual provision.

To appreciate the effects of the clause, it is helpful to consider how the good faith clause in the contract compares with its legal context.

If the applicable law to the contract does *not* contain a general duty of good faith, then it appears that the parties' intention at the time of contracting was to supplement the applicable law by *adding* obligations. This intention must be given effect by an arbitral tribunal in case of a dispute. A difficulty of interpretation may arise if the wording of the good faith clause is as vague as the applicable law. However, such problems of interpretation are the same as may arise with respect to any other substantive contractual provision.

When the applicable law *already* provides for a general duty of good faith, the arbitral tribunal should pay particular attention to the wording of the clause in order to verify whether it:

(i) simply restates obligations already arising from the applicable law; or
(ii) expands the obligations arising from the applicable law; or
(iii) seeks to reduce them. If the clause seeks to reduce or exclude the good faith obligations arising from the applicable law, a further question arises as to whether this exclusion is valid. This is not always the case, or it may only be valid to a limited extent. The UNIDROIT Principles of International Commercial Contracts 2016, for example, clearly state that it is not possible in Article 1.7:[8]
    (1) Each party must act in accordance with good faith and fair dealing in international trade.
    (2) The parties may not exclude or limit this duty.

In French law, the issue has received little interest because the Civil Code states that the requirement to perform a contract in good faith 'belongs to public policy' ('*cette*

6. E. Jolivet, La jurisprudence arbitrale de la CCI et la lex mercatoria, Gazette du Palais, n° 123 p. 36 (2001) ; Emmanuel Gaillard, Trente ans de Lex Mercatoria, (1995) 1 J.D.I. 5, 16.
7. G. Cuniberti, Three Theories of Lex Mercatoria, Columbia Journal of Transnational Law, Vol. 52, No. 1, p. 17 (2013).
8. Unidroit Principles official website: https://www.unidroit.org/instruments/commercial-contracts/unidroit-principles-2010/chapter-1/.

disposition est d'ordre public').[9] However, an author has analysed this question in detail and concluded that, although a general waiver of the whole duty of good faith would not be valid, an agreed limitation of certain sub-obligations derived from the general duty of good faith could be valid.[10]

The presence of a good faith clause in the contract will, in many cases, create very difficult conflicts between the different provisions of the same contract, with one party relying on a substantive provision and the other relying on the good faith clause to neutralize the substantive provision invoked by the other.

Such situations are very challenging. They create a tension between the effectiveness of a clear substantive provision and the duty of good faith, where both terms are equally subject to *pacta sunt servanda*. How should one resolve this conflict? It is impossible to give a general answer. Every case must be assessed on its merits; Good judgment and legal skills on the part of the arbitral tribunal will be key.

To put these theoretical considerations into perspective, it is helpful to consider a few practical examples.

A case drawn from the author's practice as counsel provides an appropriate illustration of the conflicts that may arise between substantive contractual provisions and a good faith clause. The dispute concerned a take-or-pay supply contract which was terminated by the supplier because of the buyer's failure to order the agreed quantities of a certain product. The supplier was seeking USD 700 million from the buyer on the basis of the take-or-pay provisions of the contract.

However, the buyer's failure to order or pay for the agreed quantity was due to a change of circumstances, which rendered the take-or-pay provision extremely onerous.

The contract was governed by Belgian law, which includes the CISG and a general duty of good faith in the performance of commercial contracts, clearly codified in Article 1134 of the Belgian Civil Code.

The contract further contained a very detailed good faith clause, which provided as follows:

> *Good faith*. In all matters affecting this Agreement, its interpretation and implementation, the Parties shall deal fairly with each other and act at all times in good faith. Good faith in this context includes, without limiting this duty, an obligation to cooperate, not to intentionally mislead, and to carry out this Agreement to the mutual benefit of both Parties, accepting that each is entitled to achieve its reasonable objectives. Purchaser undertakes not to disclose pricing information to third parties.

9. Article 1104 of the French Civil Code provides as follows: 'Les contrats doivent être formés et éxécutés de bonne foi. Cette disposition est d'ordre public' ('Contracts must be negotiated, formed and performed in good faith. This provision belongs to public policy' (unofficial translation)).
10. Yves-Marie Laithier, *L'obligation d'exécuter le contrat de bonne foi est-elle susceptible de clause contraire ? Réflexions comparatives*, D. 2014.33. As an example, M. Laithier considers that parties could agree on the limitation of their obligation of information, provided that such information is not mandatory under statutory law.

A party-appointed Belgian law expert analysed this clause as *expanding* the Belgian law duty of good faith. According to this expert, the Belgian law standard of good faith did not go as far as requiring the parties to 'carry out their obligations to the mutual benefit of both parties, accepting that each is entitled to achieve its reasonable objectives'. Giving effect to such a clause entailed looking carefully at whether the supplier's reliance on the take-or-pay provisions was, in light of the circumstances, compatible with these obligations.

Multiple arguments presented themselves to mitigate the harshness of the take-or-pay provisions in light of the circumstances, all of them being different variations of the principle of good faith:

- an argument based on the interpretation in good faith of the contract: the contract should be read as excluding the take-or-pay provisions in the circumstances;
- an argument based on changed circumstances/hardship derived from the good faith standard found in the applicable CISG;
- an argument based on analysing the take-or-pay provision as a penalty clause, which, under Belgian law, could be revised by the arbitral tribunal if the penalty turned out to be manifestly excessive – another application of good faith; and
- finally, the good faith clause was relied upon as a standalone basis to deny the other side the full benefit of the take-or-pay provisions.

The case settled, which can be read as an indication that the party relying on the interpretation of the clear substantive contractual provision realized that the arguments raised on the basis of the good faith principle had reasonable chances of success.

§3.03 MAY THE GOOD FAITH PRINCIPLE BE DEEMED APPLICABLE IRRESPECTIVE OF THE APPLICABLE LAW OR THE PROVISIONS OF THE CONTRACT?

Some authors argue that good faith constitutes one of the general principles of international commercial law.

The famous treatise of Professors Fouchard, Gaillard, and Goldman, which is now more than twenty years old, states that there are 'countless awards recognising the principle of good faith as a general principle of international commercial law'.[11]

11. Fouchard, Gaillard, Goldman on *International Commercial Arbitration* (Emmanuel Gaillard & John Savage eds, 1999), §1460. 'Illustrations of general principles of international commercial law found in arbitral case law naturally include rules with an extremely broad scope. This is the case of both the principle of the binding force of contracts, often expressed in arbitral awards as pacta sunt servanda, and the principle of good faith. There are now countless arbitral awards recognizing that both rules are general principles of international commercial law. In most cases, arbitrators simultaneously characterize the two rules as general principles.'

Another author has written that 'good faith is widely regarded as a general principle of law applicable in international trade and the standard is frequently applied in international commercial arbitration'.[12]

An experienced arbitrator has even suggested that arbitral tribunals quasi-systematically rely on the general principle of good faith:

> The fact that the principle of good faith appears in one form or another in the majority of arbitral awards is clear evidence of its importance in international arbitration; .... In many arbitration awards, the general principles of law and, specifically, of good faith, are not only guides, but rather the specific basis for the claims.
>
> ... the parties ... assume that [arbitrators will take] into consideration in their decision ... the general principle of law of good faith.[13]

This author's experience is different with respect to the frequency of the appearance of the concept of good faith in the reasoning of awards. However, the above citations confirm the importance of the principle of good faith in international arbitration practice and the need, therefore, for arbitrators to handle this principle with care and with due regard for the specific effects of the principle in each case, based on the contract and the applicable law.

§3.04 GOOD FAITH AS A 'SWISS ARMY KNIFE'

Apart from its importance in comparative law and its status as a general principle of international commercial law, there are other reasons why the general principle of good faith is so successful with arbitrators and so frequently relied on in the reasoning of their awards.

[A] Good Faith as a Fallback Option

In many cases, good faith is invoked in the arbitral tribunal's reasons for lack of a better option.

Indeed, arbitrators are often confronted with difficulties concerning the content or application of the applicable law to the merits. The general principle of good faith, if it is available in the contract or the applicable law, is a good way to resolve such difficulties.

These difficulties which are met by arbitrators in their application of the contract and /or the applicable law to the facts of a dispute can be sorted into three broad categories as follows:

---

12. Stefan Vogenauer, Commentary on the UNIDROIT Principles of International Commercial Contracts (2015) § 2-4, 165-166.
13. Bernardo M. Cremades, *Good Faith in International Arbitration*, 27 Am. U. Intl L. Rev. 761-788 (2012).

- situation 1: the parties' counsel have not framed their arguments in a way that makes the most sense to the arbitral tribunal; or
- situation 2: the evidence of the content of the applicable law before the arbitral tribunal is insufficient; or
- situation 3: the applicable law is simply insufficient to provide guidance to the arbitral tribunal because this law has not addressed the question at hand or has only addressed it insufficiently. There is just no answer to the question in the applicable law that the arbitral tribunal can discern. This is especially difficult when the applicable law is foreign to some or all members of the tribunal. What should happen in such a case?

In all three types of situations, reliance on a general principle of good faith, which is common to many legal systems, accepted as a general principle of international commercial law, and generally accepted as forming part of *lex mercatoria*, is very helpful.

This general principle of good faith enables the arbitral tribunal to fill in the gaps in the applicable law, or in its knowledge of the applicable law, or in the parties' submissions, and to provide reasons for the outcome that it considers to be the legally and/or morally correct, but is otherwise difficult to justify.

Another important practical consideration that helps understand arbitral tribunals' reliance on the principle of good faith relates to the way in which deliberations are conducted. It can happen that the deliberation process is protracted over time or takes place quite some time after the hearing, especially where the arbitral tribunal is composed of three busy arbitrators in different time zones, and for various reasons, deliberations could not be completed until several weeks, maybe months after the hearing or the last submissions from the parties.

In such cases, it may happen that, during the deliberations, the arbitral tribunal finds itself short with respect to the evidence of the applicable law or discovers a loophole in the arguments made by the parties .... The arbitral tribunal might then be uncomfortable reopening the debate at a late stage to ask questions, request further elements, etc. What should happen in such a case? The parties expect the award, not a reopening of the debate with yet more exchanges of submissions and evidence. The arbitral tribunal has few options, and the most appealing one is often to make do with what has been brought before it. In many cases, the good faith principle will appear somewhere and provide a flexible basis to reach the legal and commercial outcome that the arbitral tribunal considers to be correct.

Admittedly, in such cases, reliance on good faith is – strictly speaking – not very satisfactory from a purely legal standpoint. However, this approach enables the arbitral tribunal to overcome obstacles and challenges in order to reach the agreed outcome in deliberations.

In addition, the tribunal may sometimes rely on good faith in cases where there is no real consensus on the reasoning to reach that outcome. This is not rare, and when it does occur, it does not always justify separate opinions from each arbitrator. The award needs to be acceptable to all three arbitrators despite their differences of opinion on the correct legal reasoning.

In the real world, when the various options are well considered, the recourse to the good faith principle might just be the least unsatisfactory option, enabling the issuance of a unanimous award within a reasonable time to the parties, offering an adequate, definitive resolution of the dispute in terms of outcome, which is, in fact, the most important for the parties.

[B] What to Do When the General Duty of Good Faith Is Not Available to the Arbitral Tribunal but Is Necessary to Achieve the Right Outcome?

Sometimes, neither the law nor the contract contains any general principle of good faith, and the application of the law or the contract gives rise to an outcome which the arbitral tribunal considers inadequate, even unjust - for example because one party who is deemed to be manifestly in bad faith receives a benefit at the expense of the other party, who is manifestly in good faith, and who is unjustly prejudiced.

What should happen in such a case?

If the arbitral tribunal has not been granted the power to act *ex aequo et bono*, in theory, the arbitral tribunal's hands are tied. However, some arbitrators might be tempted to cheat and reintroduce good faith in a disguised way.

A leading international arbitrator provides his own view on this question:[14]

> *the arbitrator must not cheat with the law*, and if the provisions of the contract are clear, he or she must apply them.

He goes on to mention an interesting example:

> the arbitrator sometimes finds a way to avoid the catastrophic result to which a strict application of the contract would lead. I remember a case in which the contract had been drafted in such a way that, by insisting on its literal interpretation, which, unfortunately was clear, one party could cause not only the ruin of the other party, but also that of a whole sector of the industry, in the most unfair way. *No rule of law could have prevented this result. But the tribunal managed to convince the parties to settle the dispute, and the disaster was thus avoided.*

The good faith principle may help to avoid these situations when it is available. However, if it is not available - an arbitral tribunal should not cheat with the law, or with due process, and instead should find other clever ways to avoid an injustice.

§3.05 THE PITFALLS

As it transpires from the above, the application of the general principle of good faith by international arbitrators raises many challenges. Arbitrators should be aware of the potential pitfalls in order to avoid them.

14. Pierre Mayer, *Must Justice Be a Goal for the Arbitrator?*, 37 Arb. Intl 503-513 (2021) DOI: 10.1093/arbint/aiab020.

[A] First Risk: Arbitrariness

The flexibility of the principle of good faith, which causes its attraction, is a slippery slope.

There is a fine line between applying good faith in accordance with the applicable law or the contract and, as a consequence, deciding not to apply a substantive provision in accordance with its letter and deciding the dispute based on one's understanding of the equities, in breach of the arbitral tribunal's mandate to decide the dispute in law.

Arbitrators should be conscious of the risk of falling on the side of arbitrariness and should, therefore, include detailed reasoning in their award, with sufficient references to factual and legal evidence to support their findings. Being demanding with oneself and with other members of the arbitral tribunal in terms of legal and factual reasoning is usually sufficient to avoid arbitrariness.

[B] Second Risk: Sloppiness

For those parties who read through the entire award, many of them the losing party, it is enraging to lose a case based on an application of the good faith principle. In most cases, the outcome will be felt to be subjective or even arbitrary, especially if the reasons given in the award are insufficient and come across as being mostly based on the arbitral tribunal's own sense of justice, which is merely dressed up as being based in law through an artefact (i.e., the application of the general principle of good faith).

The losing party needs to be convinced that the outcome is correct in law. Indeed, in many cases, this party thought that it had a good arguable case in law. This is often why the arbitration proceeded to the end without a settlement.

Reliance on good faith to reach a desired outcome can be a convenient way to reason for the arbitral tribunal for the reasons set out above, but a good arbitral tribunal will always consider whether this is sufficient to ensure that its award will be well accepted so that it is complied with voluntarily by the losing party. After all, this is the desired outcome of every arbitration, and arbitrators should not lose sight of this objective. The case does not stop after the issuance of the award for the parties to the dispute, as it does for the arbitrators. A sloppy or inadequate reliance on good faith can defeat the effective resolution of the dispute.

The risk is real.

For example, in the ICSID case of *Klöckner v. Cameroon*, the award was found in favour of the Republic of Cameroon on the basis of the principle of 'the duty of full disclosure to a partner' (an emanation of the good faith principle) was annulled in 1985 by an ad hoc Committee on the grounds that it was not legitimate to exclusively apply general principles of law. [15]

15. *Klöckner Industrie-Anlagen GmbH and others v. United Republic of Cameroon and Société Camerounaise des Engrais*, ICSID Case No. ARB/81/2, Decision of the ad hoc Committee dated 3 May 1985.

§3.06 CONCLUSION

The sloppiness or arbitrariness that characterizes certain awards or parties' submissions should not distract from the fact that the general principle of good faith is a valid legal rule recognized in many legal systems and a popular provision in international commercial contracts. In many cases, it can validly form a standalone basis for a claim or defence.

For this reason, it is unfair to label the appearance of the general principle of good faith as a red flag of an empty case. In fact, this suggestion verges on patronizing counsel and demonstrates bias – perhaps even an issue conflict – which should always be avoided when acting as arbitrator.

The general principle of good faith is a useful tool for parties and arbitrators, which, if applied correctly with the right methodology, enables international arbitrators to reach adequate outcomes in international commercial disputes. It should be described and applied as such.

CHAPTER 4

Good Faith as an Instrument of Treaty Interpretation: Instructions for Use

Andrea Bianchi[*]

§4.01 IS GOOD FAITH LIKE LOHENGRIN?

A German legend has it that Lohengrin, Percival's son and knight of the Holy Grail, was sent to help Princess Elsa, the King of Brabant's daughter, in distress after the death of her father. Challenged to her claim to the throne by the wicked Count Telramund, Elsa finds herself in mortal danger. Luckily, Lohengrin comes to her rescue on a boat drawn by a swan and defeats Elsa's enemy. Elsa and Lohengrin fall in love, get married and have two children together. Lohengrin, however, reminds Elsa that she could never ask where he comes from, as he had made a vow to his order of knighthood to forever guard this secret. After some time, Elsa can no longer resist her own curiosity about her husband's past, and she fatally asks him the question, which causes Lohengrin to return to the Castle of the Holy Grail, never to return.

Later popularized by Richard Wagner's opera,[1] the saga of Lohengrin has become part and parcel of popular culture nowadays.[2] Widely represented in works of art and even cited in legal writings,[3] Lohengrin has come to acquire a mythical aura. He stands for justice, protection of higher values and loyalty to one's vows to the detriment of their personal well-being. But Lohengrin is also about mystery and the risk that the revelation of one's past may lead to their future demise. When the fatal question is asked of him, 'where do you come from?', Lohengrin gets on his swan-drawn boat to

* The author gratefully acknowledges Ms Zelin Li's valuable research assistance.

1. *See Wagner's Lohengrin Opera Study Guide and Libretto* (Opera Classics Library 2017).
2. Scenes from the Lohengrin saga are famously represented in the murals of Schloss Neuschwanstein in Southern Bavaria, Germany.
3. Andrea Bianchi, 'International Law and US Courts: The Myth of Lohengrin Revisited' 15 *European Journal of International Law* 751 (2004) DOI: 10.1093/ejil/15.4.751.

disappear forever. Lohengrin's elusive character and his mysterious origin do not take anything away from his powerful intervention in the affairs of the Kingdom of Brabant or from his love for Elsa, for that matter. It is just that one should not have indulged their curiosity and asked whence he came from.

Overall, the myth of Lohengrin attests to the elusive nature of good, justice, love and beauty. When one tries to know more about them, their magic may disappear at once, either literally – as in Lohengrin's case – or metaphorically. The analogy about Lohengrin and good faith in treaty interpretation naturally sprang to my mind. Also, good faith is invoked in treaty interpretation to bring about fairness and justice, avoid unreasonable and bad-faith interpretations, and protect and safeguard not just individual claims but also the legitimate expectations of the community and the international legal order. Good faith is an extremely important element in treaty interpretation that may cause the interpretive balance to tilt in one or another direction by the very power of its prestige and the perception of fairness its application inevitably entails. Yet, good faith remains rather mysterious. Legal scholars have tried to shed light on its origins and normative status. As we shall see below, opinions diverge a great deal in this respect.[4]

In many ways, good faith is just as elusive as Lohengrin. Bin Cheng famously stated that good faith eludes any *a priori* definition.[5] While its use can be illustrated by examples, its quintessential nature does indeed escape precise definition. Like most analogies, however, the one on Lohengrin and good faith has its limits. If the aura of mystery about the origins of the German legend's mythical figure must be preserved at all costs, I do not see any good reason why one should not inquire afresh what the origins and functions of the principle of good faith in treaty interpretation are. If Elsa, in Act III of Wagner's opera, faints lifeless at Lohengrin's disappearance, I believe that we all can survive knowing more about our object of investigation and, possibly, learn how to make better use of such an important tool of treaty interpretation. And to this, I will now turn.

§4.02 GOOD FAITH AS A TRAVELLING CONCEPT

In any discipline, concepts are ways of apprehending reality, the tools its members use to understand the world. They are intellectual constructs that allow for the drawing of boundaries, for classifying, orientating and creating meaning. We use concepts as categories to fit the realities surrounding us, to account for and justify them or, if need be, to contest them and advocate change. Despite their inherent vocation for bringing order by way of theoretical abstraction and systematization, concepts may be volatile. Despite the fixity and boundedness that disciplines tend to attach to them, oftentimes,

4. *See infra*, §4.05 and §4.06.
5. Bin Cheng, *General Principles of Law as Applied by International Courts and Tribunals* (Stevens 1953; reprint Cambridge University Press 1987): 'What exactly this principle (*ie good faith, editor's note*) implies is difficult to define. As an English judge once said, such rudimentary terms applicable to human conduct as "Good Faith", "Honesty", or "Malice" elude a priori definition.' (105, FN omitted)

the contours of concepts can be porous. Furthermore, concepts may travel across disciplines and adjust to different cultures and scientific paradigms. A journey almost inevitably changes the traveller, and it should not come as a surprise that this is also the case with concepts. Once they are used in contexts different from that for which they were originally designed and meant to operate, concepts may take up different connotations and discharge different functions.[6]

A good example of such versatility is the concept of good faith. Despite its legal origins being rooted in the Roman law concept of bona fides and, therefore, well known to domestic lawyers and international ones alike, the use of the concept of good faith is widespread. It cuts across different domains of life, and it presents social, legal and moral underpinnings. Good faith is expected not only of the negotiators of international agreements and of those who have to execute contractual arrangements but also of the local car dealer trying to sell you a second-hand car as well as of your fellow players in a round of poker. Or, should you be the purchaser of a valuable piece of art, good faith may be asked of you if, one day, that very same masterpiece were to be identified as a stolen one. We all believe that we have an intuitive understanding of what good faith is, but when it comes to defining its exact contours, the image gets blurred.[7]

It is quite telling that a shake of hands is the image most often associated with good faith. The image stands for mutual respect, honesty of purpose and fairness in social intercourse. Good faith is thus not merely correlated with the contract law requirement of 'good faith and fair dealing'. It is a concept that exists independently of its legal undertones. It relates to the observance of socio-legal-moral standards that set the boundaries of acceptable behaviour in any given community. Occasionally, good faith is invoked and relied upon as a synonym with, or at least as a proxy for, justice. Hence its occasional visual representation as the hammer of justice. Be that as it may, good faith is the natural antidote against any malicious or fraudulent intent. Surreptitious or self-serving behaviour and violation of fundamental standards of decency cannot withstand scrutiny against this background. Whether defined by the lawmaker, shaped up by the case law, or dictated by social or moral standards, good faith rules them all out.

§4.03 LEGAL VALIDATION: TRANSLATING CONCEPTS INTO PRINCIPLES

To determine the legal status of the concept of 'good faith' is no easy task. Particularly if one takes the traditional doctrine of the sources of international law, there is hardly any room for finding a suitable categorization. Yet, the concept of 'good faith' exists as

6. The importance of concepts in the discipline of international law has been recently foregrounded in Jean d'Aspremont & Sahib Singh (eds), *Concepts for International Law – Contributions to Disciplinary Thought* (Edward Elgar 2019).
7. The same applies to philosophical inquiries about Sartre's understanding of this term. *See* Ronald E. Santoni, *Bad Faith, Good Faith and Authenticity in Sartre's Early Philosophy* (Temple University Press 1995).

a concept on its own, as a mental representation based on the practical experience and emotional intuition of social relations. What is often overlooked in legal scholarship is that such normative concepts may exert an enormous influence on international legal processes regardless of their formal legal status. These concepts usually get 'translated' into the language of law by the term 'principles', not so much according to the meaning of 'general principles of law' in Article 38(1)(c) of the Statute of the International Court of Justice, but rather in the sense of normative prescriptions of a general character.[8]

Often relegated to the realm of irrelevance in traditional positivistic thinking, notoriously averse to what is somewhat arbitrarily defined as 'extra-legal considerations',[9] these normative concepts can only come into existence in our lawyerly world when they are translated into accepted legal categories. Unless something is expressed in a form that is couched in legal terms, it has a slim chance of being accepted within the discipline. Hence, the need to qualify as 'principles' those concepts that would otherwise have no standing in the world of legal imagery and representation.

International legal scholarship remains circumspect about investigating normativity beyond the traditional discourse on the doctrine of sources.[10] Truth be told, however, the idea of the existence of concepts and/or values that find their roots in the societal body and contemporary culture is not novel. Suffice it to mention Roberto Ago's notion of meta-legal principles of a general nature that would shape the content, interpretation and enforcement of international legal rules,[11] a notion that has been later taken up and expanded upon by Antonio Cassese.[12] Vaughan Lowe, in turn, has highlighted the existence of 'interstitial norms', which would operate in the interstices of primary rules in order to ensure that the legal system conforms with the contemporary ethos.[13] Lowe's theory has the merit of departing from the traditional doctrine of sources by providing new insights that clearly point to an increasing normative modularity in international law.[14] It would be a naivety of sorts to maintain that

8. I expressed analogous considerations about the concept of transparency in my essay 'On Power and Illusion: The Concept of Transparency in International Law', in Andrea Bianchi & Anne Peters (eds), *Transparency in International Law* (CUP 2013), 1-19, 6-7.
9. Judge Spender and Judge Fitzmaurice refer to 'considerations of a non-juridical character' in: ICJ, *South West Africa Case (Liberia and Ethiopia v. South Africa)*, Preliminary Objections, Judgment of 21 December 1962, ICJ Reports 1963, 319 (Joint Dissenting Opinion of Judge Spender and Fitzmaurice), 466. On how to distinguish 'non-legal' approaches from the so-called traditional methodology, *see*: Olivier Corten, *Méthodologie du droit international public*, UBlire Références, 8 (Brussels: Edition de l'Université de Bruxelles, 2009).
10. For an interesting exception, *see*: Joost Pauwelyn et al. (eds), *Informal International Lawmaking* (OUP 2012).
11. Roberto Ago, *Lezioni di diritto internazionale* (Milano, 1943), 65.
12. Antonio Cassese, *Diritto internazionale* (a cura di Paola Gaeta) (Il Mulino, 2006), 271-272; and even more specifically: *Diritto internazionale* (a cura di Paola Gaeta) (Il Mulino, 2003), 61. In English *see* Antonio Cassese, *International Law*, 2nd ed. (OUP, 2005), 46; and Paola Gaeta, Jorge Viñuales and Salvatore Zappalà, *Cassese's International Law*, 3rd ed. (OUP 2020), 45.
13. Vaughan Lowe, 'The Politics of Law-Making: Are the Method and Character of Norm Creation Changing?', in Michael Byers (ed.), *The Role of Law in International Politics: Essays in International Relations and International Law* (OUP 2000), 207-226.
14. Andrea Bianchi, 'Principi di diritto, modularità funzionale e relatività normativa: il concetto di precauzione nel diritto internazionale', in Andrea Bianchi/Marco Gestri (eds), *Il principio precauzionale nel diritto internazionale e comunitario* (Giuffrè, 2006), 429-459.

contemporary international law only accommodates in its normative structure binding and directly enforceable rules.[15] Some normative prescriptions accomplish different tasks in specific areas; others perform a more systemic role.[16] In many ways, these concepts or norms - almost invariably couched in terms of principles - operate as permanent connectors between law and societal realities.[17] They direct normative processes and the interpretation of legal prescriptions. Their legal relevance is self-evident, their exact qualification less so.

§4.04 ZEROING IN ON THE TARGET

Luckily, the task undertaken in this paper is less daunting than providing an overall view of the scope of the principle of 'good faith' in international law. The aim of the inquiry is to explore the role and function of 'good faith' as a principle of treaty interpretation. For once, there is hardly any controversy about good faith being an integral part of the general rule of interpretation laid down in Article 31(1) of the Vienna Convention on the Law of Treaties (VCLT). The proviso is nearly universally regarded as declaratory of customary international law, and practically no judgment, scholarly article, legal brief, or expert report on treaty interpretation would call this into question.

As is well known, good faith appears in Article 31 of the VCLT alongside ordinary meaning, context, and object and purpose as part of the composite test laid down as the general rule for the interpretation of treaties.[18] The main rule of Article 31(1) is often presented as a 'crucible' that requires a process of interpretation, in which due heed must be paid to the different criteria contained therein. Despite the apparent absence of a formal hierarchy, however, the rule accords some pre-eminence to the 'ordinary meaning of the terms', often referred to as 'plain meaning'. The International Court of Justice (ICJ) in *Libya v. Chad* clearly stated, after quoting the text of Article 31 of the

15. *See* the conservative approach of the International Law Commission (ILC) which is currently studying general principles, focussing on principles derived from national legal systems and principles formed within the international legal system and inductively inferred from conventional and customary rules (*see* the three reports prepared by Special Rapporteur Marcelo Vázquez-Bermúdez (1st report (UN Doc. A/CN.4/732, 5 April 2019); 2nd report (UN Doc. A/N.4/741, 9 April 2020); 3rd report (UN Doc. A/CN.4/753, 18 April 2022)), and the *Text and titles of draft conclusions 1,2 and 4* provisionally adopted by the Drafting Committee on 28 July 2021 (UN Doc. A/CN.4/L.955). The ILC Secretariat prepared a useful memorandum on general principles of law as background for the work of the Commission (*see* UN Doc. A/CN.4/742, 12 May 2020).
16. For Ulf Linderfalk, for example, the principle of good faith would ensure the consistency of the international legal system: *see* 'What Are the Functions of the General Principles? Good Faith and International Legal Pragmatics', 78 ZaöRV 1-31 (2018).
17. Lowe, 'The Politics of Law-Making', *supra* n. 13, 221: 'Interstitial norms are the points where general culture obtrudes most clearly into the processes of legal reasoning.'
18. Article 31 of the VCLT reads: 'A treaty shall be interpreted in good faith in accordance with the ordinary meaning to be given to the terms of the treaty in their context and in the light of its object and purpose.'

VCLT, that 'interpretation must be based above all upon the text of the treaty'.[19] This principle, deeply rooted in international case law well before the 1969 VCLT,[20] is shared by most commentators who stress that ordinary meaning is the 'starting point' for any interpretive process in international law, generally,[21] and, more particularly, in international investment law.[22] The predominance of the 'ordinary meaning of the terms' was also justified, not on grounds of any formal hierarchy, but rather on considerations of logic, by the International Law Commission (ILC) in its Commentary to then Article 27 of its draft articles (to become Article 31 of the Vienna Convention).[23]

Integrated into the general rule of Article 31, the principle of good faith is not a stand-alone criterion for the interpretation of treaties. It is rather a principle of general applicability that should inspire and guide the interpreter throughout the process of interpretation.[24] As argued by Dörr, '[a]lthough it is difficult to give precise content to the concept in general, the bottom line of it appears to be a fundamental requirement of reasonableness qualifying the dogmatism that can result from purely verbal or, for that purpose, excessively teleological analysis'.[25] While plenty of scholarly writings exist on the other criteria of Article 31, good faith remains often in the background. Maybe this is because – as the tribunal put it in *Vivendi* – 'the first criterion of Article 31 "good faith" requires no further explanation'.[26] But, does it really not?

§4.05 HETEROGENEITY OF CASE LAW AND SCHOLARLY OPINION

A cursory overview of contemporary scholarship clearly attests to the heterogeneity of views about the definition and scope of the principle of good faith in treaty

---

19. *Case Concerning the Territorial Dispute* (*Libyan Arab Jamahiriya v. Chad*), Judgment, 3 February 1994, ICJ Reports 1994, 6; § 41.
20. *Competence of the General Assembly for the Admission of a State to the United Nations*, Advisory Opinion, 3 March 1950, ICJ Reports 1950, 4, 8.
21. Oliver Dörr & Kirsten Schmalenbach (eds), *Vienna Convention on the Law of Treaties. A Commentary*, 2nd ed. (Springer Verlag 2018), 580; Mark E. Villiger, *Commentary on the 1969 Vienna Convention on the Law of Treaties* (Nijhoff 2009), 435. On the issue of how 'textualism' came to impose itself as the prevailing approach to interpretation in international law *see* Fuad Zarbiyev, 'A Genealogy of Textualism in Treaty Interpretation', in Andrea Bianchi, Daniel Peat & Matthew Windsor (eds), *Interpretation in International Law* (OUP 2015), 251.
22. August Reinisch, 'The Interpretation of International Investment Agreements', in Marc Bungenberg, Jörn Griebel, Stephan Hobe & August Reinisch (eds), *International Investment Law – A Handbook* (C.H. BECK/Hart/Nomos 2015), 372, 378; Tarcisio Gazzini, *Interpretation of International Investment Treaties* (Hart 2016), 79; Robert Kolb, *The Law of Treaties – An Introduction* (Edward Elgar 2016), 136.
23. ILC *Yearbook*, vol. II, 1966, 220.
24. Ulf Linderfalk, *On the Interpretation of Treaties. The Modern International Law as Expressed in the 1969 Vienna Convention on the law of Treaties* (Springer 2010), 44-45: 'this principle of good faith is a norm that guides the entire interpretation process. Consequently, the principle should be seen to influence not only the contents of the rules of interpretation. They should also be seen to play a part *above and beyond these rules*'(emphasis in the original).
25. Oliver Dörr, 'General Rule of Interpretation', in Oliver, Dörr & Kirsten Schmalenbach (eds), *Vienna Convention on the Law of Treaties: A Commentary*, *supra* n. 21, 559, 587-588 (emphasis in the original). *See also* Richard Gardiner, *Treaty Interpretation*, 2nd ed. (OUP 2015), 171, 176.
26. *Compañía de Aguas del Aconquija S.A. and Vivendi Universal S.A. v. Argentine Republic*, Case No. ARB/97/3, Award, 20 August 2007, § 7.4.3.

interpretation. The recent monograph by Emily Sipiorski, by far the most thorough and systematic study on the topic in recent scholarship, well illustrates the multiple functions performed by the principle of good faith in the field of treaty interpretation.[27] According to Sipiorski, at the interpretive level, the principle of good faith can be used to fill a gap in the language of treaties, legitimize decisions and connect investment arbitration to the private and public dimensions of the law as well as to the domestic and international normative levels.[28] Finally, good faith would also have a correcting function by displaying its moral and ethical underpinnings when 'acting as an unwritten, all-informing remedy to prevent unfair and unjust results'.[29] Not unlike Bin Cheng,[30] Sipiorski underscores that the principle of good faith 'acts as a natural moral barometer – a principle that cannot be applied independently but adds moral strength to the other express obligations'.[31]

Despite the difficulty of defining with accuracy the concept of good faith as it applies to treaty interpretation and to international investment arbitration, more specifically, the principle of good faith guarantees the overall consistency of the investment arbitration regime by maintaining 'the integrity and functionality of the system of dispute resolution'.[32] According to Sipiorski, while necessary to preserve the 'integrity and purpose of the system of international investment arbitration', the principle of good faith's 'results are best when its use is not detected'.[33] The principle helps interpret the law 'not only correctly but also justly'.[34] It is the responsibility of arbitrators to make sure that a treaty text is understood justly and that the act of interpretation is carried out in a fair manner.[35]

To De Brabandere and Van Damme, good faith is a '[m]eta-norm underlying all forms and methods of treaty interpretation and their use in practice'.[36] Acknowledging that it is not common to find explanations about how the principle of good faith operates in treaty interpretation, they say that it is indeed difficult 'to identify a stand-alone application of good faith in treaty interpretation'.[37] It is rather used to justify the use of other principles not expressly mentioned in the VCLT, such as the principle of effectiveness, or to give priority to some interpretive criteria over others.[38] Interestingly, the principle of good faith is also identified as a tool to limit the discretion

27. Emily Sipiorski, *Good Faith in International Investment Arbitration* (OUP 2019).
28. *Ibid.*, 13-15.
29. *Ibid.*, 15.
30. Bin Cheng, *General Principles of Law, supra* n. 5, 118.
31. Sipiorski, *Good Faith in International Investment Arbitration, supra* n. 27, 14.
32. *Ibid.*, 237.
33. *Ibid.*, 238.
34. Emily Sipiorski, 'Interpretation in Good Faith and Its Relevance in International Investment Arbitration: Addition to Justice or Ensuring Justice?', 23 *International Community Law Review* 57-78 (2021), 78 DOI: 10.1163/18719732-12341458.
35. *Ibid.*, 65.
36. Eric De Brabandere & Isabelle Van Damme, 'Good Faith in Treaty Interpretation', in Andrew D. Mitchell, Muthucumuraswamy Sornarajah & Tania Voon, *Good Faith in International Law* 37-59 (OUP 2015), 43.
37. *Ibid.*, 43.
38. *Ibid.*, 42 ff.

of judicial and quasi-judicial bodies in interpreting treaty provisions.[39] In this respect, the principle can be qualified as 'a general standard of behaviour for the interpreter, requiring the latter to act reasonably and properly'.[40]

According to Robert Kolb, good faith has mainly a double role in the interpretation of treaties.[41] On the one hand, good faith sanctions the primacy of the spirit of the treaty over an excessive reliance on its wording. This function is primarily aimed at avoiding interpretations that are absurd, or that would be made in bad faith. On the other hand, the principle of good faith can be identified with the search for a reasonable interpretation, meant as an interpretation that an honest and reasonable party would make of the mutually agreed upon text. In this respect, the principle of good faith would be a means to ensure respect for the legitimate expectations of the parties.[42] O'Connor argues instead that the principle of good faith would only become relevant when the plain meaning approach to interpretation fails, at which point 'the essence of good faith comes to the fore. The "spirit" of the Treaty which requires the Tribunal to have regard to honesty, fairness and reasonableness, takes precedence over the incomplete or ambiguous words which have failed to yield a "plain meaning"'.[43]

The extreme variety of scholarly opinions does not seem to stem from academic elucubrations or fancy theories. In fact, it reflects the diversity of international case law and arbitration practice. The over sixty cases referring to good faith in treaty interpretation, which I collected and read to write this essay, are difficult to cluster and classify. As De Brabandere and Van Damme aptly noted, 'even if it is possible to catalogue some of the tools, principles and values that are accepted in a good faith interpretation, their purpose and appeal often depend on a range of contextual elements'.[44] These factors make it difficult to theorize in general terms about the use of interpretive criteria and the principle of good faith, which remains elusive as an object of academic investigation as well as a normative interpretive standard to be applied in practice.

§4.06 THE TOWER OF BABEL AND ITS DISCONTENTS

It is not infrequent in international arbitration and international law scholarship to come across controversial issues and principles, the exact contours of which are difficult to grasp. The image of the tower of Babel springs to mind when one realizes in how many different meanings good faith can be invoked and applied in practice. People often speak at cross-purposes and risk not understanding one another, as in the biblical example. While no divine intervention can be presumed to be the cause for such a state of confusion, the difficulty of coming to a common understanding of good faith remains. Everyone believes that they are acting in conformity to good faith; it is

39. *Ibid.*, 56; 59.
40. *Ibid.*, 59.
41. Robert Kolb, *Good Faith in International Law* (Hart 2017). Kolb, however, identifies other roles that the principle of good faith would perform in the interpretation of treaties (*ibid.*, 65-67).
42. *Ibid.*, 62-63.
43. J.F. O'Connor, *Good Faith in International Law* (Darthmout Publishing 1991), 109.
44. Eric De Brabandere & Isabelle Van Damme, 'Good Faith in Treaty Interpretation', *supra* n. 36, 43.

always their opponents who do not. Paraphrasing Terry Eagleton's famous analogy of ideology to halitosis,[45] one could say that it is always the other who acts in bad faith!

As Professor Cremades aptly put it: 'It is difficult to find any international arbitration award not based on, or that does not at least mention, good faith. The omnipresence of good faith does not mean (rather quite the contrary) that it is clearly understood, that we know how to use it, or that we are able to predict how an arbitration tribunal may apply good faith in a particular case.'[46] Although not strictly limited to the use of good faith in treaty interpretation, the quote clearly attests to the mismatch between the invocation of the principle in arbitration practice and the aura of uncertainty surrounding its meaning.

Academic commentators and practitioners are often at a loss for words when they must explain to the reader, to the client or to the judge what a good argument based on, or inspired by, good faith may sound like. Besides bold and often counter-productive attacks against the alleged lack of good faith by the other party, arguments are often couched on a flimsy legal basis. Good faith is perceived to be an argument that the losing side puts forward as some sort of *extrema ratio*. Although everyone seems to have an understanding of it, good faith makes it a difficult card to play in the game of treaty interpretation.[47] Like the unskilled viewer may stand puzzled before Magritte's famous painting 'La bonne foi', not quite knowing what to make of the hat and the pipe, legal practitioners and commentators may stand baffled before the legal notion of good faith. Against this background of ambivalence and ambiguity, the crucial question for the competent professional and the critical observer remains: what can one do with the concept of 'good faith' as an instrument of treaty interpretation?

§4.07 THE GUIDING BEACON

A fairly effective way of attempting to grasp a concept which may be otherwise difficult to define is to resort to a metaphor. As I wrote in another context, '[m]etaphors are powerful tools of mediated knowledge that may help to understand reality better, particularly when they provide mental links and associations to objects and situations that we experience in our everyday life'.[48] When it comes to good faith in treaty interpretation, one of the most effective metaphors to convey the main tenets of the concept of good faith and to explain its function was put forward by the tribunal in *Sempra*. In a well-known passage, the tribunal held that '[t]he principle of good faith

45. Terry Eagleton, *Ideology: An Introduction* (Verso 1991), 2: 'ideology, like alitosis, is ... what the other person has!'
46. Bernardo M. Cremades, 'Good Faith in International Arbitration', 27 *American University International Law Review* 761 (2012), 761.
47. On the metaphor of treaty interpretation as a game *see*: Andrea Bianchi, 'The Game of Interpretation in International Law: the Players, the Cards and Why the Game Is Worth the Candle' in Andrea Bianchi, Daniel Peat & Matthew Windsor (eds), *Interpretation in International Law, supra* n. 21, 34-57; and Daniel Peat & Matthew Windsor, 'Playing the Game of Interpretation: On Meaning and Metaphor in International Law', *ibid.*, 3-33.
48. Andrea Bianchi, 'On Power and Illusion: The Concept of Transparency in International Law', supra n 8, 1, 9.

is thus relied on as the common guiding beacon that will orient the understanding and interpretation of obligations, just as happens under civil codes'.[49]

The image of a 'common guiding beacon' assisting and directing the interpretation process is very fitting to explain the role of the good faith principle in treaty interpretation. As Gazzini clearly explains, 'with regard to interpretation of treaties by investment tribunals ..., interpreting a treaty in good faith means essentially that arbitrators must follow interpreting the path defined in Articles 31-33 (of the VCLT, ed. note) with a balanced, unbiased and not preconceived attitude'.[50] This is in line with what the *Postová banka* tribunal held in its award: 'an interpretation in good faith is not simply interpretation bona fides, as opposed to the absence of mala fides, or a principle providing for the rejection of an interpretation that is abusive or that may result in the abuse of rights. It also means that the interpretation requires elements of reasonableness that go beyond the mere verbal or purely literal analysis'.[51]

The explanatory force of the 'common guiding beacon' metaphor should not be underestimated. As explained by cognitive linguists and philosophers George Lakoff and Mark Johnson in their ground-breaking book *Metaphors We Live By*, '[t]he essence of metaphors is under-standing [sic] and experiencing one kind of thing in terms of another'.[52] Since 'most of our ordinary conceptual system is metaphorical in nature', metaphors may determine 'how we perceive, how we think and what we do'.[53] To compare it to a beacon of light showing the way to sailors at sea or to pilots in an airfield is tantamount to saying that the principle of good faith provides guidance about where to go (and where not to go) in treaty interpretation. A cursory overview of international arbitration practice can help shed light on this point.

In terms of providing indications about 'where to go', arbitration practice is hardly ambiguous. Good faith is invariably invoked as a tool to provide reasonable and balanced interpretations that conform to the parties' legitimate expectations. In *Yukos*, the Hague Court of Appeal aptly underlined: '[t]hat the interpretation must be performed in good faith means that it must comply with the fundamental principle of reasonableness and must not lead to a meaning which is manifestly absurd or unreasonable'.[54] Similar considerations were expressed in *Kappes*, in which the tribunal, endorsing a scholarly opinion, held that: 'In accordance with Article 31(1) of the VCLT, a good faith interpretation must take into account the consequences that the States parties must 'reasonably and legitimately be considered to have envisaged as

49. *Sempra Energy International v. Argentina*, ICSID Case No. ARB/02/16, Award, 28 September 2007, § 67.
50. Tarcisio Gazzini, *Interpretation of International Investment Treaties*, *supra* n. 22, 61, relying on Robert Kolb, *La bonne foi en droit international public* (PUF 2009), 260 ff., cited with approval by Jan Paulsson in his individual opinion in *Hrvatska Elektroprivreda v. Slovenia*, ICSID Case No. ARB/05/24, Procedural Decision 4, Treaty Interpetation Issue, 12 June 2009, § 51.
51. *Postová banka, A.S. and Istrokapital SE v. Hellenic Republic*, ICSID Case No. ARB/13/08, Award, 30 April 2015, § 67.
52. George Lakatoff & Mark Johnson, *Metaphors We Live By*, 2nd ed. (University of Chicago Press 2003), 5.
53. *Ibid.*, 4.
54. *Yukos Universal Limited (Isle of Man) v. The Russian Federation*, PCA Case No. 2005-04/AA227, Judgment of the Hague Court of Appeal (Unofficial English Translation), § 4.2.3.

flowing from their undertakings'.[55] Similar language is used by the tribunal in *Euram*, cross-referencing the *Amco* tribunal: '... any convention, including conventions to arbitrate, should be construed in good faith, that is to say by taking into account the consequences of the commitments the parties may be considered as having reasonably and legitimately expected'.[56] The 'necessity' to provide 'a balanced interpretation' in good faith of the relevant treaty provisions was also highlighted in *El Paso*.[57]

Likewise, the beacon of good faith indicates quite clearly what type of interpretations cannot be upheld, in other words, 'where not to go'. Good faith is used as an exclusionary mechanism to set aside certain interpretations or some elements or circumstances judged incompatible with a balanced and reasonable interpretation of treaty provisions. In the set-aside proceedings in the *Natland* case,[58] for example, the Swiss Federal Tribunal held that a good faith interpretation of the relevant ECT (*Energy Charter Treaty, editor's note*) provisions implies that the host State is precluded from offering an interpretation that could result in the State's non-compliance with its international obligations, or that could defeat the meaning and purpose of the treaty.[59]

In *Vattenfall*, the tribunal relied on good faith to state that the terms of a multilateral treaty must 'have a single consistent meaning' for all the parties and that this 'need for coherence in interpretation, and for a single unified interpretation for each treaty provision' is embedded in the text of Article 31 of the VCLT, and the priority accorded therein to the text of the treaty.[60] An interpretation in good faith of the relevant treaty provisions led the tribunal in *Menzies* to rule out that Article II (MFN clause) of the GATS could provide a basis for consent to international arbitration.[61] In a similar vein, the tribunal in *Hulley* held that an interpretation in good faith of Article 21(5)(b)(i) of the ECT 'leads to the conclusion that a referral cannot be required if following the deferral procedure would clearly be futile under the circumstances of the specific case'.[62] A good faith interpretation of Article 17 of the ECT was deemed not to

55. *Daniel W Kappes and Kappes, Cassiday & Associates v. Republic of Guatemala*, ICSID Case No. ARB/18/43, Decision on Respondent's Preliminary Objections, 13 March 2020, § 84 (quoting from J Romesh Weeramantry, *Treaty Interpretation in Investment Arbitration* 47-48 (OUP 2012)).
56. *European American Investment Bank (Euram) AG (Austria) v. Slovak Republic*, PCA Case No. 2010-17, Award on Jurisdiction, 22 October 2012, § 166, quoting *Amco Asia et al. v. Indonesia*, ICSID Case No. ARB/81/1, Decision on Jurisdiction, 25 September 1983, § 14.
57. *El Paso Energy International Company v. Argentina*, ICSID Case No. ARB/03/15, Decision on Jurisdiction, 27 April 2006, § 70.
58. *G.I.H.G. Limited, Natland Group Limited, Natland Investment Group NV and Radiance Energy Holding S.A.R.L. v. Czech Republic*, PCA Case No. 2013-35.
59. Swiss Federal Tribunal, Decision of 7 February 2020 (only available in French): 'Le principe de la bonne foi implique notamment de la loyauté de la part de l'Etat contractant dans l'exécution de ses engagements ... Un Etat contractant doit proscrire tout comportement ou toute interprétation qui aboutirait à éluder ses engagements internationaux ou à détourner le traité de son sens et de son but.' (§ 3.1.2.).
60. *Vattenfall et al. v. Federal Republic of Germany*, ICSID Case ARB/12/12, Decision on the Achmea Issue, 31 August 2018, § 156.
61. *Menzies Middle East et Africa S.A. et Aviation Handling Services International Ltd c République du Senegal*, Affaire CIRDI ARB/15/21, Sentence, 5 août 2016, §§ 145-146.
62. *Hulley Enterprises Limited (Cyprus) v. The Russian Federation*, PCA Case No. AA 226, Final Award, 18 July 2014, § 1424. *Accord Yukos Universal Limited (Isle of Man) v. The Russian*

allow the tribunal in *Khan* to construe the treaty provision in such a way as to 'allow host states to lure investors by ostensibly extending to them the protection of the ECT, to then deny these protections when the investor attempts to invoke them in international arbitration'.[63]

If one may not always agree with arbitral tribunals and their choices, what emerges quite clearly from investment arbitration practice is that the function of the principle of good faith is to direct the interpretive process towards reasonable and balanced solutions and, consequently, to sweep away any element or circumstance that might hamper the attainment of such interpretations.

§4.08 ANCILLARY FUNCTION

The other noticeable and distinguishing feature of good faith in treaty interpretation is that it is almost invariably used in an accessory, secondary role. As highlighted by the ICJ, although the principle of good faith is 'one of the basic principles governing the creation and performance of legal obligations ... it is not a source of legal obligation where none would exist otherwise'.[64] Also, as a principle of treaty interpretation, good faith is often subservient to other principles and /or values and rarely plays a prominent role or provides the interpretive rule of decision in international law and international investment arbitration. It has an ancillary function.

As accurately noted by Gardiner, the attempt to demonstrate that a certain interpretation has been put forward in bad faith is no easy task, let alone to show that a judgment by an international or arbitral tribunal is rendered on the basis of an interpretation in bad faith.[65] In fact, whenever good faith is invoked to justify a given interpretation, this is almost invariably done 'to buttress some other line of reasoning without providing any obviously additional criteria'.[66]

This can be done, for example, to confirm an interpretation reached on other grounds, as in *Hrvatska*, in which the tribunal qualified the principle of good faith as 'the core principle about which all else revolves'.[67] The tribunal used good faith to confirm the interpretation at which it had arrived in such a way that the 'result does no violence, either to the Agreement's language or in its result.[68] In a similar vein, the principle has been used to buttress (and provide further justification for) the other

Federation, PCA Case No. AA 227, Final Award, 14 July 2014, § 1424; and *Veteran Petroleum Limited (Cyprus) v. The Russian Federation*, PCA Case No. AA 228, Final Award, 18 July 2014, § 1424.

63. *Khan Resources Inc. et al. v. The Government of Mongolia*, PCA Case No. 2011-09, Decision on Jurisdiction, 25 July 2012, § 429.
64. ICJ, *Border and Transborder Armed Activities (Nicaragua v. Honduras)*, Judgment on Jurisdiction and Admissibility, ICJ Reports 1988 105, § 94, quoted with approval in: *Land and Maritime Boundary between Cameroon and Nigeria*, Judgment on Preliminary Objections, ICJ Reports 1998, 275; § 39. *Contra* Robert Kolb, *Good Faith in International Law*, *supra* n. 41, 245-246.
65. Gardiner, *Treaty Interpretation*, *supra* n. 25, 168.
66. *Ibid.*
67. *Hrvatska Elektropriveda D.D. v. The Republic of Slovenia*, ICSID Case No. ARB/05/24, Decision on Treaty Interpretation, 12 June 2009, § 191.
68. *Ibid.*

components of Article 31 of the VCLT's general rule of interpretation. In *Alps Finance*, the tribunal used good faith to qualify ordinary meaning ('good faith ordinary meaning') and used the principle to interpret the meaning of the adjective 'real' in the expression 'real economic activities' in order to determine whether the claimant could be qualified as an investor.[69] Reference to good faith to reinforce the object of the treaty is made in *Al-Warraq*, where the tribunal opted for an interpretation of the relevant BIT provisions 'that favours the object of investment promotion and protection'.[70]

In *PV Investors*, the tribunal used good faith to strengthen all the other components of Article 31 of the VCLT by stating that '... a good faith interpretation of the ordinary meaning of Article 26 (*of the Energy Charter Treaty, editor's note*) suggests that no "special" or "dual" consent is required for the institution of arbitral proceedings in aggregate form beyond the express jurisdictional requirements contained in Art. 26. Neither does the context in which the offer of consent is placed nor the object and purpose of the Treaty suggest a different conclusion'.[71]

In yet another string of cases, the principle of good faith has been used by arbitral tribunals to provide a normative basis and, therefore, a legal justification for the use of the *effet utile* principle. In *Fraport*, the tribunal held that the principle of good faith 'encompasses the principle of effet utile'.[72] By a very similar wording, the tribunal in *Postova Banka* maintained that an interpretation in good faith of treaty provisions 'embodies the principle of effectiveness'.[73] The link between the principle of good faith and the principle of effectiveness was also acknowledged by the tribunal in *Orascom*,[74] whereas in *Urbaser*, the tribunal noted that 'the principle of *effet utile* "is given effect within Article 31 (1) of the Vienna Convention by virtue of the requirement to interpret in good faith"'.[75]

A cursory overview of the practice of interpretation of arbitral tribunals attests to the ancillary role of the principle of good faith in treaty interpretation. If it were to compete for the Academy Awards, the much-celebrated Oscars, good faith would most likely be nominated in the 'best supporting actress' category. Quite interestingly, in the Oscars regulations, no distinction between leading and supporting roles in acting is

---

69. *Alps Finance and Trade AG v. The Slovak Republic*, UNCITRAL Arbitration, Award (redacted version), 5 March 2011, § 226.
70. *Hesham Talaat M. Al-Warraq v. The Republic of Indonesia*, Award on Respondent's Preliminary Objections to Jurisdiction and Admissibility of the Claim, 21 June 2012, § 82.
71. *The PV Investors v. The Kingdom of Spain*, (UNCITRAL Arbitration), Preliminary Award on Jurisdiction, 13 October 2014, § 98.
72. *Fraport AG Framkfurt Airport Services Worldwide v. The Republic of the Philippines*, ICSID Case No. ARB/11/12, Award, 10 December 2014, § 329.
73. *Postova Banka A.S. and Istrokapital SE v. The Hellenic Republic*, *supra* n. 51, § 293: 'The interpretation in good faith, be it considered alone or in conjunction with the object and purpose of the treaty, embodies the principle of effectiveness' (*ut res magis valeat quam pereat*).
74. *Orascom TMT Investment S.à.r.l. v. People's Democratic Republic of Algeria*, ICSID Case No. ARB/12/35, Award, 31 May 2017, § 288: 'The principle of effectiveness plays an important role in the interpretation of treaties ... this canon of interpretation is normally linked to the object and purpose of the treaty and to the principle of good faith' (footnote omitted).
75. *Urbaser S.A. et al. v. The Argentine Republic*, ICSID Case No. ARB/07/26, Award, 8 December 2016, § 1190.

made.[76] In fact, the eligibility criteria for this category are not specified, and the determination of whether or not an actress should be put into the leading role category or in the supporting role category is made directly by the voting members at the time of balloting, depending on how central to the story being told in the movie each role is. The analogy to the role played by good faith in treaty interpretation is striking, if somewhat unorthodox, in our lawyerly circles.

§4.09 INSTRUCTIONS FOR USE: RECAP

'Instructions for use' is generally meant to refer to the information leaflet provided by the manufacturer to inform the user of a device's intended purpose and proper use as well as of any precautions to be taken, if any. I thought that at the end of this cursory overview of the principle of good faith in treaty interpretation, a short recap might come in handy to the readers and potential users (academics, practitioners, counsel, judges, negotiators, and decision-makers).

First and foremost, the principle of good faith is no hard-and-fast rule of interpretation. In fact, it is hardly ever an autonomous, stand-alone principle of interpretation, just as it is almost never a source of obligation outside the realm of interpretation. As an interpretive principle, the principle of good faith is like a beacon of light that shows the direction in which the interpretive process should lean in terms of fair and reasonable outcomes.

By showing where to go, good faith impliedly warns against where not to go. It is suggested that the principle of 'good faith', and its flip-side 'bad faith', should not be used too aggressively or in a confrontational way, for the connotation of moral stigma that the qualification of 'bad faith' attached to an argument or an interpretation of the law brings about may yield unintended effects and backfire. By the same token, taking the moral high ground is not recommended either, as this posture is often associated with a sense of superiority and arrogance that may backlash against its proponent. Good faith is there to temper and, occasionally, to pre-emptively strike against an unfavourable/unfair/unjust interpretive solution, not to vilify or express contempt towards the party invoking it. For the very same reason, arbitral tribunals rarely endorse accusations of interpretations allegedly made in bad faith by one of the parties against the other.

The principle of good faith is to be used parsimoniously to show that a given interpretation conforms to professionally and socially shared understandings of reasonableness and fairness. After all, as highlighted above, it is not by chance that the image most often associated with good faith is a shake of hands! The principle allows excluding the negativity of an interpretation based on bad faith or bias or leading to an unreasonable or manifestly unjust result.

76. *See* the *95th Oscars Complete Rules* approved by the Academy of Motion Picture Arts and Sciences, particularly Rule Six 'Special rules for the Acting Awards', para. 4, available at: https://www.oscars.org/sites/oscars/files/95th_oscars_complete_rules.pdf.

Indeed, in terms of persuasive force, the principle of good faith is more effective when used in a systemic way rather than in an adversarial way. This communal orientation of the principle goes hand in hand with the practice of using it together with other interpretive principles to establish a sense of fairness and reasonableness of the adopted interpretive solution. This rationale can be embedded in different normative contexts. For instance, in international trade law, the principle of good faith may be associated with the need to meet the legitimate expectations of the parties,[77] whereas in international law it may resonate better when used in connection with the need to respect the intention of the parties and the undertakings they made when they adopted the treaty.[78]

The normative value of the principle of good faith may be highly contextual, but its strategic argumentative use is extremely valuable. Regardless of the user's perspective (counsel's, expert's or arbitrator's), its invocation and/or application has great potential for conveying to the audience convincing interpretive outcomes. Its moral and ethical underpinnings carry much weight in terms of persuasion, particularly when good faith complements and/or supports interpretations based on other rules and principles (so-called ancillary function). If one learns how to tame the principle and how to use its nuanced normativity smoothly, its potential for providing justification and legitimation to interpretive solutions can be remarkable indeed.

In a way, good faith is part and parcel of our perennial quest for equitable and impartial solutions, the quest for the Holy Grail of justice and governance, in fairness to all. The art of using its argumentative benefits largely offsets the need for articulating a 'theory' or investigating where it comes from. After all, the initial analogy to Lohengrin might be appropriate. Let us not allow Lohengrin to go back to the castle of the Holy Grail, and let us keep (good) faith in our interpretive tool kit and its varied content. Sooner or later, it will come in handy.

77. For an overview of good faith in the interpretation of WTO Agreements, *see* Marion Panizzon, *Good Faith in the Jurisprudence of the WTO: The Protection of Legitimate Expectations, Good Faith Interpretation and Fair Dispute Settlement* (Hart Publishing 2006), particularly 'Chapter 7: Good Faith Interpretation of the WTO Agreements', 197 ff.; Chapter 8: Good Faith Non-interpretation by the WTO Appellate Body', 233 ff.; and 'Chapter 9: Towards a WTO-Specific Good Faith Interpretation?', 261 ff. *See also* Graham Cook, 'Good Faith', *A Digest of WTO Jurisprudence on Public International Law Concepts and Principles* (Cambridge University Press 2015) section 8.3, 157-170.

78. *See*, however, Robert Kolb, *Good Faith in International Law*, *supra* n. 41, 64-66, who considers the protection of legitimate expectations as 'a corollary and essential criterion' of the principle of good faith (65).

CHAPTER 5

The Definition of Investment in International Investment Law: The Future of Good Faith Investments

Emily Sipiorski

§5.01 INTRODUCTION

Clarifying the scope of a good faith investment is critical to maintaining the system of international investment protection, particularly in a moment of disruption and reconsideration.[1] This clarity ensures consistency and stability of expectations for investors, states, as well as civil society and other relevant actors. Questions regarding securing and maintaining an investment in good faith are usually limited to disputes where allegations arise as to the contrary. An intentional disregard for host state laws or a misuse of economic power may result in the examination of whether the investment was made in good faith – or, more strongly, whether there was an abuse of the treaty protections. The manipulation of ownership to secure the protection of a treaty might further extend these questions of good faith. While there is rarely (although increasingly) an express obligation for the investment to be made in good faith, those obligations arise in both domestic as well as public international law. An expansion, however, in the relevance of good faith in the analysis of investment may be opening as corporate actors are now understood to have the capacity for making both positive and negative impacts within the broader context of sustainable development.

1. *See generally*, United Nations Commission on International Trade Law, Working Group III: Investor-State Dispute Settlement Reform; *The Backlash Against Investment Arbitration: Perceptions and Reality* (Michael Waibel, Asha Kaushal, Kwo-Hwa Chung and Claire Balchin, eds, Kluwer Law International 2010).

One of the central criticisms of the system of international investment protection points to the disconnect between state's obligations and investor's rights.[2] The system of international investment protection sits in a hybrid space of international law: the actors are a complex mix of public and private.[3] The treaties are concluded within the system of public international law - even if an agreement to arbitrate is beyond the scope of public international law and more properly positioned as a contractual agreement between the host state and the investor.[4] Corporate actors often play a key role in enabling foreign direct investment, while public international law lacks the ability to create obligations for non-state actors.[5] Namely, an investor is not obliged to maintain responsibilities that arise out of public international law. Relevant in that context are obligations with respect to the environment[6] and human rights.[7] This disconnect has been recognized more generally in the space of human rights law with the drafting of soft law instruments intended to connect business and human rights.[8] Moreover, these developments are embodied on the international level within the

2. David Gaukrodger, *Addressing the Balance of Interests in Investment Treaties: The Limitation of Fair and Equitable Treatment Provisions to the Minimum Standard of Treatment under Customary International Law*, OECD Working Papers on International Investment, No. 2017/03 (OECD) (discussing the issue of balance from the perspective of government action that seeks to balance investment protection alongside the right to regulate, specifically applied through the fair and equitable treatment provision).
3. Julie A. Maupin, *Public and Private in International Investment Law: An Integrated Systems Approach*, 54(2) Virginia Journal of International Law 367, 373 et seq. (2014) (identifying the public-private debate in investment law as part of a larger debate in international law).
4. *Tradex Hellas (Greece) v. Republic of Albania*, ICSID Case No. ARB/94/2, Decision on Jurisdiction, 24 December 1996, (1999) 14 ICSID Rev. - Foreign Inv. L.J., pp. 186-187; *Emilio Agustín Maffezini v. The Kingdom of Spain*, ICSID Case No. ARB/97/7, Decision of the Tribunal on Objections to Jurisdiction, 25 January 2000, para. 23 ('In determining whether Spain conditioned its acceptance of the Centre's jurisdiction and the Tribunal's competence on the prior exhaustion of domestic remedies, the Tribunal notes that in ratifying the ICSID Convention, Spain did not attach any such condition to its acceptance of Article 26'); *Wintershall Aktiengesellschaft v. Argentine Republic*, ICSID Case No. ARB/04/14, Award 8 December 2008, paras 190 et seq. *See also* Makane Moïse Mbengue, *Consent to Arbitration Through National Investment Legislation* (Investment Treaty News, 19 July 2012), available at https://www.iisd.org/itn/en/2012/07/19/consent-to-arbitration-through-national-investment-legislation/.
5. Regarding corporate obligations: Markos Karavias, *Corporate Obligations under International Law* (Oxford Univ. Press 2013) 17 (providing that '[s]ince corporate activities have been perceived as challenging State sovereignty, States have been sceptical, if not hostile, about the idea of utilizing international law to regulate corporate activities, with the notable exception of international rules governing the treatment of foreign investors. And even in this case, international law has historically been criticized as accommodating the interests of corporations and of their home States'.).
6. Maristella Svampa, *Resource Extractivism and Alternatives: Latin American Perspectives on Development, in Beyond Development: Alternative Visions from Latin America* (M. Lang & D. Mokrani eds, Transnational Institute 2013), pp. 117-43; Diana M. Liverman & Silvina Vilas, *Neoliberalism and the Environment in Latin America*, 31 Annual R. of Env't & Res. 327, 334 (2006) DOI: 10.1146/annurev.energy.29.102403.140729.
7. Kate Miles, *The Origins of International Investment Law: Empire, Environment and the Safeguarding of Capital* (Cambridge Univ. Press 2013), 2 et seq.; Nathalie Bernasconi-Osterwalder & Edith Brown Weiss, *International Investment Rules and Water: Learning from the NAFTA Experience*, in *Fresh Water and International Economic Law* (Edith Brown Weiss, Laurence Boisson de Chazournes & Nathalie Bernasconi-Osterwalder eds, Oxford Univ. Press 2005).
8. United Nations, Guiding Principles on Business and Human Rights (2011); Organisation for Economic Cooperation and Development OECD Guidelines for Multinational Enterprises (2000).

framework of the United Nations Sustainable Development Goals and are progressing in some domestic jurisdictions towards hard law.[9] Yet, a divide lingers within investment protection despite significant discussion on this connection.[10] This residual fragmentation is being approached through the reform efforts within the context of UNCITRAL as well as in the drafting of the most recent treaties.

An argument, however, can be made that the solution lies within the definition of investment itself. More specifically, the solution lies within the conceptualization of a good faith investment that adheres to the higher ideal of contribution to the economic development of the host state – within a framing that economic development has now come to be understood as sustainable economic development.[11] This contribution intends to examine the future of investment, but more pointedly, the factors that would need to be included in a good faith investment of the future. As states' obligations towards the environment grow, will a parallel development occur in the interpretation of 'investment', thus requiring that investments – in the least – do not degrade the environment? As soft law business and human rights principles grow, will similar obligations be implied within a good faith investment? Most structurally, as economic development becomes conceptualized as *sustainable* economic development, growing in parallel with the United Nations Sustainable Development Goals, will the obligations for an investment to be made for the promotion of the development of the host state similarly incorporate that element of sustainability? As such, this contribution pushes the analysis of an investment towards the future by questioning the shape of a good faith investment and its reality as the language of treaties takes on a more integrated perspective on obligations and incorporates – at least in the preambular language – contributions to sustainable development generally and environmental and human rights more specifically. It further explores how changing commitments within the realm of public international law and European Union (EU) law may reconfigure and reconceptualize the understanding of good faith (and thus covered) investments.

These questions above point to substantive questions regarding a good faith investment. In tandem, the role of good faith interpretation pursuant to the Vienna Convention on the Law of Treaties (VCLT), Article 31, may be required to create this level of systemically integrated richness to the definition of investment. How does a tribunal use its discretion in a dispute in a way that aligns with good faith interpretation?

9. European Parliament Resolution of 10 March 2021 with Recommendations to the Commission on Corporate Due Diligence and Corporate Accountability (2020/2129(INL)).
10. Tarcisio Gazzini, *Bilateral Investment Treaties and Sustainable Development*, 15 J. of World Inv. & Trade 936 (2014) DOI: 10.1163/22119000-01506008; Philippe Sands, Jacqueline Peel, Adriana Fabra & Ruth Mackenzie, *Principles of International Environmental Law* (Cambridge Univ. Press 2012); Marie-Claire Cordonier Segger, Markus Gehring & Andrew Newcombe eds, *Sustainable Development in World Investment Law* (Kluwer Law International 2011).
11. Andrew Newcombe, *Sustainable Development and Investment Treaty Law*, 8 J. World Inv. & Trade 357, 402 (2007) DOI: 10.1163/221190007x00071 ('In my view, the IIA regime does not act as an impediment to or subvert principles of sustainable development. Under the IIA regime, states retain plenary regulatory authority to promote economic development and engage in economic, social and environmental regulation.').

This contribution proposes a reflection on the definition and scope of investment as central to re-aligning the system within the realities of transnational law and maintaining a system of investment protection in compliance with environmental and human rights norms. Taking into account the available language in the treaties, the mechanisms available for interpretation in the VCLT, and the discretion of arbitral panels, the tools may be available to recognize the foundational intention of investment protection and apply those intentions in a systemically coherent manner. Ultimately, the question lies in whether the 'backlash' and imbalance are merely a matter of application and interpretation, absorbed unnecessarily by guiding precedent further complicated by its conceptualization as a system.[12]

The contribution first identifies and frames the object and purpose of investment treaties as contributions towards economic development. The next section (§5.03) returns to the basics: what is an investment, and why does good faith matter? Section §5.04 examines changing commitments, from both the perspective of treaty language, public international law, and EU law specifically, as a case study for the incorporation of possible increased corporate responsibility within the context of the environment and human rights, and in that context explores potential impacts on the shape of a good faith investment. The final section (§5.05) gives a perspective on future developments and their limitations.

§5.02 FRAMING ECONOMIC DEVELOPMENT AND THE OBJECT AND PURPOSE OF INVESTMENT TREATIES

To a large extent, the current system of investment protection was created out of a moment when development was closely linked to cooperation in trade and investment,[13] centralized in economic development theories.[14] In the post-World War II global economic environment in which foreign investment was encouraged, economic cooperation was identified as key to peaceful global cooperation. The movement of foreign capital and the transfer of wealth was realized in part through foreign direct

12. Irene M. Ten Cate, *The Costs of Consistency: Precedent in Investment Treaty Arbitration*, 51 Colum. J. Transnat'l L. 418, 474 et seq. (2013); *see also* more generally on investment law as a system of law, Stephan W. Schill, *The Multilateralization of International Investment Law* 15 (Cambridge Univ. Press 2009).
13. Jeswald Salacuse, *The Law of Investment Treaties* (Oxford Univ. Press 2010), 80; Kenneth Vandevelde, *Bilateral Investment Treaties: History, Policy and Interpretation* (Oxford Univ. Press 2009), 22; Christian Tietje & Emily Sipiorski, *The Evolution of Investment Protection Based on Public International Law Treaties: Lessons to Be Learned, in International Investment Law and Soft Law* 202 (Andrea K. Bjorklund & August Reinisch, eds, Edward Elgar 2012).
14. From the economic perspective, *see* Robert Gilpin, *Global Political Economy: Understanding the International Economic Order* (Princeton Univ. Press 2001); Adam Szirmai, *The International Economic and Political Order Since 1945, in The Dynamics of Socio-Economic Development* 515 (Adam Szirmai ed., Cambridge Univ. Press 2012); Robert E. Lipsey, *The Role of Foreign Direct Investment in International Capital Flows*, NBER Working Paper Series, Working Paper 7094 (April 1999); Allen T. Bonnell, *The Post-War International Economic Order*, 9(1) Southern Econ. J. 46, 46 (1942) DOI: 10.2307/1052481.

investments.[15] International investment agreements were designed, negotiated, and implemented as a mechanism for safeguarding those investments.[16] Even today, this approach to engaging in economic cooperation remains vital to the conclusion of agreements on investment protection and trade, as recently evidenced in the Kenya-United Kingdom Economic Partnership agreement, among other examples, providing in the preamble: 'Recognising that substantial investment is required to uplift the standards of living of the EAC [East African Community] Partner State(s).'[17] While questions have arisen over whether foreign direct investment brought development[18] as well as whether investment treaties brought foreign direct investment,[19] economic development remains central to the object and purpose of the treaties.

Economic gain is integrated into the development ideal, but simultaneously, the ideals of economic cooperation have been influenced by the rhetoric of sustainable development – now prominently incorporated into the development dialogue.[20] Where economic cooperation was once seen as key to peaceful global cooperation, it is now more recognized that cooperation also requires environmental and social considerations.[21] Sustainability has emerged as a development ideal, to a certain extent updating and replacing the previous singular emphasis only on economic growth.[22] In particular, the idea of a healthy environment has become more embedded in the understanding of the term.[23] Beyerlin notes the interest in balancing the needs of

15. Raymond J. MacDermott, *Environmental Regulations and the Flow of Foreign Direct Investment: A Review of the Pollution Haven Hypothesis, in Foreign Direct Investment* (Harrison G. Blaine ed., Nova Science Publisher 2009); Rachel McCulloch, *New Perspectives on Foreign Direct Investment, in Foreign Direct Investment* (Kenneth A. Froot ed., Univ. of Chicago Press 1994).
16. Kenneth J. Vandevelde, *The First Bilateral Investment Treaties: U.S. Postwar Friendship, Commerce, and Navigation Treaties* (Oxford Univ. Press 2017).
17. Economic Partnership Agreement between the United Kingdom of Great Britain and Northern Ireland, of the one part, and the Republic of Kenya, a Member of the East African Community, of the other part (8 December 2020).
18. Maria Carkovic & Ross Levin, *Does Foreign Direct Investment Accelerate Economic Growth, in Does Foreign Direct Investment Promote Development?* 196 et seq. (Theodore Moran, Edward Graham & Magnus Blomstrom eds, Peterson Institute for International Economics 2005) (providing a conclusion critical to an association between FDI and economic growth).
19. Jason Webb Yackee, *Do Bilateral Investment Treaties Promote Foreign Direct Investment? Some Hints from Alternative Evidence,* 51 Va. J. Int'l L. 397, 426-431 (2011) DOI: 10.2139/ssrn.1594887; Muhammad Zubair Mumtaz & Zachary Smith, *Do Bilateral Investment Treaties Promote Foreign Direct Investment Inflows in Asian Countries?* (2018) XVIII (2) Islamabad Policy Research Institute 78-110, 108 (concluding that there are mixed results for states dependent in part on their size and location); Eric Neumayer, *Self-Interest, Foreign Need, and Good Governance: Are Bilateral Investment Treaty Programs Similar to Aid Allocation?* 2(3) Foreign Pol'y Analysis 245 (2006) DOI: 10.1111/j.1743-8594.2006.00029.x.
20. UN General Assembly, *Transforming our World: The 2030 Agenda for Sustainable Development,* 21 October 2015, A/RES/70/1.
21. Ulrich Beyerlin, *Sustainable Development,* in *Max Planck Encyclopedia of International Law,* para. 11.
22. The 1987 Brundtland Commission Report described sustainable development as 'development that meets the needs of the present without compromising the ability of future generations to meet their own needs'.
23. *See, e.g.,* Beyerlin, *supra* n. 21, para. 11 ('Today, [Sustainable Development] is broadly understood as a concept that is characterized by (1) the close linkage between the policy goals of economic and social development and environmental protection; (2) the qualification of environmental protection as an integral part of any developmental measure, and vice versa; and

developing economies and environmental interests.[24] With that said, the lack of normativity in the characterization of sustainable development limits guidance towards state's environmental policy decisions under sustainable development commitments.[25]

§5.03 DEFINING INVESTMENT AND THE RELEVANCE OF GOOD FAITH

This emerging understanding of development connects directly to how 'investment' is interpreted by tribunals. Namely, following the leading cases where the definition of 'investment' was discussed, contribution to the economic development of the state is frequently identified as one element.[26] This construction in the case law and interpretation of treaties follows the fact that the definition of investment can be expanded or limited by contracting states to a treaty,[27] enabling the sovereignty of states during the negotiation of international investment agreements.[28] Treaty parties may view this vagueness of the definition of 'investment' differently – some with a greater desire for legal certainty within the treaty language.[29] In that sense, the definition of investment has both the benefit and the detriment of being left undefined in the ICSID Convention[30] and broadly defined in most bilateral investment agreements.[31] At the time of the

(3) the long-term perspective of both policy goals, that is the States' inter-generational responsibility.'); *see also* F. Racioppi et al., *Reaching the Sustainable Development Goals Through Healthy Environments: Are We on Track?*, 30 Eur. J. Pub. Health i14, i15 (1 March 2020) DOI: 10.1093/eurpub/ckaa028.

24. Beyerlin, *supra* n. 21, at para. 12: 'equitable balance between the competing interests of development and environmental protection presupposes their equivalence in substance. This conclusion appears to be all the more convincing since there is no evidence for assuming that development prevails over environmental protection, or vice versa. Developing countries which internally face economic deficiencies and social disruption are tempted to give preference to developmental needs over environmental ones, while industrialized States are inclined to take the opposite view. However, the concept of SD ultimately does not lend support to either of the positions. Thus, in any individual case a fair, or equitable, compromise between both the developmental and environmental needs has to be reached'.
25. Beyerlin, *supra* n. 21, at para. 19.
26. *Salini Costruttori S.p.A. and Italstrade S.p.A. v. Kingdom of Morocco [I]*, ICSID Case No. ARB/00/4, Decision on Jurisdiction (French Original: 129 Journal du droit international 196 (2002)) (English translation: 42 ILM 609 (2003), 6 ICSID Rep. 400 (2004)); *Phoenix v. Czech Republic*, ICSID Case No. ARB/06/5, Award (15 April 2009), para. 100.
27. Michael Hwang & Jennifer Lee Cheng Fong, *Definition of Investment – A Voice from the Eye of the Storm*, 1 Asian J. Int'l L. 99, 101 (2011) DOI: 10.1017/s2044251310000378; Prabhash Ranjan, *Definition of Investment in Bilateral Investment Treaties of South Asian Countries and Regulatory Discretion*, 26 J. Int'l Arb. 217 (2009) DOI: 10.54648/joia2009011.
28. Emily Sipiorski, *Good Faith in International Investment Arbitration* para. 4.08 (Oxford Univ. Press 2019); Julian David Mortenson, *The Meaning of 'Investment': ICSID's Travaux and the Domain of International Investment Law*, 51(1) Harv. Int'l L.J. 257 (2010).
29. James Maxeiner, *Legal Certainty: A European Alternative to American Legal Indeterminacy?*, 15 Tul. J. Int'l & Comp. L. 54 (2007).
30. ICSID Convention, Art. 25, providing '(1) The jurisdiction of the Centre shall extend to any legal dispute arising directly out of an investment, between a Contracting State (or any constituent subdivision or agency of a Contracting State designated to the Centre by that State) and a national of another Contracting State, which the parties to the dispute consent in writing to submit to the Centre. When the parties have given their consent, no party may withdraw its consent unilaterally.'

drafting of the ICSID Convention, that vagueness was intentional albeit debated, namely from a development perspective.[32] Some states with developing economies argued for a more restrictive approach to the issue of defining investment.[33]

This decision to maintain a vaguely construed definition and the continued decisions during negotiation and drafting to leave investment broad in treaty language can result in substantial space for the discretionary involvement of investment tribunals.[34] How much discretion should be transferred to a decision-maker is complex and debatable.[35] Tribunals have come to varied conclusions regarding the breadth and application of the term 'investment'.[36] Thus, the vagueness intentionally constructed

31. *See, e.g.*, US Model Bilateral Investment Treaty (2012), Art. 2 providing '1. This Treaty applies to measures adopted or maintained by a Party relating to: (a) investors of the other Party; (b) covered investments; and (c) with respect to Articles 8 [Performance Requirements], 12 [Investment and Environment], and 13 [Investment and Labor], all investments in the territory of the Party.'; Agreement between the Government of the State of Israel and the Government of the United Arab Emirates on Promotion and Protection of Investments (20 October 2020), section A: 'covered investment' means, with respect to a Party, an investment: (a) in its territory; (b) directly or indirectly owned or controlled by an investor of the other Party; and (c) existing on the date of entry into force of this Agreement, or made or acquired thereafter; Agreement on the Encouragement and Reciprocal Protection of Investments between the Kingdom of the Netherlands and the Sultanate of Oman (17 January 2009), Art. 1: 'For the purposes of the present Agreement: (a) the term "investment" shall comprise every kind of asset whether directly or indirectly owned, such as share of capital; movable and fixed assets; rights derived from shares, bonds and other kinds of interests in companies and joint ventures; title to any performance having an economic value; rights in the fields of intellectual property, technical processes and know-how. (b) the term "investment" also includes rights granted under public law and agreed upon by special agreements between the concerned parties, which may include rights to prospect, explore, extract and win natural resources.'; Dutch Model BIT (2019), Art. 1.
32. Christoph Schreuer, *The ICSID Convention: A Commentary* 82 (Cambridge Univ. Press 2d ed. 2009); Antonio R. Parra, *The History of ICSID* 71-72 (Oxford Univ. Press 2d ed. 2017) ('the jurisdiction of the Centre was the subject of much debate at Legal Committee meetings. Opinion was again divided between experts, mainly from developing countries, who thought that the jurisdiction of the Centre should be more strictly circumscribed and experts who favored a more flexible, open approach'). *See also* Antoine Romanetti, *Defining Investors: Who Is Eligible to Claim?*, 29(3) J. Int'l Arb. 231 (2012) DOI: 10.54648/joia2012015.
33. Felix O. Okpe, *The Definition of Investment and the ICSID Convention: Matters Arising under the Nigerian Investment Promotion Act and International Investment Law*, 8 J. Sustainable Dev. L. & Pol'y 133, 154 (2017) (noting the particular complexity for developing countries 'caught off guard because of the amorphous definition of investment'); Julian David Mortenson, *The Meaning of 'Investment': ICSID's Travaux and the Domain of International Investment Law*, 51(1) Harv. Int'l L. J. 307 (2010) DOI: 10.4314/jsdlp.v8i2.7.
34. Jean Ho, *The Meaning of 'Investment' in ICSID Arbitrations*, 26 Arbitration Int'l 633 (2010) DOI: 10.1093/arbitration/26.4.633. *See generally*, Sebastián A. Reyes Molina, *Judicial Discretion as a Result of Systemic Indeterminacy*, 33 Can. J. L. & Jur. 369 (2020) DOI: 10.1017/cjlj.2020.7; Kent Greenawalt, *Vagueness and Judicial Responses to Legal Indeterminacy*, 7(4) Legal Theory 433 (2001) DOI: 10.1017/s1352325201704077; Timothy Endicott, *Vagueness in Law* (Oxford Univ. Press 2000); David O. Brink, *Legal Interpretation, Objectivity and Morality*, *in Objectivity in Law and Morals* 12 (Brian Leiter ed., Cambridge Univ. Press 2001).
35. H.L.A. Hart, *The Concept of Law* 126-136 (Oxford Univ. Press 3d ed. 2012); Ronald Dworkin, *The Model of Rules*, 35 U. Chi. L. Rev. 14 (1967) DOI: 10.2307/1598947; Ronald Dworkin, *A Matter of Principle* 119 et seq. (Harvard Univ. Press 1985).
36. *Phoenix Action, Ltd. v. The Czech Republic*, ICSID Case No. ARB/06/5, Award (15 April 2009), para. 100; *Gustav F W Hamester GmbH & Co KG v. Republic of Ghana*, ICSID Case No. ARB/07/24, Award (18 June 2010), para. 123.

in the definition in the ICSID Convention, Article 25, may create uncertainty[37] but also enables interpretation to enter into the term during the course of an investment dispute.[38] The vagueness and openness of the term, as included in the ICSID Convention, have allowed a turn to both general principles in the interpretation process[39] as well as the object and purpose of the treaty.[40] It is that openness and capacity for input that makes good faith an especially useful principle in the process of understanding 'investment', including in the understanding of economic development.[41] This vagueness, however, also leaves the process of interpreting whether an investment exists to layers of questions, including temporal implications that often rely on good faith in the analysis.[42]

For over a decade, there have been recommendations to limit the scope of 'investment' to those investments which contribute to the development of the host state's economy.[43] As noted above, this proposal is in line with the most widely cited definitions drawn from arbitral decisions.[44] The *Salini* decision provides that the investment must include a contribution for a certain duration with an element of risk and with a 'contribution to the economic development of the host State of the investment'.[45] These criteria have been criticized as too broadly construed[46] and have

37. Okpe, *supra* n. 33, at 134 (referring to the Nigerian Investment Promotion Act, the author notes that the 'amorphous definition [...] creates uncertainty in view of the lack of a precise definition of the term in the ICSID Convention').
38. Salacuse, *supra* n. 13, at 162-163 (providing for consideration of the object and purpose when interpreting provisions of investment treaties); Trinh Hai Yen, *The Interpretation of Investment Treaties* (Brill 2014), 76 (noting the - at times - disregard for rules of treaty interpretation in investment disputes).
39. Andreas Kulick, *From Problem to Opportunity?: An Analytical Framework for Vagueness and Ambiguity in International Law*, 59 German Yearbook Int'l L. (2016).
40. Oliver Doerr, *Article 31, in Vienna Convention on the Law of Treaties: A Commentary* 557-616 (Oliver Doerr & Kirsten Schmalenbach eds, 2d ed. Springer 2018).
41. Hwang & Fong, *supra* n. 27, at 128.
42. Engela C. Schlemmer, *Investment, Investor, Nationality, and Shareholders, in The Oxford Handbook of International Investment Law* (Peter Muchlinski, Federico Ortino & Christoph Schreuer eds, Oxford Univ. Press 2008) 51 ('There are [...] situations arising out of the source of consent to ICSID arbitration where one will have to determine whether the transaction in the midst of the dispute is indeed an investment. The first of these is if there is a national law dictating special requirements for a transaction in order to be accepted as an investment.').
43. United Nations Conference on Trade and Development, *Scope and Definition, UNCTAD Series on Issues in International Investment Agreements II* (UNCTAD 2011), 2-3.
44. *Salini Costruttori S.p.A. and Italstrade S.p.A. v. Kingdom of Morocco [I]*, ICSID Case No. ARB/00/4, Decision on Jurisdiction (French Original: 129 Journal du droit international 196 (2002)) (English translation: 42 ILM 609 (2003), 6 ICSID Rep. 400 (2004)).
45. *Salini Costruttori S.p.A. and Italstrade S.p.A. v. Kingdom of Morocco*, *supra* n. 44, initially noting that the issue of the definition of investment had not yet been adequately examined by previous tribunals: 'The Tribunal notes that there have been almost no cases where the notion of investment within the meaning of Article 25 of the Convention was raised. However, it would be inaccurate to consider that the requirement that a dispute be "in direct relation to an investment" is diluted by the consent of the Contracting Parties. To the contrary, ICSID case law and legal authors agree that the investment requirement must be respected as an objective condition of the jurisdiction of the Centre.' Cf. Laurence Burger, *The Trouble with Salini*, 31 ASA Bull. 521, 522 (2013) (stating that 'despite its importance in practice, the Salini test has been considerably criticized and has in particular generated much opposition from tribunals who prefer the competing subjectivist theory which attributes primary importance to the definition of investments in BITs.').

not been consistently applied by tribunals – with some further restricting and others expanding. The *Phoenix* tribunal added two additional elements, indicating that in order for the tribunal to assume jurisdiction over the dispute, the investment was required to both be made within the laws of the host state and bona fide.[47] Michael Hwang and Jennifer Lee Cheng Fong suggest that good faith should be 'subsumed' under the economic development criterion.[48]

The relevance of good faith in defining investment can be drawn from both substantive and interpretative perspectives. It also sits at the balance between public international law and private contract law. States have obligations to uphold their treaty commitments pursuant to the VCLT, Article 26. From the private perspective of commitments, most domestic legal systems have a requirement (or a relatively equivalent concept) for negotiation of contracts in good faith.[49] The tribunal bears the burden with respect to interpretation: 'A treaty shall be interpreted in good faith in accordance with the ordinary meaning to be given to the terms of the treaty in their context and in the light of its object and purpose',[50] including the definition of investment. Moreover, states can re-assume that interpretative power through authentic interpretations.[51]

§5.04 CHANGING COMMITMENTS: IMPACTING THE DEFINITION OF GOOD FAITH

[A] Treaty Language

The definition of 'investment', however, may be transforming explicitly in the treaties and implicitly through good faith interpretation. The element of contribution to the development of the host state – as well as the variations – is important as the conceptualization of the idea of development has transformed over the course of the past fifty years. While development at the inception of the ICSID Convention was closely drawn to a purely post-war economic integration and revitalization model, development is now understood as pointing more towards sustainable development. This has been expressly addressed in recent Bilateral Investment Treaties (BITs).

46. Laurens J.E. Timmer, *The Meaning of 'Investment' as a Requirement for Jurisdiction Ratione Materiae of the ICSID Centre*, 29(4) J. Int'l Arb. 363, 367 (2012) DOI: 10.54648/joia2012024.
47. *Phoenix Action, Ltd. v. The Czech Republic*, ICSID Case No. ARB/06/5, Award (15 April 2009), para. 100.
48. Hwang & Fong, *supra* n. 27, at 128.
49. Sipiorski, *supra* n. 28, at paras 2.67 et seq.
50. Vienna Convention on the Law of Treaties (23 May 1969), 1155 U.N.T.S. 331; 8 I.L.M. 679 (1969), Art. 31(1).
51. Tarcisio Gazzini, *Authentic (or Authoritative) Interpretation of Investment Treaties by the Treaty Parties* (EJIL: Talk!, 17 August 2020), https://www.ejiltalk.org/authentic-or-authoritative-interpretation-of-investment-treaties-by-the-treaty-parties/ (indicating that '[a]uthentic interpretations are an important tool in the hands of States to improve the accuracy of treaty interpretation and enhance the coherence and consistency of investment arbitration'.).

The difficulty in re-negotiating and updating existing BITs means that much of the language of the treaties remains stagnant in a previous era of development.[52] However, some investment treaties expressly point to this transformation in ideals of development. Nearly all of the more recent investment agreements or investment chapters in trade agreements acknowledge the importance of sustainable development in the preambular language. The Dutch Model BIT, while showcasing the classically broad definition of 'investment', provides in the preamble that:

> Desiring to strengthen their traditional ties of friendship and to extend and intensify economic relations between them by creating conditions with a view to attract and promote responsible foreign investment of the Contracting Parties in their respective territories that contribute to sustainable economic development;
>
> Recognizing that fostering an open and transparent policy environment and protecting investments of investors of one Contracting Party in the territory of the other Contracting Party are conducive to the stimulation of mutually beneficial economic activity and intensification of economic cooperation;
>
> Reaffirming their commitment to sustainable development and to enhancing the contribution of international trade and investment to sustainable development.

The Nigeria-Morocco BIT (2016) – which has not yet been ratified – represents an innovative example of a more forward reform to the language and approach to investment protection. The concept of sustainable development is included in the preamble – but here, three times:

> [...] RECOGNIZING the important contribution investment can make to the sustainable development of the state parties, including the reduction of poverty, increase of productive capacity, economic growth, the transfer of technology, and the furtherance of human rights and human development; SEEKING to promote, encourage and increase investment opportunities that enhance sustainable development within the territories of the state parties; UNDERSTANDING that sustainable development requires the fulfillment of the economic, social and environmental pillars that are embedded within the concept.

The implications for this inclusion are dynamic, creating a simple link within the treaties' object and purpose to a range of soft laws and more normatively developed frameworks regarding environmental, social, and human rights.

52. On the issue of treaty reform, *see, e.g.*, Catharine Titi, *Most-Favoured-Nation Treatment, Survival Clauses and Reform of International Investment Law*, 33(5) J. Int'l Arb. 425, 426 (2016) DOI: 10.54648/joia2016034 ('Reform requires a reconciliation of competing interests, which is generally so difficult to achieve that it is often unclear whether an option constitutes 'reform' or unwanted change. Sometimes, contracting parties amend investment treaty provisions in order to counteract non-envisaged and unintended interpretations advanced by claimant investors or adopted by arbitral tribunals'); Federico M. Lavopa, Lucas E. Barreiros & Victoria Bruno, *How to Kill a BIT and Not Die Trying: Legal and Political Challenges of Denouncing or Renegotiating Bilateral Investment Treaties*, 16 J. Int'l Econ. L. 869, 885 (2013) DOI: 10.2139/ssrn.2102683 (discussing the difficulty of renegotiation and amending treaties); Federico M. Lavopa et al., *The Challenges of Denouncing BITs: Why It Is Better to Renegotiate*, UNCTAD Investment Policy Hub Featured Discussion (12 February 2013), https://investmentpolicy.unctad.org/blogs/19/the-challenges-of-denounci
ng-bits-why-it-is-better-to-renegotiate.

With respect to the definition of investment, the Nigeria-Morocco BIT provides that:

> 'Investment' means an enterprise within the territory of one State established, acquired, expanded or operated, in *good faith*, by an investor of the other State in accordance with law of the Party in who territory the investment is made taken together with the asset of the enterprise which *contribute sustainable development* of that Party and has the characteristics of an investment involving a commitment of capital or other similar resources, pending profit, risk-taking and certain duration. (emphasis added)

Notably, the criteria explicitly include that the investment is made in good faith but also in line with the ideals of sustainable development. This points to and incorporates within the language and obligations transforming ideas of economic development. Could this be the good faith investment of the future? If investment law is read as a system, should these changing elements of sustainable development be recognized across the system? How might this affect the way that investment is understood? Also, how might this be broadened to the various stages of the investment?

Taking this expansion of contribution to development to include sustainable development, the implications for the types of investments that should be covered are significant. While sustainable development in itself is a complex balance of economics, development, and the environment, there is a growing understanding of that balance and a growing development of its conceptualization in international law.[53] The growing reference to it - if not reliance on it - in relevant decisions of international tribunals[54] provides a legitimacy for investment tribunals to similarly accept its role in the larger dimensions of the international investment system. This, however, does not imply that every tribunal will go to the preamble in addressing the definition of 'investment'.

This express inclusion of a sustainable development element to the definition of 'investment' has potential implications at several stages of the investment. In the pre-investment stage, there may be a higher level of accountability placed on both the host state and the investor to engage in environmental impact assessments and other preliminary assessments. During the investment, supply chain issues could become an element of an investment conducted within the parameters of sustainable development. Even after an investor has decided to leave an investment, there may be a heightened level of accountability toward environmental standards of conduct derived from other areas of international law.

53. Phillipe Sands, *International Law in the Field of Sustainable Development*, 65 British Yearbook Int'l L. 303 (1994); Winfried Lang, *Sustainable Development and International Law* (Graham & Trotman 1995).
54. *See, inter alia*, *Lac Lanoux (France v. Spain)*, Award, [1957] 12 R.I.A.A. 281; *Pulp Mills on the River Uruguay (Argentina v. Uruguay)*, Judgment, [2010] ICJ Reports 14, paras 160-168; *Whaling in the Antarctic (Australia v. Japan, New Zealand intervening)*, Judgment, [2014] ICJ Reports 226, paras 74-246; *United States – Measures Concerning the Importation, Marketing and Sale of Tuna and Tuna Products*, WT/DS381/RW/USA, WT/DS381/AB/RW2, 14 December 2018, Report of the Appellate Body, para. 6.84; *Dispute Concerning the Delimitation of the Maritime Boundary between Bangladesh and Myanmar in the Gulf of Bengal* (14 March 2012).

[B] Public International Law

While the potential lack of normativity implied in the most recent international environmental treaties, in particular the Paris Agreement under the United Nations Framework Convention on Climate Change, leaves the application of international environmental laws rather unreachable within the context of investment protection, environmental issues have already arisen within investment disputes in a number of ways, including as counterclaims[55] and also an environmental claim against a state for failure to maintain a protected environment.[56] The international framework for environmental protection may also further enlighten the interpretation of sustainable development or other preambular language; significant domestic legislation also impacts investments. The enactment of environmentally forward energy law has enabled foreign investments.[57] In the case of the heightening of domestic environmental law, unanticipated changes in the regulatory environment may lead to a claim against a state for breach of legitimate expectations. While the limitations on the application of such laws are recognized, domestic environmental laws, however, may find their way into the definition of investment through several avenues. The first route involves the definition as provided by the *Phoenix* tribunal and with the layered good faith interpretation of those requirements. The requirement that the investment be made within the laws of the host state enables – at least should the laws exist when the investment is made – respect for these domestic environmental norms. The obvious limitation arises after the investment is made. Any strengthening of the environmental law could result in a regulatory change that may lead to a breach of the fair and equitable treatment provision of the investment treaty. This approach returns directly to the problems of the right to regulate.[58]

The existence of other soft law mechanisms within the sphere of international law provides further basis for intersection with investment law generally and the definition of investment more specifically. While the UN Guiding Principles on Business and Human Rights provided the foundation for implementing a transnational regime for corporate responsibility,[59] the open-ended intergovernmental working

55. *Burlington Resources Inc. v. Republic of Ecuador*, ICSID Case No. ARB/08/5, Decision on Ecuador's Counterclaims, 7 December 2017, para. 77; *Perenco Ecuador Ltd v. Republic of Ecuador*, ICSID Case No. ARB/08/6, Award, 27 September 2019, paras 423 et seq., 489.
56. *David R. Aven and Others v. Republic of Costa Rica*, ICSID Case No. UNCT/15/3, Award of the Tribunal, 18 September 2018, paras 447 et seq. (analysis of whether Cost Rica breached the investor's legitimate expectations as a result of changes to development restrictions in a protected wetland area).
57. European Union Energy Action, 2020 Climate and Energy Package; European Commission, Press Release, *REPowerEU: Joint European action for more affordable, secure and sustainable energy* (8 March 2022).
58. Yulia Yevoshova, *The Right of States to Regulate in International Investment Law: The Search for Balance Between Public Interest and Fair and Equitable Treatment* 26 (Kluwer 2019) ('Disputes in the area of the environment and public health have instigated a discussion on the extent to which investment agreements are able to limit a state's internal sovereignty.'); Catharine Titi, *The Right to Regulate in International Investment Law* (Nomos/Hart 2014).
59. In particular, Principle 8 calls for policy coherence which is significantly relevant in the context of investment law as it bridges the domestic and international spheres.

group on transnational corporations and other business enterprises with respect to human rights (OEIGWG) has provided further room for incorporation and integration of obligations. In particular, the current draft of the Legally Binding Instrument to Regulate, in International Human Rights Law, the Activities of Transnational Corporations and other Business Enterprises[60] includes the express intention for applicability to 'business activities of a transnational character'.[61] Article 14.5 provides that:

> States Parties shall ensure that: a. All existing bilateral or multilateral agreements, including regional or sub-regional agreements, on issues relevant to this (Legally Binding Instrument) and its protocols, including trade and investment agreements, shall be interpreted and implemented in a manner that does not undermine or restrict their capacity to fulfill their obligations under this (Legally Binding Instrument) and its protocols, if any, as well as other relevant human rights conventions and instruments. b. All new bilateral or multilateral trade and investment agreements shall be compatible with the States Parties' human rights obligations under this (Legally Binding Instrument) and its protocols, as well as other relevant human rights conventions and instruments.

[C] European Union: Legal Developments on Investors

Furthermore, certain regional (or supra-national) commitments have also created a layer of deference to sustainable development, even beyond express implications for it in the treaty law. In particular, the EU has made significant inroads in this respect, possibly impacting the manner in which the agreements are concluded by the EU.[62] The European Parliament has identified this gap in obligations for corporate actors and the role of these actors in potential violations of human rights and environmental protections; it has begun the process of developing due diligence laws requiring corporate compliance in the supply chain.[63] The intersection between this potential legal requirement within the EU and the current framework of investment law leaves significant questions to be answered regarding how such legal regimes would interact in an investment dispute, whether its relevance would be identified, and whether a tribunal would possess authority under the respective agreements to take such a decision on an investor's obligations.

60. Third Review Draft, 17 August 2021.
61. Draft Art. 3.
62. J. Robert Basedow, *The European Union's New International Investment Policy and the United Nation's Sustainable Development Goals: Integration as a Motor of Substantive Policy Change?, in International Trade, Investment, and the Sustainable Development Goals* (Cosimo Beverelli, Jürgen Kurtz & Damian Raess eds, Cambridge Univ. Press 2020).
63. European Parliament, Briefing, *Towards a mandatory EU system of due diligence for supply chains* (22 October 2020), https://www.europarl.europa.eu/thinktank/en/document/EPRS_BRI(2020)659299; Beata Faracik, *Implementation of the UN Guiding Principles on Business and Human Rights*, European Parliament, DG External Policies, External Study (February 2017), https://www.europarl.europa.eu/RegData/etudes/STUD/2017/578031/EXPO_STU(2017)578031_EN.pdf; European Commission, Directorate-General for Justice and Consumers, Francisca Torres-Cortés et al., *Study on Due Diligence Requirements Through the Supply Chain: Final Report* (EU Publications Office 2020), https://data.europa.eu/doi/10.2838/39830.

The proposed EU laws on due diligence in the supply chain suggest an expansion of these requirements for contribution to sustainable development.[64] The possibility of this normative development implies that the definition of 'investment' – should it be read with a requirement of contribution to the sustainable development of the home state – may further demand consideration of these types of obligations. These developments could be read and explored in parallel with the EU's power to conclude international investment agreements.[65]

§5.05 CONCLUSION: THE FUTURE OF GOOD FAITH INVESTMENTS

This discussion on how to understand a good faith investment in light of changing conceptualizations of development leaves states as well as investors on unstable ground. International investment policy has traditionally been focused on the stability of the investor in the host state. It draws on the pre-conceptions that the lack of stability in the judicial systems of host states and the lack of predictability in the legal developments can only be remedied through an additional layer of protection, through the investment protection agreements. While the discussion on the right of the host state has now re-animated how that legal stability and predictability should be understood, using mechanisms available in public international law to further engage in a layering of what qualifies as an investment may step too far from those intentions. These interpretations may be seen as veering off the course of the contractual protections that are enabled by the investors' right to take a host state to an arbitral tribunal. This may be seen as facilitating a level of judicial activism by the tribunal.

On the other hand, some may argue that the inclusion of sustainable development, requirements to invest in good faith, potential obligations arising out of supply chain legislation and the accompanying trajectories of protection regarding human rights and the environment that may be implied in such language are a mere show, changing nothing but the rhetoric. The fact that the Nigeria-Morocco BIT, one of few with such expansive language, is not yet in force leaves significant room for speculation. How would a host state invoke such investor *obligations*? Would this requirement for investment contributing to sustainable development instead place the burden on the host state in making investment decisions and when making concessions? In short, would the responsibility, because of the nature of investment protection, place the burden on the state, thus resulting in no changes for the investor in making an investment abroad?

While these treaties have been written with the intention to be predictable, binding, and enforceable, re-aligning the definition of 'investment' with changing norms of development through the application of good faith is one potential approach to the system's limitations.

---

64. European Parliament, Briefing, *supra* n. 63; Faracik, *supra* n. 63; Torres-Cortés, et al., *supra* n. 63.
65. Basedow, *supra* n. 62.

CHAPTER 6

Good Faith in Investor-State Arbitration: Is There Room for a Positive Basis to Claims and Good Pack Hunting?

Mohamed S. Abdel Wahab

> Ignorance cannot lead to evil, misconceptions lead to evil. It is not what people do know, it's what they pretend they do – *Jean Jacques Rousseau*

(A Calendar of Wisdom by Leo Tolstoy – Translated from Russian by Peter Sekirin, 1997)

§6.01 PROLOGUE

The notion of good faith attracts much controversy in comparative and international laws. National and international courts and tribunals are often asked to address arguments and determine issues pertinent to the principle of good faith. Parties, scholars and practitioners battle over the meaning, scope and implications of good faith, and investor-State arbitration is not immune to such controversy.

Whilst it is generally accepted that good faith is acknowledged as a principle of international law, divergent views exist as to its definition, scope, role and limitations. This paper aims to tackle only one aspect of good faith, that is, its role as a possible positive basis for claims in investor-State arbitration. That said, the author shall start by disambiguating the notion of good faith and will then move to address good faith as a possible basis for advancing positive claims in investor-State dispute settlement (ISDS).

§6.02 DISAMBIGUATING GOOD FAITH: CONCEPTIONS AND MISCONCEPTIONS

A stringent and narrow application of the law may sometimes lead to unjust outcomes. This has led diverse legal systems across the globe to develop and adopt legal principles that play a pivotal role in mitigating the rigid application of the law and in proposing various comprehensive remedies for controversial issues and to achieve justice.[1] One of these leading principles is good faith, the application of which is intended to bring about harmonisation and consistency in both international law and domestic law without compromising on legal certainty and predictability.[2]

The principle of good faith exists in all legal systems (belonging to both the civil and common law traditions) in order to ensure, to varying degrees, that all parties perform their legal obligations in accordance with the letter and spirit of the law and the parties' bargains and dealings. In *Phoenix Action Ltd v. Czech Republic*, the arbitral tribunal stated that:

> The principle of good faith is also recognized in most, if not all, domestic legal systems. It appears therefore as a kind of 'Janus concept', with one face looking at the national legal order and one at the international legal order. And in most cases, but not in all, a violation of the international principle of good faith and a violation of the national principle of good faith go hand in hand.[3]

The principle of good faith forms part of customary international law and is also a general principle of law.[4] In *TECO Guatemala Holdings, LLC v. Republic of Guatemala*, the arbitral tribunal stated that '[t]here is no doubt in the eyes of the Arbitral Tribunal that the principle of good faith is part of customary international law as established by Article 38.1(b) of the Statute of the International Court of Justice'.[5]

---

1. Andrew D Mitchell, M Sornarajah, and Tania Voon, *Good Faith in International Economic Law* 1-2 (Oxford University Press 2015). *See also* Anthea Roberts, *Power and Persuasion in Investment Treaty Interpretation: The Dual Role of States*, American Journal of International Law, Vol. 104, 214 (2010), available at SSRN: https://ssrn.com/abstract=1514410 (DOI: 10.5305/amerjintelaw.104.2.0179).
2. Andrew D. Mitchell, M. Sornarajah, and Tania Voon, *Good Faith in International Economic Law* 3 (Oxford University Press 2015). *See also* Emily Sipiorski, *Good Faith International in Investment Arbitration* 236-238 (Oxford University Press 2019).
3. *Phoenix Action Ltd v. Czech Republic*, ICSID Case No. ARB/06/5, Award, 15 April 2009, para. 109.
4. *Phoenix Action Ltd v. Czech Republic*, ICSID Case No. ARB/06/5, Award, 15 April 2009, para. 106 ('In the Tribunal's view, States cannot be deemed to offer access to the ICSID dispute settlement mechanism to investments not made in good faith. The protection of international investment arbitration cannot be granted if such protection would run contrary to the general principles of international law, among which the principle of good faith is of utmost importance'); *M.C.I. Power Group, L.C. and New Turbine, Inc. v. Republic of Ecuador*, ICSID Case No. ARB/03/6, Award, 31 July 2007, para. 115 ('With regard to the other relevant case cited by the Claimants, the Tribunal notes that in Opel Austria v. Council of the European Union the Court of First Instance of the European Union held that the principle of good faith is a rule of customary international law which was codified in Article 18 of the Vienna Convention'). *See also* Emily Sipiorski, *Good Faith in International Investment Arbitration* 2 (Oxford University Press 2019).
5. *TECO Guatemala Holdings, LLC v. Republic of Guatemala*, ICSID Case No. ARB/10/23, Award, 19 December 2013, para. 456.

However, in as much as good faith represents an overarching general principle of law in many jurisdictions and in international law, it lacks a universally agreed and binding definition given its linkage to moral and relative concepts such as fairness, loyalty, trustworthiness, and justice.[6] Numerous attempts have been made by scholars, courts and arbitral tribunals to give good faith a workable definition. For example, in *Inceysa v. El Salvador*, the arbitral tribunal described good faith as follows:

> Good faith is a supreme principle, which governs legal relations in all of their aspects and content. Concerning the scope and content of the principle of good faith, it is necessary to take into account the following comments: 'The Latin expression bona fide is used in the original or translated into various languages, in Spanish "*buena fe*," to indicate the spirit of loyalty, respect for the law and fidelity, in other words, absence of dissimulation or fraud in relations between two or several parties in a legal act.' In the contractual field, good faith means absence of deceit and artifice during the negotiation and execution of instruments that gave rise to the investment, as well as loyalty, truth and intent to maintain the equilibrium between the reciprocal performance of the parties.[7]

In *Phoenix Action, Ltd. v. Czech Republic*, the arbitral tribunal emphasized the significance of good faith by stating that:

> The principle of good faith has long been recognized in public international law, as it is also in all national legal systems. This principle requires parties 'to deal honestly and fairly with each other, to represent their motives and purposes truthfully, and to refrain from taking unfair advantage ....'[74] This principle governs the relations between States, but also the legal rights and duties of those seeking to assert an international claim under a treaty. Nobody shall abuse the rights granted by treaties, and more generally, every rule of law includes an implied clause that it should not be abused.[8]

That said, sceptics about good faith and its role have argued that the principle of good faith leads to unpredictable consequences, given the absence of a universally agreed definition, the variability of good faith across jurisdictions and its connectedness to notions of fairness and loyalty, which involve subjective biases.[9] This has led those sceptics to argue that the principle of good faith could be a basis for manipulation and misinterpretation.[10]

Lord McNair called upon States not to abuse good faith by attempting to rely on an ambiguity in order to misinterpret treaty provisions. He stated:

6. Andrew D. Mitchell, M. Sornarajah, and Tania Voon, *Good Faith in International Economic Law* 11 (Oxford University Press 2015).
7. *Inceysa Vallisoletana S.L. v. Republic of El Salvador*, ICSID Case No. ARB/03/26, Award, 2 August 2006, paras 230-231.
8. *Phoenix Action, Ltd. v. Czech Republic*, ICSID Case No. ARB/06/5, Award, 15 April 2009, para. 107.
9. Andrew D. Mitchell,. M Sornarajah, and Tania Voon, *Good Faith in International Economic Law* 101 (Oxford University Press 2015).
10. Andrew D. Mitchell, M. Sornarajah, and Tania Voon, *Good Faith in International Economic Law* 1 (Oxford University Press 2015).

> The performance of treaties is subject to an over-riding obligation of mutual good faith. This obligation is also operative in the sphere of the interpretation of treaties, and it would be a breach of this obligation for a party to make use of an ambiguity in order to put forward an interpretation which it was known to the negotiators of the treaty not to be the intention of the parties.[11]

Nevertheless, good faith remains a welcomed overarching principle that is respected and used to fulfil the ends of justice. In *Ioan Micula v. Romania*, the arbitral tribunal stated that '[g]ood faith is a standard that is flexible. A requirement of good faith is prevalent in all fields of the law and will arise in various matters, such as the interpretation of treaties (Article 31 of the VLCT), the prohibition to abuse rights, and the protection of legitimate expectation'.

Similarly, in *Hrvatska Elektroprivreda D.D. v. Republic of Slovenia*, the arbitral tribunal held that 'VCLT Article 31 mandates that treaties be interpreted "in good faith." That is the core principle about which all else revolves.'[12]

It is in this spirit that good faith has been described as a "Swiss army knife"[13] where it can be used and abused, and it is for the decision-makers to harness and channel its positive energy to fall on the side of law and justice. Good faith, as a prevailing principle of law, is not intended to circumvent the law and/or revoke agreements or obligations; it aims to properly apply the law and to correctly implement and construe the parties' bargains, rights and obligations in accordance with the parties' common intention and the duties of cooperation, trust and confidence that ought to prevail between contracting parties.

§6.03 GOOD FAITH AS A SOURCE OF POSITIVE OBLIGATIONS

This section addresses the issue of whether good faith can be a source of positive obligations and focuses on the obligation of the host State to act in good faith in light of the minimum standards of international investment law, such as the standard of fair and equitable treatment (FET), full protection and security, non-discrimination, the protection of legitimate expectations of foreign investors, and expropriation. Moreover, it casts light on the consequences of breaching the principle of good faith in the assessment of damages and cost allocation in investment arbitration.

International law recognises the principle of good faith and imposes an obligation on States to comply with it. Article 2(2) of the United Nations Charter states that 'All Members, in order to ensure to all of them the rights and benefits resulting from

11. Lord Arnold McNair, *The Law of Treaties* 465 (Clarendon Press 1961).
12. *Hrvatska Elektroprivreda D.D. v. Republic of Slovenia*, ICSID Case No. ARB/05/24, Decision on the Treaty Interpretation Issue, 12 June 2009, para. 191.
13. Andrew D. Mitchell, M. Sornarajah, and Tania Voon, *Good Faith in International Economic Law* 11 (Oxford University Press 2015). ('In international dispute settlement, good faith has a firm place as both a facilitating and a restraining agent: it helps, on the one hand, to infuse predictability and reasonableness into state behaviour, furthers due process, and serves as an interpretative tool for international courts and tribunals, while on the other hand it restrains legal formalism and arbitrariness. With all these virtues incorporated in one principle, good faith could be characterized as the "Swiss army knife" among international legal principles.')

membership, shall fulfil in good faith the obligations assumed by them in accordance with the present Charter'.[14] In addition, Article 26 of the Vienna Convention on the Law of Treaties (VCLT) reads as follows: '[e]very treaty in force is binding upon the parties to it and must be performed by them in good faith'.[15] Furthermore, Article 18 VCLT states that a State which has signed or ratified a treaty has an obligation to refrain from acts which would defeat the object and purpose of that treaty prior to its entry into force.[16]

Moreover, the principle of good faith is integrated into investment law and investment treaty protections.[17] Article 34 of the Convention on the Settlement of Investment Disputes between States and Nationals of Other States (ICSID) reads as follows: '[t]he parties shall cooperate in good faith with the Commission in order to enable the Commission to carry out its functions, and shall give their most serious consideration to its recommendations'.[18] Similarly, Rule 23 of the ICSID *Conciliation Rules* imposes an obligation on the parties to cooperate in good faith with the Commission concerning providing documents, information, and explanations to assist

---

14. United Nations, Charter of the United Nations, 24 October 1945, 1 UNTS XVI.
15. *Vienna Convention on the Law of Treaties* (1969), adopted on 23 May 1969, Art. 26. *See ILC (International Law Commission) Draft Articles on Responsibility of States for Internationally Wrongful Acts*, adopted on 9 June 2001, Art. 52(4).
16. *Vienna Convention on the Law of Treaties* (1969), adopted on 23 May 1969, Art. 18.
17. *See, e.g., World Bank (World Bank Group) Guidelines on the Treatment of Foreign Direct Investment* (1992), adopted on 21 September 1992, IV (1) ('A State may not expropriate or otherwise take in whole or in part a foreign private investment in its territory, or take measures which have similar effects, except where this is done in accordance with applicable legal procedures, in pursuance in good faith of a public purpose, without discrimination on the basis of nationality and against the payment of appropriate compensation'). *Convention establishing the Multilateral Investment Guarantee Agency*, 11 October 1985, 1508 U.N.T.S.99 (I-26012) (entered into force 12 April 1988), Article 3(d) ('The parties shall cooperate in good faith with the conciliator and shall, in particular, provide him with all information and documentation which would assist him in the discharge of his functions; they shall give their most serious consideration to his recommendations.'). *North American Free Trade Agreement*, adopted on 17 December 1992, Art. 1109(4) and (5), Art. 1111(2), and Art. 2104 (2)(b). *The Energy Charter Treaty*, adopted on 17 December 1994, Article 14(4) ('a Contracting Party may protect the rights of creditors, or ensure compliance with laws on the issuing, trading and dealing in securities and the satisfaction of judgements in civil, administrative and criminal adjudicatory proceedings, through the equitable, non-discriminatory, and good faith application of its laws and regulations'). *See also* Energy Charter Secretariat, *The Energy Charter Treaty and Related Documents: A Legal Framework for International Energy Cooperation (2005)*, at 157. *ASEAN Comprehensive Investment Agreement*, adopted on 26 February 2009, Art. 13(3) and Art. 20(2). *Central America-Dominican Republic-United States Free Trade Agreement (DR-CAFTA)*, adopted on 5 August 2004, Art. 10.8(4), and Art. 10.14(2). *Agreement between the Republic of Turkey and Turkmenistan concerning the Reciprocal Promotion and Protection of Investments*, adopted on 2 May 1992, Art. IV(1). *Agreement between the Government of the Argentine Republic and the Government of the United Mexican States for the Promotion and Reciprocal Protection of Investments*, adopted on 13 November 1996, Art. 4(3). Agreement between the Government of the United Kingdom of Great Britain and Northern Ireland and the Government of the Arab Republic of Egypt for the Promotion and Protection of Investments, adopted on 11 June 1975, Art. 6(1).
18. *Convention on the Settlement of Investment Disputes between States and Nationals of Other States*, adopted on 18 March 1965, Art. 34(1).

the Tribunal in hearing the witnesses and the experts.[19] According to Article 2(2)(c) of the Charter of Economic and Political Duties of States, States in their economic and political relations shall fulfil their international obligations in good faith. However, it is worth noting that observing the requirements of good faith is a two-way process, with the result that investments not made in good faith may not benefit from treaty protections. It is in this respect that the arbitral tribunal in the *Phoenix* case held that:

> The purpose of the international mechanism of protection of investment through ICSID arbitration cannot be to protect investments made in violation of the laws of the host State or investments not made in good faith, obtained, for example, through misrepresentations, concealments or corruption, or amounting to an abuse of the international ICSID arbitration system. In other words, the purpose of international protection is to protect legal and bona fide investments.[20]

The United Nations General Assembly also stated that '[h]owever, upon agreement by sovereign States and other parties concerned, settlement of the dispute should be made through arbitration or international adjudication ... Foreign investment agreements freely entered into by or between sovereign States shall be observed in good faith'.[21]

Accordingly, States are expected to establish coherent legal frameworks to protect and support bona fide foreign investments and assure investors of the State's full compliance with the principle of good faith and other protections granted under the concerned treaties. In *Salini v. Jordan*, the arbitral tribunal decided that a State is required to 'create and maintain in its territory a legal framework apt to guarantee to investors ... the compliance in good faith, of all undertakings assumed with regard to each specific investor'.[22]

Given the existing international framework that supports an overarching obligation of good faith, what remains to be considered is whether good faith can be a source of positive obligations.

Whilst the International Court of Justice (ICJ) in the *Nuclear Tests case* stated that '[o]ne of the basic principles governing the creation and performance of legal obligations, whatever their source, is the principle of good faith. Trust and confidence are inherent in international co-operation, in particular in an age when this co-operation in

19. *ICSID (International Centre for Settlement of Investment Disputes) Rules of Procedure for Conciliation Proceedings (2003)*, adopted in 2003, Rule 23(1) ('The parties shall cooperate in good faith with the Commission and, in particular, at its request furnish all relevant documents, information and explanations as well as use the means at their disposal to enable the Commission to hear witnesses and experts whom it desires to call. The parties shall also facilitate visits to and inquiries at any place connected with the dispute that the Commission desires to undertake.').
20. *Phoenix Action Ltd v. Czech Republic*, ICSID Case No. ARB/06/5, Award, 15 April 2009, para. 100.
21. UN General Assembly, *Permanent sovereignty over natural resources*, 17 December 1973, A/RES/3171, available at https://www.ohchr.org/sites/default/files/Documents/Professional Interest/resources.pdf.
22. *Salini Costruttori S.p.A. and Italstrade S.p.A. v. Hashemite Kingdom of Jordan*, ICSID Case No. ARB/02/13, Award, 31 January 2006, para. 30.

many fields is becoming increasingly essential'.[23] Justice Read, in the *Certain Norwegian Loans case*, stated, in his dissenting opinion, that 'I should be disinclined to bring notions of "good faith" and *abus de droit* into the question. Practically speaking, it is, I think, impossible for, an international tribunal to examine a dispute between two sovereign States on the basis of either good or bad faith or of abuse of law'.[24] Similarly, the ICJ in the *Land and Maritime Boundary Case* stated that the principle of good faith is 'one of the basic principles governing the creation and performance of legal obligations ... it is not in itself a source of obligation where none would otherwise exist'.[25] In addition, in the *Border and Transborder Armed Actions case*, the ICJ held that 'good faith is not in itself a source of obligation where none would otherwise exist'.[26]

Thus, according to the ICJ, it may be argued that the principle of good faith 'has no teeth in the absence of another valid legal obligation and cannot be treated as a self-standing clause of international law equipped with its own remedy'.[27] However, In *FYR Macedonia and Greece over the name of Macedonia*, the ICJ had to consider the principle of good faith in the context of negotiations.[28] The Court stated that 'although Article 5, paragraph 1, contains no express requirement that the Parties negotiate in good faith, such obligation is implicit under this provision'.[29] For purposes of dispute settlement, the Court imposed an obligation on States to conduct meaningful negotiations, and this obligation to negotiate is not only to enter negotiations but also to pursue them with a view to concluding agreements.[30] To put it differently, States are required to enter meaningful negotiations and must do so in good faith.

23. *Nuclear Tests (Australia v. France)* ICJ Rep 253, Judgment, 20 December 1974, para. 46.
24. *Certain Norwegian Loans (France v. Norway)* ICJ Rep 9, Dissenting Opinion of Judge Read, 6 July 1957, p. 94.
25. *Land and Maritime Boundary between Cameroon and Nigeria (Cameroon v. Nigeria: Equatorial Guinea intervening)* ICJ Rep 275, Judgment - Preliminary Objections, 11 June 1998, para. 39.
26. *Border and Transborder Armed Actions (Nicaragua v. Honduras)* ICJ Rep 1988, Judgment - Jurisdiction of the Court and Admissibility of the Application, 20 December 1988, para. 94.
27. Sanja Djajic, *Mapping the Good Faith Principle in International Investment Arbitration: Assessment of Its Substantive and Procedural Value*, 207-233 (2012), available at https://ssrn.com/abstract=3502511.
28. *Application of the Interim Accord of 13 September 1995 (The Former Yugoslav Republic of Macedonia v. Greece)* ICJ Rep 2011, Judgment, 5 December 2011.
29. *Application of the Interim Accord of 13 September 1995 (The Former Yugoslav Republic of Macedonia v. Greece)* ICJ Rep 2011, Judgment, 5 December 2011, para. 131 ('the Court notes that although Article 5, paragraph 1, contains no express requirement that the Parties negotiate in good faith, such obligation is implicit under this provision (*see* 1969 Vienna Convention, Art. 26; *see also* Delimitation of the Maritime Boundary in the Gulf of Maine Area (Canada/United States of America), Judgment, I.C.J. Reports 1984, p. 292, para. 87; Fisheries Jurisdiction (United Kingdom v. Iceland), Merits, Judgment, I.C.J. Reports 1974, pp. 33-34, paras 78-79; Fisheries Jurisdiction (Federal Republic of Germany v. Iceland), Merits, Judgment, I.C.J. Reports 1974, p. 202, para. 69; Nuclear Tests (Australia v. France), Judgment, I.C.J. Reports 1974, p. 268, para. 46; Nuclear Tests (New Zealand v. France), Judgment, I.C.J. Reports 1974, p. 473, para. 49; North Sea Continental Shelf (Federal Republic of Germany I Denmark; Federal Republic of Germany I Netherlands), Judgment, I.C.J. Reports 1969, pp. 46-47, para. 85').
30. *Application of the Interim Accord of 13 September 1995 (The Former Yugoslav Republic of Macedonia v. Greece)* ICJ Rep 2011, Judgment, 5 December 2011, para. 132.

In light of the above, the ICJ appears to have imposed a duty of good faith on the parties when conducting negotiations. Thus, according to the ICJ, whilst the good faith principle is not regarded as a source of autonomous self-standing obligations, it can serve as an ancillary mechanism to deploy implied obligations to support and give effect to existing obligations.[31] Be that as it may, it seems that the ICJ's jurisprudence remains unchanged as to good faith, which can guide the decision-making process,[32] but does not serve as a self-standing source of positive obligations, absent an express legal basis to elevate its role in creating positive obligations that are non-ancillary to already existing ones.

In *Sempra v. Argentina*, the arbitral tribunal held that:

> The principle of good faith is thus relied on as the common guiding beacon that will orient the understanding and interpretation of obligations, just as happens under civil codes.[33]

Having considered the principle of good faith in general, it is now important to deepen the analysis by considering the role of good faith in the specific contexts of: (i) the FET treatment standard; (ii) the principle of legitimate expectations; (iii) the full protection and security standard; (iv) expropriation; and (v) damages and allocation of costs, before making a few concluding remarks.

[A] Fair and Equitable Treatment

The standard of FET forms part of international investment law and provides foreign investors with fair and equitable remedies.[34] In the *Oil Platforms case,* Justice Higgins stated that 'the key terms "fair and equitable treatment to nationals and companies" and "unreasonable and discriminatory measures" are legal terms of art well known in

31. Sanja Djajic, *Mapping the Good Faith Principle in International Investment Arbitration: Assessment of Its Substantive and Procedural Value*, 207-233 (2012), available at https://ssrn.com/abstract=3502511.
32. Steven Reinhold, *Good Faith in International Law*, UCL Journal of Law and Jurisprudence, Vol. 2, 40 63 (2015), available at https://discovery.ucl.ac.uk/id/eprint/1470678/1/2UCLJLJ40%20-%20Good%20Faith.pdf.
33. *Sempra Energy International v. Argentine Republic*, ICSID Case No. ARB/02/16, Award, 28 September 2007, para. 297. *See also* Rudoff Dolzer, *Fair and Equitable Treatment: A Key Standard in Investment Treaties*, 39 Int'l L. 87-106 (2005), available at https://scholar.smu.edu/til/vol39/iss1/6. *See* Andrew D. Mitchell, M. Sornarajah, and Tania Voon, *Good Faith in International Economic Law* 11 (Oxford University Press 2015). ('Good faith plays ... a role in international law comparable to that of a catalyst in a chemical reaction. Alone, the catalyst is completely passive. It must be added to other elements for a reaction to occur; without it, nothing will happen, even if all the necessary components are present in sufficient quantities. It is a bit the same with good faith ... It is always related to specific behavior or declarations and it invests them with legal significance and legal effects').
34. Rumana Islam, *The Fair and Equitable Treatment (FET) Standard in International Investment Arbitration Developing Countries in Context* 9 (Springer 2018). *See generally* Martins Paparinskis, *The International Minimum Standard and Fair and Equitable Treatment* (Oxford University Press 2013).

the field of overseas investment protection, which is what is there addressed'.[35] The standard of fair and equitable treatment has no specific definition. One commentator argued that the standard in question should be determined on a case-by-case because of its evolutionary nature.[36] Similarly, in *Siag v. Egypt*, the arbitral tribunal stated that '[t]he fair and equitable treatment ("FET") standard is broad requirement, the application of which depends on the particular facts of each case'.[37] In *Suez v. Argentina*, the arbitral tribunal held that:

> *An effort to determine the ordinary meaning of 'just' or 'fair and equitable treatment' does not result in an answer of great precision and specificity.* At the outset, it should be noted that neither of the BITs applicable to this case define the three key words: 'fair', 'equitable', and 'treatment'. 'Treatment', according to the Oxford English Dictionary, is 'Conduct, behaviour; action or behaviour towards a person.' In its Decision on Jurisdiction in this case, the Tribunal stated the following with respect to the meaning of 'treatment': '"The word "treatment" is not defined in the treaty text. However, the ordinary meaning of that term within the context of investment includes the rights and privileges granted and the obligations and burdens imposed by a Contracting State on investments made by investors covered by the treaty.' The Tribunal will continue to employ that definition for purposes of this decision on the merits of the Claimants' case.[38]

In light of the above, there appears to be a clear correlation between the principle of good faith and the standard of FET. If a State or an investor does not act in accordance with the requirements of good faith, a breach of the standard of FET will be triggered. This is further analysed below in the context of some important decisions rendered by international tribunals in investment treaty cases.

In *TECO Guatemala Holdings, LLC v. Republic of Guatemala*, the arbitral tribunal captured and emphasised the direct relationship between good faith and the FET standard when it held that:

> The Arbitral Tribunal also considers that the minimum standard is part and parcel of the international principle of good faith. There is no doubt in the eyes of the Arbitral Tribunal that the principle of good faith is part of customary international law as established by Article 38.1(b) of the Statute of the International Court of

35. *Oil Platforms (Iran v. United States)* (Preliminary Objections) ICJ Rep 803, Separate Opinion of Judge Higgins, para. 39.
36. Roland Kläger, *Fair and Equitable Treatment in International Investment Law* 122 (Cambridge Press 2011).
37. *Waguih Elie George Siag and Clorinda Vecchi v. Arab Republic of Egypt*, ICSID Case No. ARB/05/15, Award, 1 June 2009, para. 450.
38. *Suez, Sociedad General de Aguas de Barcelona S.A., and InterAgua Servicios Integrales del Agua S.A. v. The Argentine Republic*, ICSID Case No. ARB/03/17, Decision on Liability, 30 July 2010, para. 195; *Saluka Investments BV v. The Czech Republic*, PCA Case No. 2001-04, Partial Award, 17 March 2006, para. 297 ('The "ordinary meaning" of the "fair and equitable treatment" standard can only be defined by terms of almost equal vagueness. In MTD, the tribunal stated that: In their ordinary meaning, the terms "fair" and "equitable" [...] mean "just", "even-handed", "unbiased", "legitimate". On the basis of such and similar definitions, one cannot say much more than the tribunal did in S.D. Myers by stating that an infringement of the standard requires treatment in such an unjust or arbitrary manner that the treatment rises to the level that is unacceptable from the international perspective. This is probably as far as one can get by looking at the "ordinary meaning" of the terms of Article 3.1 of the Treaty').

> Justice, and that a lack of good faith on the part of the State or of one of its organs should be taken into account in order to assess whether the minimum standard was breached.[39]

In *S.D. Myers Inc. v. Canada*,[40] the issue was whether Canada's export ban, which was considered to violate the principle of good faith under international law, was therefore discriminatory against SDMI and US PCB disposal companies and in favour of Canadian PCB remediation business.[41] Under Article 1105 of NAFTA, Canada is obliged to treat foreign investors in accordance with international law, including FET and to perform that treaty obligation in good faith.[42] In other words, Canada must treat foreign investors fairly and equally and must perform that treaty obligation in good faith. On the facts of the case, Canada issued an export ban that affected SDMI and US PCB disposal companies in favour of US agencies operating in Canada. SDMI, the claimant, argued that the export ban was discriminatory and unfair and violated the principle of good faith under international law. The arbitral tribunal found that Canada did not act in good faith, as it issued an export ban that affected SDMI's interests and favoured the interests of US companies operating in Canada.[43] Thus, the arbitral tribunal found that Canada's breach of the principle of good faith triggered the breach of the standard of FET and that the export ban was discriminatory and violated good faith under international law.[44]

In this specific case, it is worth noting that the arbitral tribunal did not state that Canada acted in bad faith because acting in bad faith (allegations of unlawful conduct

39. *TECO Guatemala Holdings, LLC v. Republic of Guatemala*, ICSID Case No. ARB/10/23, Award, 19 December 2013, para. 456. *Merril & Ring Forestry LP v. Canada* (Award) (Ad Hoc Arbitral Tribunal, UNCITRAL, 31 March 2010) para. 187 ('Good faith and the prohibition of arbitrariness are no doubt an expression of such general principles and no tribunal today could be asked to ignore these basic obligations of international law. The availability of a secure legal environment has a close connection too to such principles and transparency, while more recent, appears to be fast approaching that standard').
40. *S.D. Myers, Inc. v. Government of Canada*, Partial Award (Merits), 13 November 2000, paras 15-27. Canada prohibited the export of PCB (highly toxic substance) to the US without prior consent of the US Environmental Protection Agency (EPA). Later, the EPA, without notifying Canada, changed its policy and allowed imports of PCB into the US by discretionary exemptions under the Toxic Substances Control Act. SDMI, the claimant and a US company disposing of PCB waste, was granted a discretionary exemption. However, the Canadian Minister of Environment issued an export ban that prohibited the export of PCB waste to the US except from U.S. agencies operating in Canada. SDMI claimed that the export ban breached Canada's obligations under NAFTA as it was discriminatory, and it was issued to protect the Canadian PCB remediation business. Canada argued that the export ban was issued for environmental protection, not for other purposes. The arbitral tribunal found that the export ban was discriminatory against SDMI and US PCB disposal companies in favour of Canadian PCB remediation business. Canada acted in a bad faith towards SMID which triggered the breach of the FET.
41. *S.D. Myers, Inc. v. Government of Canada*, Partial Award (Merits), 13 November 2000, paras 15-27.
42. *North American Free Trade Agreement*, adopted on 17 December 1992, Art. 1105(1) ('Each Party shall accord to investments of investors of another Party treatment in accordance with international law, including fair and equitable treatment and full protection and security.').
43. *S.D. Myers, Inc. v. Government of Canada*, Partial Award (Merits), 13 November 2000, paras. 134-136.
44. *S.D. Myers, Inc. v. Government of Canada*, Partial Award (Merits), 13 November 2000, paras. 134-136.

attributed to the State or the investor) is not necessarily equivalent to breaching the principle of good faith. A finding of bad faith appears to be a high threshold that is not needed when assessing breaches of the requirements of good faith. More specifically, establishing outright bad faith is not required to prove a breach of the FET standard.[45]

In *Cargill v. Mexico,* Cargill, Inc., the claimant and a US company resorted to arbitration against Mexico on behalf of its wholly owned subsidiary, Cargill de Mexico S.A de C.V. The claimant argued that the purpose of Mexico's 2002 adoption of a tax on high fructose corn syrup had been the protection of Mexico's domestic sugar producers; therefore, Mexico's tax on high fructose corn syrup breached the minimum standard of treatment obligation under NAFTA's Article 1105.[46] The arbitral tribunal set a criterion to determine whether an action or a policy satisfied the requirement of the FET standard.[47] The arbitral tribunal held that the action must be unjust, unfair, arbitrary, etc., to trigger a breach of a fair and equitable standard. Moving more specifically to the arbitral tribunal's point concerning bad faith, it held that a finding of bad faith is not a required element to establish a breach of the standard of FET under NAFTA. However, this position is not limited to NAFTA arbitrations. In *Loewen Group, Inc. and Raymond L. Loewen v. United States of America,* the arbitral tribunal held that: 'Neither State practice, the decisions of international tribunals nor the opinion of commentators support the view that bad faith or malicious intention is an essential element of unfair and inequitable treatment or denial of justice amounting to a breach

45. Jeswald W. Salacuse, *The Law of Investment Treaties* 322 (Oxford University Press 2021). *See also* Emily Sipiorski, *Good Faith in International Investment Arbitration* 182-183 (Oxford University Press 2019).
46. *Cargill, Incorporated v. United Mexican States,* ICSID Case No. ARB(AF)/05/2, Award, 18 September 2009, paras. 1-5.
47. *Cargill, Incorporated v. United Mexican States,* ICSID Case No. ARB(AF)/05/2, Award, 18 September 2009, para. 296 ('In summation, the Tribunal finds that the obligations in Article 1105(1) of the NAFTA are to be understood by reference to the customary international law minimum standard of treatment of aliens. The requirement of fair and equitable treatment is one aspect of this minimum standard. To determine whether an action fails to meet the requirement of fair and equitable treatment, a tribunal must carefully examine whether the complained of measures were grossly unfair, unjust or idiosyncratic; arbitrary beyond a merely inconsistent or questionable application of administrative or legal policy or procedure so as to constitute an unexpected and shocking repudiation of a policy's very purpose and goals, or to otherwise grossly subvert a domestic law or policy for an ulterior motive; or involve an utter lack of due process so as to offend judicial propriety. The Tribunal observes that other NAFTA tribunals have expressed the view that the standard of fair and equitable treatment is not so strict as to require "bad faith" or "willful neglect of duty". The Tribunal agrees. However, the Tribunal emphasizes that although bad faith or willful neglect of duty is not required, the presence of such circumstances will certainly suffice.'); *Waste Management v. United Mexican States (II),* ICSID Case No. ARB(AF)/00/3, Award, 30 April 2004, para. 138 ('the minimum standard of treatment of fair and equitable treatment is infringed by conduct attributable to the State and harmful to the claimant if the conduct is arbitrary, grossly unfair, unjust or idiosyncratic, is discriminatory and exposes the claimant to sectional or racial prejudice, or involves a lack of due process leading to an outcome which offends judicial propriety - as might be the case with a manifest failure of natural justice in judicial proceedings or a complete lack of transparency and candour in an administrative process. In applying this standard it is relevant that the treatment is in breach of representations made by the host State which were reasonably relied on by the claimant').

of international justice.'[48] Nevertheless, the presence of bad faith does trigger a breach of the FET standard.[49] In *Ioan Micula, Viorel Micula and others v. Romania (I)*, the arbitral tribunal stated that '[t]here is no dispute that conduct that is substantively improper, whether because it is arbitrary, manifestly unreasonable, discriminatory or in bad faith, will violate the fair and equitable treatment standard'.[50]

In *Tecnicas Medioambientales, TECMED SA v. Mexico*, Tecmed, the claimant, alleged to have lost its investments in a waste landfill because Mexican authorities did not renew a licence necessary for the operation of that landfill. Under the Spain-Mexico BIT, each party to the BIT agreed to provide the investments of an investor of another party with a FET according to international law. The arbitral tribunal interpreted this treaty obligation in light of the good faith principle and found that the contracting parties must meet the basic expectations taken into account by foreign investors before investing in the host State.[51] The arbitral tribunal stated that foreign investors expect the host State:

- To act consistently, without ambiguity, and with total transparency in such a way that they can be aware of the relevant rules and regulations that will govern its investments, goals of the relevant policies, and directives so that they can comply with them.
- Not to deprive them of their investments without proper compensation.
- Not to revoke any pre-existing decisions or permits issued by the host State relied on by them to launch their commercial and business activities.[52]

The arbitral tribunal concluded that Mexico's actions were not consistent with the requirements of good faith and its behaviour amounted to a violation of FET, especially given the fact that Mexico assured Tecmed that it could operate the landfill

48. *Loewen Group, Inc. and Raymond L. Loewen v. United States of America*, ICSID Case No. ARB(AF)/98/3, Award, 26 June 2003, para. 132.
49. *Glamis Gold Ltd. v. United States of America*, Award, 8 June 2009, para. 616 ('It therefore appears that, although situations may be more varied and complicated today than in the 1920s, the level of scrutiny is the same. The fundamentals of the Neer standard thus still apply today: to violate the customary international law minimum standard of treatment codified in Article 1105 of the NAFTA, an act must be sufficiently egregious and shocking – a gross denial of justice, manifest arbitrariness, blatant unfairness, a complete lack of due process, evident discrimination, or a manifest lack of reasons – so as to fall below accepted international standards and constitute a breach of Article 1105(1). The Tribunal notes that one aspect of evolution from Neer that is generally agreed upon is that bad faith is not required to find a violation of the fair and equitable treatment standard, but its presence is conclusive evidence of such. Thus, an act that is egregious or shocking may also evidence bad faith, but such bad faith is not necessary for the finding of a violation. The standard for finding a breach of the customary international law minimum standard of treatment therefore remains as stringent as it was under Neer, it is entirely possible, however that, as an international community, we may be shocked by State actions now that did not offend us previously.').
50. *Ioan Micula, Viorel Micula and others v. Romania (I)*, ICSID Case No. ARB/05/20, Final Award, 11 December 2013, para. 522.
51. *Técnicas Medioambientales Tecmed, S.A. v. United Mexican States*, ICSID Case No. ARB(AF)/00/2, Award, 29 May 2003, para. 154.
52. *Técnicas Medioambientales Tecmed, S.A. v. United Mexican States*, ICSID Case No. ARB(AF)/00/2, Award, 29 May 2003, para. 154.

until the relocation was conducted and that new land would be provided together with licenses to operate the new landfill, and, yet, denied the renewal of the license. The arbitral tribunal found such behaviour to be ambiguous, uncertain, and prejudicial to the investor. It held that:

> It cannot be ignored, *in light of the good faith principle* (Articles 18 and 26 of the Vienna Convention), that the conduct of the Respondent between the date of execution of the Agreement (in view of the Respondent's determination to ratify it subsequently) and the effective date thereof, is incompatible with the imperative rules deriving from Article 4(1) of the Agreement as to fair and equitable treatment.[53]

It should be noted, however, that the principles of non-discrimination[54] and FET are distinct from each other, although they may cross paths. For example, whilst a breach of non-discrimination may trigger a breach of the standard of FET, a breach of the FET does not necessarily result in a breach of non-discrimination. In *Noble Ventures v. Romania*, the arbitral tribunal held that:

> Considering the place of the fair and equitable treatment standard at the very beginning of Art. II(2), one can consider this to be a more general standard which finds its specific application in *inter alia* the duty to provide full protection and security, the prohibition of arbitrary and discriminatory measures and the obligation to observe contractual obligations towards the investor. *As demonstrated above, none of those obligations or standards has been breached. While this in itself cannot lead to the conclusion that the more general fair and equitable treatment standard has not been breached.*[55]

Various bilateral investment treaties refer to non-discrimination in their provisions as a standalone autonomous obligation.[56] In *Azurix v. Argentina (I)*, the arbitral tribunal stated that: 'the Tribunal agrees with the interpretation of the Claimant that a measure needs only to be arbitrary to constitute a breach of the BIT. This interpretation has not been contested by the Respondent and it follows from the alternative way in

53. *Técnicas Medioambientales Tecmed, S.A. v. United Mexican States*, ICSID Case No. ARB(AF)/00/2, Award, 29 May 2003, para. 172.
54. *Elettronica Sicula S.p.A. (ELSI) (United States of America v. Italy)*, Judgment, 20 July 1989, para. 128 ('Arbitrariness is not so much something opposed to a rule of law, as something opposed to the rule of law. This idea was expressed by the Court in the *Asylum* case, when it spoke of "arbitrary action" being "substituted for the rule of law" *(Asylum, Judgment, I.C.J. Reports 1950*, p. 284). It is a wilful disregard of due process of law, an act which shocks, or at least surprises, a sense of juridical propriety. Nothing in the decision of the Prefect, or in the judgment of the Court of Appeal of Palermo, conveys any indication that the requisition order of the Mayor was to be regarded in that light.').
55. *Noble Ventures, Inc. v. Romania*, ICSID Case No. ARB/01/11, Award, 12 October 2005, para. 182.
56. *Agreement Between the Government of the Republic of Cuba and the Government of the Kingdom of Denmark Concerning the Promotion and Reciprocal Protection of Investments*, adopted on 19 February 2001, Art. 6(1). Agreement Between the Government of the United Arab Emirates and the Government of the People's Republic of Bangladesh for the Promotion and Reciprocal Protection of Investment, adopted on 17 January 2011, Art. 5(1).

which the term "measures" is qualified by the adjectives "arbitrary or discriminatory"'.[57] The arbitral tribunal was referring to Article II(2)(b), which refers only to non-discrimination.[58]

Concerning the relationship between the principle of good faith and non-discrimination, the arbitral tribunal, in *Cargill v. Mexico*, decided that Mexico violated Article 1102 of NAFTA as the investor was subject to discrimination because of its nationality.[59] Mexico imposed import permit requirements for High Fructose Corn Syrup (HFCS) from the US to pay higher MFN tariffs.[60] Mexico wanted to compel the US to live up to its NAFTA obligations.[61] The arbitral tribunal established that:

> the requirement was an intentional targeting of Claimant's investment that was designed specifically so that Claimant would not receive a permit. Likewise, the issue is not whether there was poor administration of government leading to arbitrary acts. In this instance, the administration by the government of the import permit requirement was quite effective. Finally, the Tribunal does not, and need not, rest its holding on the import permit requirement being *domestically unlawful given its conclusion that the requirement is manifestly unjust and akin to an act in bad faith.*[62]

However, in *Parkerings v. Lithuania*, the arbitral tribunal relied on the circumstances of the case with regard to discrimination and did not rely on good (bad) faith. The arbitral tribunal held that:

> Discrimination is to be ascertained by looking at the circumstances of the individual cases. Discrimination involves either issues of law, such as legislation affording different treatments in function of citizenship, or issues of fact where a State unduly treats differently investors who are in similar circumstances. *Whether discrimination is objectionable does not in the opinion of this Tribunal depend on subjective requirements such as the bad faith or the malicious intent of the State*: at least, Article IV of the Treaty does not include such requirements. However, to violate international law, *discrimination must be unreasonable or lacking proportionality, for instance, it must be inapposite or excessive to achieve an otherwise legitimate objective of the State.* An objective justification may justify differentiated

57. *Azurix Corp. v. The Argentine Republic (I)*, ICSID Case No. ARB/01/12, Award, 14 July 2006, para. 391.
58. *Treaty between United States of America and the Argentine Republic Concerning the Reciprocal Encouragement and Protection of Investment*, adopted on 14 November 1991, Art. II(2)(b) ('Neither Party shall in any way impair by arbitrary or discriminatory measures the management, operation, maintenance, use, enjoyment, acquisition, expansion, or disposal of investments. For the purposes of dispute resolution under Articles VII and VIII, a measure may be arbitrary or discriminatory notwithstanding the opportunity to review such measure in the courts or administrative tribunals of a Party.').
59. *Cargill, Incorporated v. United Mexican States*, ICSID Case No. ARB(AF)/05/2, Award, 18 September 2009, para. 554.
60. *Cargill, Incorporated v. United Mexican States*, ICSID Case No. ARB(AF)/05/2, Award, 18 September 2009, para. 104.
61. *Cargill, Incorporated v. United Mexican States*, ICSID Case No. ARB(AF)/05/2, Award, 18 September 2009, para. 213.
62. *Cargill, Incorporated v. United Mexican States*, ICSID Case No. ARB(AF)/05/2, Award, 18 September 2009, para. 303.

treatments of similar cases. It would be necessary, in each case, to evaluate the exact circumstances and the context.[63]

Considering all of the above, it is clear that a breach of the principle and requirements of good faith is a fact-sensitive exercise, and if such breach is established, it would trigger a breach of the FET standard in investor-State disputes, and it may even trigger a further breach of the non-discrimination standard if applicable. However, in any event, there seems to be a consensus that a finding of a breach of the requirement of good faith does not necessitate proving bad faith (which requires a higher threshold) and that the breach of good faith in this context may constitute a positive basis for claiming a breach of the FET standard.

[B] Legitimate Expectations

Turning to legitimate expectations, which remains topical in investment law and international investment disputes, it is worth noting that investors frequently invoke the doctrine of legitimate expectations to allege investment treaty breaches on the basis that certain expectations existed at the time they considered and made, their investment in the host State.

Apart from the global debate over the existence and scope of such doctrine, legitimate expectations are generated when the host State makes certain assurances to the investor, on the basis of which the latter proceeds with its investment. In addition, the legal and business framework of the host State plays a significant role in enticing investors to invest in the host State. Consequently, and to the extent certain legitimate expectations exist and are established, they merit protection, and the principle of good faith kicks in to bind the host State to act in good faith, observe those expectations and fulfil its promises towards the investment.

In *Siag v. Egypt*, the arbitral tribunal captured and emphasised the relationship between good faith and legitimate expectations when it held that '[n]umerous arbitral tribunals have held that, in international investment arbitration, the host State's duty to respect the investor's legitimate expectations arises from its more general duty to act in good faith towards foreigners'.[64] This is further analysed below with reference to further international investment awards.

---

63. *Parkerings-Compagniet AS v. Republic of Lithuania*, ICSID Case No. ARB/05/8, Award, 11 September 2007, para. 368.
64. *Waguih Elie George Siag and Clorinda Vecchi v. Arab Republic of Egypt*, ICSID Case No. ARB/05/15, Award, 1 June 2009, para. 450. It is important to note that the standard of fair and equitable treatment and legitimate expectations are intertwined: if a host State does not live up to its assurances to foreign investors, then a breach of the standard of fair and equitable treatment will be triggered; *El Paso Energy International Company v. Argentine Republic*, ICSID Case No. ARB/03/15, Award, 31 October 2011, para. 348 ('the legitimate expectations of the investors have generally been considered central in the definition of FET, whatever its scope. There is an overwhelming trend to consider the touchstone of fair and equitable treatment to be found in the legitimate and reasonable expectations of the Parties, which derive from the obligation of good faith. [...]').

In *South American Silver v. Bolivia*, South American Silver Limited (SAS), the claimant and a Canadian company, focusing on the development and exploitation of silver mining projects in South America, were investing in Bolivia for eighteen years because of the Bolivian government's encouragement and support.[65] SAS owned the majority shares in Compañía Minera Malku Khota (CMMK), a company in Bolivia that acquired ten mining concessions. The areas of the concessions were inhabited by indigenous communities. In 2010, according to the indigenous communities, CMMK was responsible for, among other things, environmental pollution, deceiving and threatening community members, and abuse of authority.[66] Because of the confrontations between the indigenous communities and CMMK, Bolivia issued Supreme Decree No. 1308 (the Reversal Decree), by which Bolivia reversed the ownership of the mining concessions to Bolivia. Article 1 of the Reversal Decree stated that '*the following Special Transitory mining Authorizations shall revert back to the original ownership of the State:* [(b) "Jalsuri", "Alkasi", "Cobra", "Viento," "Takhuani", "Takhaua", "Daniel", "Antacuna", "Norma", And "Silluta,"] [...]'.[67] The claimant argued that Bolivia failed to protect SAS's legitimate expectations and did not act in good faith and in a transparent and predictable manner.[68] After the arbitral tribunal examined the standard of protection of legitimate expectations, it determined two prerequisites to the protection of the legitimate expectations of investors under investment treaties. The arbitral tribunal held that:

> First, several international investment tribunals have established that the investor is entitled to protection of its legitimate expectations provided (i) that it exercised due diligence, and (ii) that its legitimate expectations were reasonable in light of the circumstances. The circumstances to be taken into consideration by the investor are not merely legal in nature, but they should also include the social, cultural, and economic environment of the host State of the investment, amongst other factors. According to the *Duke Energy v. Ecuador* tribunal, '[t]*he assessment of the reasonableness or legitimacy* [of the investor's expectations] *must take into account all circumstances, including not only the facts surrounding the investment, but also the political, socioeconomic, cultural and historical conditions prevailing in the host State.*'[69]

The arbitral tribunal established that the investor's legitimate expectations must be reasonable considering the circumstances, and all the circumstances must be considered collectively.[70] The arbitral tribunal held that Bolivia did not breach its

65. *South American Silver Limited v. The Plurinational State of Bolivia*, PCA Case No. 2013-15, Award, 22 November 2018, para. 86.
66. *South American Silver Limited v. The Plurinational State of Bolivia*, PCA Case No. 2013-15, Award, 22 November 2018, paras 112-118.
67. *South American Silver Limited v. The Plurinational State of Bolivia*, PCA Case No. 2013-15, Award, 22 November 2018, para. 169.
68. *South American Silver Limited v. The Plurinational State of Bolivia*, PCA Case No. 2013-15, Award, 22 November 2018, para. 642.
69. *South American Silver Limited v. The Plurinational State of Bolivia*, PCA Case No. 2013-15, Award, 22 November 2018, para. 648.
70. *South American Silver Limited v. The Plurinational State of Bolivia*, PCA Case No. 2013-15, Award, 22 November 2018, para. 633 ('Safeguarding legitimate expectations requires the State to guarantee the stability of the legal and business framework and to act "*consistently, i.e.,*

obligation to provide FET under Article 2(2) of the Agreement between the Government of the United Kingdom of Great Britain and Northern Ireland and the Government of the Republic of Bolivia for the Promotion and Protection of Investments.[71] Accordingly, Bolivia did not fail to protect the claimant's legitimate expectations. Having considered all the circumstances of the host State, the arbitral tribunal found that the claimant knew or should have known that indigenous communities inhabit the mining areas, and the advisors of CMMK recommended that specific measures be adopted to deal with the situation from the outset.[72] Furthermore, the claimant's actions escalated the tensions within the indigenous communities and aggravated the social conflict; therefore, the government had to intervene to restore public order and protect the lives of both CMMK's employees and the population in the area.[73] There was no breach of good faith or acts of bad faith that could be attributed to Bolivia in the circumstances of the case.

In *International Thunderbird Gaming Corporation v. United Mexican States*, Thunderbird, a Canadian gaming company, wished to establish gaming and entertainment facilities in Mexico. The claimant fully disclosed its intended business activities to Mexico and sought an official opinion attesting to the legality of these business activities. Mexico approved the legality of the claimant's gaming operations, and consequently, the claimant relied on this official opinion and started its investments in Mexico. After a change of government, Mexico reversed course and reneged upon its prior approval of the claimant's investments. The issue was whether Mexico's official opinion created a legitimate expectation to the effect that it brought the claimant's claim under Article 1105 NAFTA. The arbitral tribunal relied upon the principle of good faith to determine the relevance of the legitimate expectation standard to the case and whether Mexico was bound by it. The arbitral tribunal found that Mexico was under an obligation to meet the claimant's expectations and concluded that:

> Having considered recent investment case law and the good faith principle of international customary law, the concept of "legitimate expectations" relates, within the context of the NAFTA framework, to a situation where a Contracting Party's conduct creates reasonable and justifiable expectations on the part of an investor (or investment) to act in reliance on said conduct, such that a failure by the NAFTA Party to honour those expectations could cause the investor (or investment) to suffer damages.[74]

without arbitrarily revoking any preexisting decisions or permits issued [...] *that were relied upon by the investor to assume its commitments as well as to plan and launch its commercial and business activities'*).

71. *South American Silver Limited v. The Plurinational State of Bolivia*, PCA Case No. 2013-15, Award, 22 November 2018, para. 674. *Agreement between the Government of the United Kingdom of Great Britain and Northern Ireland and the Government of the Republic of Bolivia for the Promotion and Protection of Investments*, adopted on 24 May 1988, Art. 2(2).
72. *South American Silver Limited v. The Plurinational State of Bolivia*, PCA Case No. 2013-15, Award, 22 November 2018, para. 655.
73. *South American Silver Limited v. The Plurinational State of Bolivia*, PCA Case No. 2013-15, Award, 22 November 2018, para. 656.
74. *International Thunderbird Gaming Corporation v. The United Mexican States*, Arbitral Award, 26 January 2006, para. 147.

In light of the above, it is clear that legitimate expectations and good faith go hand-in-hand. First, the existence of certain legitimate expectations presupposes that the parties are acting in good faith. Second, the existence of a duty of good faith to guide the analysis and scope of the principle of legitimate expectations appears to be of assistance to arbitral tribunals, and the emphasis on 'legitimate' does appear to imply a duty to act in good faith; otherwise, the expectations may not be dubbed as 'legitimate'. Third, upon conducting a factual and legal analysis, arbitral tribunals may find a breach of the requirements of good faith, which may trigger a further breach of the legitimate expectations of the investor. Thus, a breach of good faith in this context may also constitute a positive basis for claiming a breach of the legitimate expectations standard.

[C] The Standard of Full Protection and Security

With respect to the standard of full protection and security (FPS), it imposes an obligation on the host State to protect investments from private parties and acts attributable to the host State.[75] To that extent, the principle of good faith remains fully relevant and useful since a duty to protect and secure necessitates the undertaking of certain acts and omissions in good faith; otherwise, a breach could be inferred and established from the absence of good faith. This is further analysed below.

In *Frontier v. Czech Republic*, the arbitral tribunal stated that 'the guarantee of full protection and security is the host state's obligation to "take active measures to protect the investment from adverse effects that stem from private parties or from the host state and its organs"'.[76] In this case, the issue was whether the Czech Republic breached its obligations under the Canada-Czech Republic BIT because the Czech courts refused to recognise and enforce an international arbitration award on the grounds of public policy under the New York Convention.[77] The arbitral tribunal found that the host State is obligated to provide full protection and security to the investor; however, that obligation is not limited to providing a system of courts but extends to providing a legal framework that contains legal provisions for the protection of the investment. The arbitral tribunal added that not every failure to obtain a remedy could be considered a

75. *Rumeli Telekom A.S. and Telsim Mobil Telekomunikasyon Hizmetleri A.S. v. Republic of Kazakhstan*, ICSID Case No. ARB/05/16, Award, 29 July 2008, para. 668 ('ICSID tribunals have recognized that in international law, the full protection and security obligation is one of "due diligence" and no more. More recently, in Saluka, the Tribunal also decided that "the "full security and protection" clause is not meant to cover just any kind of impairment of an investor's investment, but to protect more specifically the physical integrity of an investment against interference by use of force'); *Biwater Gauff (Tanzania) Limited v. United Republic of Tanzania*, ICSID Case No. ARB/05/22, Award, 24 July 2008, para. 730 ('The Arbitral Tribunal also does not consider that the "full security" standard is limited to a State's failure to prevent actions by third parties, but also extends to actions by organs and representatives of the State itself.').
76. *Frontier Petroleum Services Ltd. v. The Czech Republic*, PCA Case No. 2008-09, Final Award, 12 November 2010, para. 261.
77. *Frontier Petroleum Services Ltd. v. The Czech Republic*, PCA Case No. 2008-09, Final Award, 12 November 2010, para. 378.

breach of the FPS standard, provided that the courts have 'acted in good faith' and have reached decisions that are reasonably tenable. The arbitral tribunal concluded that:

> In this Tribunal's view, where the acts of the host state's judiciary are at stake, '"full protection and security' means that the state is under an obligation to make a functioning system of courts and legal remedies available to the investor. On the other hand, not every failure to obtain redress is a violation of the principle of full protection and security. Even a decision that in the eyes of an outside observer, such as an international tribunal, is 'wrong' would not automatically lead to state responsibility *as long as the courts have acted in good faith and have reached decisions that are reasonably tenable*. In particular, the fact that protection could have been more effective, procedurally or substantively, does not automatically mean that the full protection and security standard has been violated.[78]

The arbitral tribunal did not elaborate much on the good faith standard; it only imposed an obligation on the host State to act in good faith to avoid State responsibility for breaching the FPS standard. It also seems that the arbitral tribunal considered the principle of good faith as a guideline for the host State to follow in complying with the FPS standard in order to evidence reasonableness. In short, the arbitral tribunal relied on good faith as a guiding beacon to interpret and understand the host State's FPS obligation.

In *Tecmed v. Mexico*, the arbitral tribunal tied the FPS standard with good faith from a different perspective when it held that the guarantee of FPS is not absolute; it is an obligation of good faith efforts (i.e., to exercise due care in good faith) and not to guarantee a specific result.[79] This has been emphasised by the United Nations Conference on Trade and Development (UNCTAD), which stated that:

> [...] *In essence, while not an obligation of result, an obligation of good faith efforts to protect the foreign-owned property has been established by these recent cases,* without special regard for the resources available to do so. This has been referred to as a standard of 'due diligence' on the part of the host country. As a result, this standard should be understood as being very much a 'living' one. It places a clear premium on political stability, and the obligation of host countries to ensure that any instability does not have negative effects on foreign investors, even above the ability to protect foreign investors.[80]

In *Wena Hotels v. Egypt*, two hotels were seized by a State entity (EHC). Article 2(2) of the Agreement for the Promotion and Protection of Investments between Egypt and the United Kingdom (IPPA) states that 'Investments of nationals or companies of either Contracting Party shall at all times be accorded FET and shall enjoy full

78. *Frontier Petroleum Services Ltd. v. The Czech Republic*, PCA Case No. 2008-09, Final Award, 12 November 2010, para. 273.
79. *Técnicas Medioambientales Tecmed, S.A. v. United Mexican States*, ICSID Case No. ARB(AF)/00/2, Award, 29 May 2003, para. 177.
80. UNCTAD, *Investor-State Disputes Arising from Investment Treaties: A Review* (United Nations, New York/Geneva 2005) pp. 40-41, available at https://unctad.org/system/files/official-document/iteiit20054_en.pdf.

protection and security in the territory of the other Contracting Party.'[81] The arbitral tribunal established that Egypt breached both standards of FET and FPS. The arbitral tribunal held that:

> The Tribunal agrees with Wena that Egypt violated its obligation under Article 2(2) of the IPPA to accord Wena's investment 'fair and equitable treatment' and 'full protection and security'. Although it is not clear that Egyptian officials other than officials of EHC directly participated in the 1 April 1991 seizures, there is substantial evidence that Egypt was aware of EHC's intentions to seize the hotels and took no actions to prevent EHC from doing so. Moreover, once the seizures occurred, both the police and the Ministry of Tourism took no immediate action to restore the hotels promptly to Wena's control. Finally, Egypt never imposed substantial sanctions on EHC or its senior officials, suggesting Egypt's approval of EHC's actions.[82]

Whilst the arbitral tribunal, quite interestingly, did not expressly refer to the principle of good faith in the *Wena Hotels v. Egypt*'s award, one can easily infer that the arbitral tribunal's decision was motivated by an understanding that Egypt did not act in accordance with the requirements of good faith in the specific context of that dispute because the award referred to: (a) Egypt's awareness of EHC's intentions to seize the hotel and yet did not adopt any preventative measures to stop EHC; (b) both the Egyptian police and the Ministry of Tourism not taking any immediate action to restore the hotels to Wena's control; and (c) Egypt not imposing any sanctions on EHC or its officials. In brief, the arbitral tribunal highlighted all the elements that led to its award and which evidenced, from the arbitral tribunal's perspective, conduct that falls short of meeting the requirements of good faith.

In conclusion, good faith also remains very relevant in the context of FPS. Two specific dimensions can be traced in arbitral decisions; these include: (a) providing protection and security necessitates taking acts and omissions in good faith to evidence the reasonableness of the host State's conduct and fulfilment of their obligations to the investor; and (b) protection and security is a dynamic standard that need not achieve a specific result, but it entails exercising due care and diligence in safeguarding the investors' rights, which, in turn, requires acts and omissions to be undertaken in good faith to demonstrate the level of care required in this context. Thus, a breach of good faith in this context may constitute a positive basis for claiming a breach of FPS.

[D] Expropriation

Good faith considerations are equally relevant in the context of expropriation, which involves the taking of the property of the foreign investor by the State, noting the

81. *Agreement between the Government of the United Kingdom of Great Britain and Northern Ireland and the Government of the Arab Republic of Egypt for the Promotion and Protection of Investments*, adopted on 11 June 1975, Art. 2(2).
82. *Wena Hotels Limited v. Arab Republic of Egypt*, ICSID Case No. ARB/98/4, Award, 8 December 2000, para. 84.

possible distinctions between expropriation, nationalisation, confiscation and requisition. By way of illustration, 'nationalisation' refers to the large-scale takings of private property in economic sectors, which are motivated by policy considerations to accomplish complete State control of the economy or certain segments thereof.[83] However, 'expropriation' relates to enterprise-specific takings where the property remains with the State or is transferred to a third party.[84] In *Saint-Gobain v. Venezuela*, the arbitral tribunal highlighted the main features of expropriation as follows: 'the term *"expropriation"* is clearly characterized by a number of elements, including: (i) the act of a State; (ii) in relation to a person's property; (iii) consisting in a de jure or de facto taking of the property; and (iv) to the benefit of the State or of a third party'.[85] It must be emphasized that expropriation has no universal binding definition, and Bilateral Investment Treaties do not necessarily define with specificity what constitutes expropriation in their provisions. In *Lauder v. Czech Republic*, the arbitral tribunal established a general definition of expropriation:

> The Bilateral Investment Treaties (hereinafter: 'BITs') generally do not define the term of expropriation and nationalization, or any of the other terms denoting similar measures of forced dispossession ('dispossession', 'taking', 'deprivation', or 'privation'). Furthermore, the practice shows that although the various terms may be used either alone or in combination, most often no distinctions have been attempted between the general concept of dispossession and the specific forms thereof. In general, expropriation means the coercive appropriation by the State of private property, usually by means of individual administrative measures. Nationalisation involves large-scale takings on the basis of an executive or legislative act for the purpose of transferring property or interests into the public domain.[86]

As known to many, expropriation can be 'direct' or 'indirect'. States generally tend to avoid direct expropriation as it involves 'forcible appropriation by the State of the tangible or intangible property of individuals by means of administrative or legislative action', which may well result in losing the confidence of foreign investors in the host State.[87] Thus, indirect expropriation is more common and takes place 'when the expropriated party is deprived of the control and benefits of its investment but retains a formal title over the assets in question'.[88]

83. UNCTAD, Expropriation, *UNCTAD Series on Issues in International Investment Agreements II*, United Nation, New York and Geneva, 2012, pp. 5-6.
84. UNCTAD, Expropriation, *UNCTAD Series on Issues in International Investment Agreements II*, United Nation, New York and Geneva, 2012, pp. 5-6.
85. *Saint-Gobain Performance Plastics Europe v. Bolivarian Republic of Venezuela*, ICSID Case No. ARB/12/13, Decision on Liability and the Principles of Quantum, 30 December 2016, para. 443.
86. *Ronald S. Lauder v. Czech Republic*, Award, 3 September 2001, para. 200.
87. *LG&E Energy Corp., LG&E Capital Corp. and LG&E International Inc. v. Argentine Republic*, ICSID Case No. ARB/02/1, Decision on Liability, 3 October 2006, para. 187.
88. *Bank Melli Iran and Bank Saderat Iran v. The Kingdom of Bahrain*, PCA Case No. 2017-25, Final Award, 9 November 2021, para. 748.

Expropriation is normally executed in accordance with the domestic legal procedures of the host State,[89] and a lawful expropriation must satisfy the following requirements: (a) investment has to be taken for a public purpose; (b) in a non-discriminatory manner; (c) in accordance with due process of law; and (d) against the payment of adequate compensation.[90] That said, it is arguable that good faith iterations do feature in the context of the non-discrimination element as well as the due process element, which examines whether the procedure by which the property is taken is lawful.[91] Given that we have already discussed the connection between good faith and non-discrimination when analysing the FET standard, it seems reasonable to now focus on the nexus between good faith and due process considerations with respect to expropriation.

In the specific context of due process, investment arbitral tribunals have resorted to the principle of good faith to assess whether the State's expropriation was lawful or not.[92] The UNCTAD laid down the following test to assess the legality of the regulatory (*indirect expropriation*) measure(s):

> If a measure is of a regulatory nature or is an enforcement of existing regulation, one would need to ask the following questions: *Does the measure contain the characteristics of a bona fide exercise of police powers by the host State?* Is it taken in pursuance of a genuine public purpose, in a non-discriminatory manner and in accordance with the due process of law? Was there a transfer of benefit of the investment of the State or any private party? Is there a manifest disproportionality between the aims pursued and the harm inflicted on the investor?[93]

Naturally, the default presumption is that a party, whether a sovereign State or a private investor, acts in good faith. The UNCTAD notes that '[t]he venerable innocent-before-proven-guilty presumption is not one that shapes action and reaction only among individuals in the criminal law sphere. It has its equivalents, and rightly so, on

89. *Agreement Between the Government of the People's Republic of China and the Government of the Republic of Uzbekistan on the Promotion and Protection of Investments*, adopted on 19 April 2011, Art. 6(1)(b). *China-United Republic of Tanzania BIT* (2013), adopted on 24 March 2013, Art. 6(1)(b).
90. UNCTAD, Expropriation, *UNCTAD Series on Issues in International Investment Agreements II*, United Nation, New York and Geneva, 2012, p. 1.
91. Emily Sipiorski, *Good Faith in International Investment Arbitration* 168 (Oxford University Press 2019).
92. Emily Sipiorski, *Good Faith in International Investment Arbitration* 168-169 (Oxford University Press 2019). *See also* UNCTAD, Expropriation, *UNCTAD Series on Issues in International Investment Agreements II*, United Nation, New York and Geneva, 2012, pp. 104-105 ('As a preliminary matter, one needs to establish whether the measure is attributable to the respondent State and if so, whether the latter acted in its sovereign capacity. Secondly, it is important to correctly identify the investment at issue and, in particular, to understand whether it should be considered as part of the investor's overall investment in the host State or whether it is capable of being expropriated separately. Moving on to the impact of the measure on investment, it needs to be determined whether the State conduct has resulted in a total or near-total deprivation of the investor's investment (loss of investment's value or of investor's control over the investment) and whether the effect of the measure is permanent. An additional factor to be considered here is whether the investor had a legitimate expectation (arising from a written commitment of the host State) that the State would not act the way it did.').
93. UNCTAD, Expropriation, *UNCTAD Series on Issues in International Investment Agreements II*, United Nation, New York and Geneva, 2012, p. 105.

the international plane'.[94] Thus, regulatory measures are generally expected to be undertaken in good faith, and it is upon the party contesting the legality or bona fide nature of such measure(s) to establish the absence of good faith or the illegality of the measure in question. In any event, the host State must also demonstrate that its acts are non-discriminatory and legally adopted according to due process and for a public purpose.[95]

In *ConocoPhillips v. Venezuela*, ConocoPhillips, a US claimant, invested in three projects which involved the production and refining of extra-heavy oils from the Orinoco Oil Belt area.[96] In 2007, Venezuela issued Decree Law 5200, which called for the transformation of the three projects into mixed companies.[97] The Decree Law also established that the affiliates of Petróleos de Venezuela, S.A. (PDVSA), Venezuela's State-owned oil company, would hold 60% of the shares of the mixed companies.[98] Furthermore, Article 4 of the Decree Law 5200 provided the claimant with four months to agree to the terms of its possible participation in the new mixed companies.[99] Before and after the enactment of Decree Law 5200, negotiations took place between the claimant and the respondent concerning transforming the three projects into mixed companies.[100] There were also negotiations regarding the payment of compensation for the claimant's rights in the three projects. These negotiations were unsuccessful, and the claimant did not receive compensation.[101] The four-month period expired, and Venezuela took the claimant's interests in the three projects.[102] The arbitral tribunal questioned whether the respondent negotiated with the claimant in good faith regarding the taking of the claimants' investment in order to decide on the legality of Venezuela's expropriation. The arbitral tribunal asked the following question:

---

94. UNCTAD, Expropriation, *UNCTAD Series on Issues in International Investment Agreements II*, United Nation, New York and Geneva, 2012, p. 92, available at https://unctad.org/system/files/official-document/unctaddiaeia2011d7_en.pdf.
95. UNCTAD, Expropriation, *UNCTAD Series on Issues in International Investment Agreements II*, United Nation, New York and Geneva, 2012, p. 93.
96. *ConocoPhillips Petrozuata B.V., ConocoPhillips Hamaca B.V. and ConocoPhillips Gulf of Paria B.V. v. Bolivarian Republic of Venezuela*, ICSID Case No. ARB/07/30, Decision on Jurisdiction and Merits, 3 September 2013, paras 2-3.
97. *ConocoPhillips Petrozuata B.V., ConocoPhillips Hamaca B.V. and ConocoPhillips Gulf of Paria B.V. v. Bolivarian Republic of Venezuela*, ICSID Case No. ARB/07/30, Decision on Jurisdiction and Merits, 3 September 2013, paras 277, 280.
98. *ConocoPhillips Petrozuata B.V., ConocoPhillips Hamaca B.V. and ConocoPhillips Gulf of Paria B.V. v. Bolivarian Republic of Venezuela*, ICSID Case No. ARB/07/30, Decision on Jurisdiction and Merits, 3 September 2013, para. 203.
99. *ConocoPhillips Petrozuata B.V., ConocoPhillips Hamaca B.V. and ConocoPhillips Gulf of Paria B.V. v. Bolivarian Republic of Venezuela*, ICSID Case No. ARB/07/30, Decision on Jurisdiction and Merits, 3 September 2013, para. 204.
100. *ConocoPhillips Petrozuata B.V., ConocoPhillips Hamaca B.V. and ConocoPhillips Gulf of Paria B.V. v. Bolivarian Republic of Venezuela*, ICSID Case No. ARB/07/30, Decision on Jurisdiction and Merits, 3 September 2013, para. 205.
101. *ConocoPhillips Petrozuata B.V., ConocoPhillips Hamaca B.V. and ConocoPhillips Gulf of Paria B.V. v. Bolivarian Republic of Venezuela*, ICSID Case No. ARB/07/30, Decision on Jurisdiction and Merits, 3 September 2013, para. 206.
102. *ConocoPhillips Petrozuata B.V., ConocoPhillips Hamaca B.V. and ConocoPhillips Gulf of Paria B.V. v. Bolivarian Republic of Venezuela*, ICSID Case No. ARB/07/30, Decision on Jurisdiction and Merits, 3 September 2013, para. 277.

> did the Respondent in the negotiations with the Claimants concerning the compensation payable in respect of the taking of the Claimants' investments negotiate in good faith in accordance with the standard stated in Article 6(c) of market value of the investments immediately before the measures were taken or the impending measures became public knowledge, whichever is the earlier, and were its actions accordingly lawful?[103]

By majority, the arbitral tribunal held that 'the Respondent breached its obligation to negotiate in good faith for compensation for its taking of the ConocoPhillips assets in the three projects on the basis of market value as required by Article 6(c) of the BIT, and that the date of the valuation is the date of the Award'.[104] The majority relied on good faith to decide on the unlawfulness of Venezuela's expropriation. Had it not been for a finding of the absence of good faith, the expropriation could have been lawful, and the claimant would not have been granted compensation.[105]

On a different note, States have also relied on considerations of good faith to justify expropriation and its related regulation. In *Glamis Gold v. USA*, the arbitral tribunal held that 'A State is not responsible, however, for loss of property or for other economic disadvantage resulting from bona fide ... regulation ... if it is not discriminatory.'[106]

That said, it is clear that good faith considerations do play a notable role in assessing the lawfulness of expropriation, namely with respect to: (a) the rationale for the State's regulatory measure and whether it was undertaken in a non-discriminatory and proportionate manner; and (b) scrutinizing the due process element of expropriation and whether it was undertaken for a public purpose and against adequate compensation. Thus, a breach of the principle and requirements of good faith would taint expropriation with illegality and trigger the liability of the breaching party.

---

103. *ConocoPhillips Petrozuata B.V., ConocoPhillips Hamaca B.V. and ConocoPhillips Gulf of Paria B.V. v. Bolivarian Republic of Venezuela*, ICSID Case No. ARB/07/30, Decision on Jurisdiction and Merits, 3 September 2013, para. 334. *See Agreement on encouragement and reciprocal protection of investments between the Kingdom of the Netherlands and the Republic of Venezuela*, adopted on 22 October 1991, Art. 6(c) ('the measures are taken against just compensation. Such compensation shall represent the market value of the investments affected immediately before the measures were taken or the impending measures became public knowledge, whichever is the earlier, it shall include interest at a normal commercial rate until the date of payment and shall, in order to be effective for the claimants, be paid and made transferable, without undue delay, to the country designated by the claimants concerned and in the currency of the country of which the claimants are nationals or in any freely convertible currency accepted by the claimants').
104. *ConocoPhillips Petrozuata B.V., ConocoPhillips Hamaca B.V. and ConocoPhillips Gulf of Paria B.V. v. Bolivarian Republic of Venezuela*, ICSID Case No. ARB/07/30, Decision on Jurisdiction and Merits, 3 September 2013, paras 401, 404.
105. Emily Sipiorski, *Good Faith International in Investment Arbitration* 172 (Oxford University Press 2019).
106. *Glamis Gold Ltd. v. United States of America*, Award, 8 June 2009, para. 354; *Methanex Corporation v. United States of America*, Final Award of the Tribunal on Jurisdiction and Merits, 3 August 2005, para. 7 ('But as a matter of general international law, a non-discriminatory regulation for a public purpose, which is enacted in accordance with due process and, which affects, inter alios, a foreign investor or investment is not deemed expropriatory and compensable.').

[E] Damages and Allocation of Costs

Whilst it is arguable that good faith may have a limited role to play with respect to the quantification of damages, it may play some role with respect to the allocation of costs, subject to the agreed and applicable legal standards that ought to be observed by an arbitral tribunal. However, it is claimed that the assessment of damages and allocation of costs should be subject to special considerations given the role of good faith.[107] Nevertheless, it is important to take into account the scarcity of cases establishing a direct correlation or causation between the breach of good faith and award of damages.

In *Parkerings-Compagniet AS v. the Republic of Lithuania*, Lithuania, the respondent signed an agreement with Parkerings-Compagniet AS, the claimant and a Norwegian company, according to which the claimant would design and build a parking system in Lithuania.[108] Under Article VI of Lithuania-Norway BIT, 'the investment cannot be expropriated nationalized or subject to measures having a similar effect except for a public purpose, in a non-discriminatory manner, upon payment of compensation and in accordance with domestic laws'.[109] On the facts of the case, the claimant argued that the government's legislative and administrative interference with the agreement deprived Baltijos Parkingas UAB (BP), the claimant's wholly owned Lithuanian subsidiary, of the legal security afforded by the agreement.[110] BP was destroyed when the respondent prevented the execution and demanded full performance of the agreement at the same time and then repudiated the agreement.[111] Because the assets of BP were taken by the respondent, which was the sole purpose of BP's existence, BP became 'a company with assets, but without business'.[112] In addition, the arbitral tribunal found that the host State adopted a '*blatant contradictory ambiguous position*' concerning the parking plan, refused to renegotiate in good faith, and then terminated the agreement unlawfully,[113] and so breached its obligations under Article VI of Lithuania-Norway BIT by failing to compensate the aggrieved party. The arbitral tribunal concluded that:

> The Claimant further argues that any diminution of value attributable to or associated with Lithuania's conduct should be discarded. The purpose of this rule is to preclude the host State from using its executive, legislative or judicial branches to progressively reduce the value of an asset and then expropriate it. This is of particular importance in the present case where Lithuania gradually eroded

107. Julien Chaisse, Leïla Choukroune, and Sufian Jusoh, *Handbook of International Investment Law and Policy* 152 (Springer 2021).
108. *Parkerings-Compagniet AS v. Republic of Lithuania*, ICSID Case No. ARB/05/8, Award, 11 September 2007, paras 51-52.
109. *Parkerings-Compagniet AS v. Republic of Lithuania*, ICSID Case No. ARB/05/8, Award, 11 September 2007, para. 432.
110. *Parkerings-Compagniet AS v. Republic of Lithuania*, ICSID Case No. ARB/05/8, Award, 11 September 2007, para. 433.
111. *Parkerings-Compagniet AS v. Republic of Lithuania*, ICSID Case No. ARB/05/8, Award, 11 September 2007, para. 432.
112. *Parkerings-Compagniet AS v. Republic of Lithuania*, ICSID Case No. ARB/05/8, Award, 11 September 2007, para. 433.
113. *Parkerings-Compagniet AS v. Republic of Lithuania*, ICSID Case No. ARB/05/8, Award, 11 September 2007, para. 296.

> the value of BP, first by litigating and legislating away the legal framework of the investment, *then by refusing to either perform or renegotiate the Agreement in good faith*, and finally by unlawfully terminating the Agreement. Thus, *full compensation of the fair market value of BP on 21 January 2004 requires the Tribunal to disregard any diminution in the value of BP that might have been caused by each of these various steps leading up to the destruction of BP.*[114]

It is worth noting that because the host State's acts were not consistent with good faith and it refused to either perform or renegotiate the agreement in good faith, the arbitral tribunal granted the claimant full compensation of the fair market value of BP and disregarded any diminution of value.

With respect to the costs of arbitration, it is important to recall that Article 61(2) of the ICSID Convention states:

> In the case of arbitration proceedings, the Tribunal shall, except as the parties otherwise agree, assess the expenses incurred by the parties in connection with the proceedings, and shall decide how and by whom those expenses, the fees and expenses of the members of the Tribunal and the charges for the use of the facilities of the Centre shall be paid. Such decision shall form part of the award.[115]

It is argued that once a breach of the principle of good faith is established, arbitral tribunals tend to refer to this finding and order a measure of costs against the unsuccessful party.[116] During the drafting of the ICSID Convention, there was a debate over the provision that became Article 61(2).[117] On the one hand, some asserted that costs should be awarded against the unsuccessful party.[118] On the other hand, others argued that the arbitral tribunal should have the discretion to undertake such an assessment according to the specific circumstances of the case. The ultimate view that prevailed was to leave the matter to the discretion of the deciding arbitral tribunal. More to the point of good faith, it is argued that the arbitral tribunal would award costs against the party who instituted the proceedings frivolously or in bad faith.[119]

In *Libananco v. Turkey*, the arbitral tribunal held that 'Article 61(2) of the ICSID Convention gives it the power to award costs (defined to include legal fees, out of pocket expenses as well as costs of the arbitration) and the discretion to decide at what level to do so. This view has also been expressed by other ICSID tribunals.'[120]

---

114. *Parkerings-Compagniet AS v. Republic of Lithuania*, ICSID Case No. ARB/05/8, Award, 11 September 2007, para. 210.
115. *Convention on the Settlement of Investment Disputes between States and Nationals of Other States* (ICSID), adopted on 18 March 1965, Art. 61(2).
116. Julien Chaisse, Leïla Choukroune, and Sufian Jusoh, *Handbook of International Investment Law and Policy* 152 (Springer 2021).
117. Christoph H. Schreuer, *The ICSID Convention: A Commentary* 1228 (Cambridge University Press 2009).
118. Christoph H. Schreuer, *The ICSID Convention: A Commentary* 1228 (Cambridge University Press 2009).
119. Christoph H. Schreuer, *The ICSID Convention: A Commentary* 1228 (Cambridge University Press 2009).
120. *Libananco Holdings Co. Limited v. Republic of Turkey*, ICSID Case No. ARB/06/8, Award, 2 September 2011, para. 560.

In light of the above, it also appears that good faith may have far-reaching effects in relation to the measure of damages to be awarded and/or the allocation of costs in case bad faith is established or it is proven that a party's conduct was not consistent with the requirements of good faith. It is also clear that arbitral tribunals do retain a degree of discretion to ascertain and assess the parties' conduct and whether its inconsistency with the requirements of good faith warrant further implications as to the award of damages and/or costs.

§6.04 CONCLUDING REMARKS

Whilst it is clearly challenging to define and determine the scope of the principle of good faith with full precision and specificity across all legal cultures and traditions, it is clear that there is a degree of consensus that good faith qualifies as a general principle of customary international law, though it may require the support of other doctrines and principles to give it far-reaching effects.[121] In investment arbitration proceedings, good faith has been a useful tool to construe and interpret legal texts and the rights and obligations of the parties in dispute. It also serves to define the legal parameters of performance of legal obligations. However, using good faith as a source of positive obligations to create rights and claim relief purely on the basis of good faith remains a contentious issue, with proponents and opponents of good faith raising valid arguments in support of either position.

Analysis of prevailing cases and ISDS awards appears to suggest that good faith usually 'hunts in a pack', such that a breach of good faith considerations may likely trigger breaches of the FET, FPS, non-discrimination, legitimate expectations and/or expropriation standards. In other words, when breaches of the good faith requirements are established, this is usually coupled with invoking concurrent breach(es) of other treaty-based or international law obligations, and together, these would constitute the basis of a positive claim by an aggrieved party. Moreover, whilst there is relative paucity in awards that establish a correlation or causation between the measure of awarded damages and allocation of costs and breaches of good faith, the view remains that arbitral tribunals have reasonable discretion to assess damages and allocate costs in light of the specificities of each case, taking into consideration the bona fide (or *mala fide*) conduct of either or both parties.

By and large, whilst good faith plays a pivotal role in ascertaining, construing and performing obligations in international law disputes, it remains to be seen whether the new generation of international investment agreements and treaties, which expressly refer to certain obligations of good faith, will result in a new trend whereby good faith could, on its own, serve as a basis for a positive claim and a source of positive obligations that are not ancillary to other obligations. In other words, the future will tell whether good faith will continue to hunt in a pack (*in tandem* with others) or will develop new techniques and gears to be able to hunt *viritim*.

---

121. Steven Reinhold, *Good Faith in International Law*, UCL Journal of Law and Jurisprudence, Vol. 2, p. 63 (2015).

CHAPTER 7

Good Faith as a Form of Admissibility Defence in Investor-State Arbitration

Natalie L. Reid[*]

§7.01 INTRODUCTION

The notion of 'good faith' appears in many investor-State decisions in cases arising under both contracts and treaties. At the highest level of generality, 'good faith' in investor-State arbitration can arise in four distinct contexts: as a matter of procedure, jurisdiction, admissibility, and merits.

As a procedural matter, it is said that the parties have a duty to arbitrate in good faith, a duty that the parties owe to each other and to the arbitral tribunal.[1]

As a jurisdictional matter, especially in treaty cases, good faith can serve as an interpretative tool of a particular treaty provision going to jurisdiction,[2] or the notion of good faith may be used to imply certain jurisdictional requirements.[3]

---

* This chapter is based on remarks delivered on 4 February 2022 at the 2022 ASA Winter Conference. The author would like to thank her colleagues Romain Zamour, Perpétua B. Chéry, and Caitlin Kim for their assistance. The views expressed in this chapter are the author's alone and do not represent the views of her firm or any of its clients.

1. *See Libananco Holdings Co. Limited v. Republic of Turkey*, ICSID Case No. ARB/06/8, Decision on Preliminary Issues, June 2008, para. 78 ('[P]arties have an obligation to arbitrate fairly and in good faith and ... an arbitral tribunal has the inherent jurisdiction to ensure that this obligation is complied with; this principle applies in all arbitration, including investment arbitration, and to all parties, including States.').
2. *See* Vienna Convention on the Law of Treaties [VCLT], 23 May 1969, U.N.T.S. vol. 1155, p. 331, *entered into force* 27 January 1980, Art. 31(1) ('A treaty shall be interpreted *in good faith* in accordance with the ordinary meaning to be given to the terms of the treaty in their context and in the light of its object and purpose.') (emphasis added).
3. *See Gustav F W Hamester GmbH & Co KG v. Republic of Ghana*, ICSID Case No. ARB/07/24, Award, 18 June 2010, para. 123 ('[a]n investment will not be protected if it has been created in violation of national or international principles of good faith'); *see also ibid.*, para. 124 ('These are general principles that exist independently of specific language to this effect in the Treaty.').

As to the merits, the potential applications of good faith are numerous and multi-faceted. In contract cases, the dispute is normally governed by a specified body of domestic law chosen in the contract. Good-faith principles under domestic law can then impact the interpretation and application of the contract in question. In treaty cases, good faith may again serve as an interpretative tool of particular substantive treaty clauses or inform the application of a given treaty requirement.[4]

This article focuses on good faith in the admissibility context – that is, when the arbitral tribunal considers not whether it *has* jurisdiction to hear and decide a particular claim but whether it should *exercise* that authority under the circumstances.

The difficulty with the notion of good faith is that it is so widespread and multi-faceted – so often invoked and in so many different contexts – that it is sometimes hard to say when 'good faith' as a defence actually has real substantive content or serves as a rule of decision to dismiss claims, as opposed to being mere rhetorical gloss. And when it does serve as a rule of decision, it is hard to articulate clearly and consistently how it operates.

This article aims to demonstrate that, when it comes to admissibility, good faith has a distinct and potentially outcome-determinative role. Yet it is not 'good faith' itself that does the work, but narrower principles that derive from good faith: what could be referred to as 'emanations' or 'manifestations' of the good faith principle. This article focuses on two such examples: good faith as a form of illegality defence (typically invoked as 'unclean hands' or 'transnational public policy') and good faith in the context of alleged litigant abuse, whether as 'abuse of rights' or as 'abuse of process'. In the next section, the article describes the application of these principles in investor-State arbitration cases. The following section then dissects the conceptual underpinnings of these manifestations of the principle of good faith.

§7.02 APPLICATION OF GOOD FAITH EMANATIONS IN THE ADMISSIBILITY CONTEXT

[A] Good Faith as a Form of the Illegality Defence

The illegality defence in investor-State arbitration has evolved along two distinct axes: a jurisdictional/temporal axis and an admissibility/claim axis. This was cogently explained in *Bank Melli v. Bahrain*:[5] while 'for the purposes of the jurisdictional legality

4. *Rumeli Telekom A.S. and Telsim Mobil Telekomunikasyon Hizmetleri A.S. v. Republic of Kazakhstan*, ICSID Case No. ARB/05/16, Award, 29 July 2008, para. 609 ('the fair and equitable treatment standard encompasses *inter alia* the following concrete principles: ... the State is obliged to act in good faith'); *see also Waguih Elie George Siag and Clorinda Vecchi v. The Arab Republic of Egypt*, ICSID Case No. ARB/05/15, Award, 1 June 2009, para. 450 ('It is ... widely recognised that the principle of good faith underlies fair and equitable treatment.').
5. *Bank Melli Iran (Iran) and Bank Saderat Iran (Iran) v. The Kingdom of Bahrain*, PCA Case No. 2017-25, Final Award, 9 November 2021, paras 351 et seq.

requirement, the violation must taint the making of the *investment* ..., when it comes to admissibility, what matters is whether the unlawful conduct taints the *claims*'.[6]

The jurisdictional/temporal axis goes to the definition of the investment through so-called legality requirements.[7] Thus, the weight of the authority suggests that the key question is *when* the illegality occurred. If it occurred at the time of the making of the investment, then the legality requirement is potentially engaged. If it occurred subsequently, then it cannot be. That is because once the investment is considered lawfully made, 'the Contracting States have consented to give the treaty tribunal the competence to adjudicate the disputes arising out of such investment, including disputes about alleged subsequent illegal activities and their consequences'.[8] While this temporal limitation might yield curious results in practice, it is said to be 'based on the text of the treaty'.[9]

In the admissibility/claim axis, the reasoning is different: it is said that a certain claim cannot be heard or is inadmissible because the claim itself is tainted or vitiated by an underlying illegality.[10] This does not go to the definition of investment, and therefore, there is no equivalent temporal restriction.[11]

---

6. *Ibid.*, para. 370 (emphasis added); *see also ibid.* ('While the two instances often overlap in practice, they are conceptually distinct.').
7. *See ibid.*, para. 355 ('The ordinary meaning of this formulation leaves no doubt that it requires that investments be "*invested*", or in other words *made* in accordance with local law.') (emphasis in the original).
8. *Ibid.*, para. 356; *see also Tethyan Copper Company Pty Limited v. Islamic Republic of Pakistan*, ICSID Case No. ARB/12/1, Decision on the Respondent's Application to Dismiss the Claims (with reasons), 10 November 2017, para. 348 ('an act of corruption in the performance of the investment would not be relevant in the context of the Tribunal's jurisdictional analysis of whether Claimant has made an 'investment' within the meaning of Article 1(1)(a) of the Treaty'); *Bank Melli*, PCA Case No. 2017-25, Final Award, para. 357 n. 294 (collecting authorities and citing to *Gavrilovic and Gavrilovic d.o.o. v. Republic of Croatia*, ICSID Case No. ARB/12/39, Award, 26 July 2018, para. 303; *Vladislav Kim and others v. Republic of Uzbekistan*, ICSID Case No. ARB/13/6, Decision on Jurisdiction, 8 March 2017, paras 374-377; *Quiborax S.A., Non Metallic Minerals S.A. and Allan Fosk Kaplún v. Plurinational State of Bolivia*, ICSID Case No. ARB/06/2, Decision on Jurisdiction, 27 September 2012, para. 266; *Vannessa Ventures Ltd v. Bolivarian Republic of Venezuela*, ICSID Case No. ARB(AF)/04/6, Award, 16 January 2013, para. 167; *Urbaser S.A. and Consorcio de Aguas Bilbao Biskaia, Bilbao Biskaia Ur Partzuergoa v. Argentine Republic*, ICSID Case No. ARB/07/26, Decision on Jurisdiction, 19 December 2012, para. 260).
9. *Bank Melli*, PCA Case No. 2017-25, Final Award, para. 358 ('The temporal limitation of the legality clause is not an arbitrary requirement, but one based on the text of the treaty.').
10. *See, e.g., ibid.*, para. 365 ('The reason why serious violations such as a breach of international public policy may bar the admissibility of claims is that international adjudicatory bodies have a duty not to entertain claims tainted by violations of certain universally accepted norms *pursuant to general principles of good faith* and *nemo auditur propiam turpitudinem allegans*.') (emphasis added) (citing to *Fraport AG Frankfurt Airport Services Worldwide v. Republic of the Philippines (I)*, ICSID Case No. ARB/03/25, Dissenting Opinion of Mr. Bernardo M. Cremades (Award), 16 August 2007, para. 40(2); *Churchill Mining and Planet Mining Pty Ltd v. Republic of Indonesia*, ICSID Case Nos ARB/12/40 and 12/14, Award, 6 December 2016, paras 507-508).
11. *Ibid.*, para. 365 ('the rationale for the temporal restriction of the jurisdictional legality defence ... does not apply to an admissibility defence under the doctrines of international public policy and unclean hands.'); *see also ibid.*, at paras 366-368 (discussing the reasoning at *World Duty Free Company Limited v. The Republic of Kenya*, ICSID Case No. ARB/00/7, Award, 4 October 2006, paras 178-189 and at Zachary Douglas, *The Plea of Illegality in Investment Treaty Arbitration*, 29(1) ICSID Rev., 155, 180 (2014) DOI: 10.1093/icsidreview/sit040.

This is said to be a manifestation of the principle of good faith, though tribunals and commentators cannot seem to agree on what precise principle is at play.[12] Some refer to 'good faith", pure and simple; others to unclean hands; others to Latin maxims; and yet others to transnational or international public policy, or even all of the above.[13] Yet, the same reasoning and approach are at play in each case.[14]

Two cases, among many others, illustrate this terminological and conceptual ambiguity.

The first of the two cases is the landmark 2006 decision in *World Duty Free v. Kenya*. This was the first ICSID decision to dismiss a claim on the basis of a finding of corruption.[15] In that case, the tribunal's jurisdiction and the claimant's causes of action were based on a contract in which the arbitration agreement called for English law and the choice-of-law clause for Kenyan law.[16]

In the arbitration, the claimant's CEO submitted a witness statement describing a USD 2 million 'donation' he had made to then-President Moi.[17] Shortly thereafter, Kenya filed an application seeking dismissal of the claims on the ground that a contract procured by bribery was unenforceable[18] and declared the contract avoided.[19]

Following its analysis of the facts, the tribunal concluded that the payment 'must be regarded as a bribe made in order to obtain the conclusion of the [contract]'[20] and dismissed the claims. The tribunal identified three distinct legal grounds for this result: (*i*) the contract-law doctrine of avoidance in English and Kenyan law;[21] (*ii*) 'public policy both under English law and Kenyan law';[22] and (*iii*) 'transnational public policy'.[23]

As to the second ground, public policy, the tribunal concluded that the claimant was 'not legally entitled to maintain any of its pleaded claims in these proceedings on the ground of *ex turpi causa non oritur actio* [no action can arise from an illegal act]'.[24]

12. *Bank Melli*, PCA Case No. 2017-25, Final Award, para. 369 ('*In one form or another*, scholars and adjudicators have recognized that adjudicatory bodies must not aid a party that engages in unlawful conduct, if the claims are affected by severe wrongdoings. Based on the analysis of the decisions of international courts and tribunals, Kreindler concludes that the rules that "[n]o one should be allowed to reap advantages from his own wrong" and that "an unlawful act cannot serve as the basis of an action in law" are *manifestations of the general principle of good faith*.') (emphasis added); *see also ibid.*, nn. 303-304 (collecting authorities).
13. *Ibid.*, para. 375 ('As described above, international tribunals have commonly recognized that claims tainted by serious wrongful conduct are inadmissible, be it under the doctrine of clean hands, international public policy, or other general principles such as good faith, *ex turpi causa non oritur actio[]*, or *nemo auditur propiam turpitudinem allegans*.').
14. *Ibid.* (referring to 'the common rationale behind these principles').
15. *World Duty Free Company Limited v. The Republic of Kenya*, ICSID Case No. ARB/00/7, Award dated 4 October 2006.
16. *Ibid.*, paras 6, 158. The tribunal generally 'consider[ed] the two legal systems to have the same material effect as applied to th[at] case.' *Ibid.*, para. 159.
17. *Ibid.*, para. 130.
18. *Ibid.*, paras 41, 105.
19. *Ibid.*, para. 109.
20. *Ibid.*, para. 136.
21. *World Duty Free*, ICSID Case No. ARB/00/7, Award, paras 183, 188.
22. *Ibid.*, para. 179.
23. *Ibid.*, para. 157.
24. *Ibid.*, para. 179.

The tribunal quoted the famous statement of Lord Mansfield in *Holman v. Johnson*: 'The principle of public policy is this: *ex dolo malo non oritur actio* [no action can arise out of fraud or deceit]. No court will lend its aid to a man who founds his cause of action upon an immoral or illegal act. If, from the plaintiff's own stating or otherwise, the cause of action appears to arise *ex turpi causa*, or the transgression of a positive law of this country, there the court says he has no right to be assisted'.[25]

As to the third ground, the tribunal came to the famous conclusion that 'bribery is contrary to the international public policy of most, if not all, States or, to use another formula, to transnational public policy'.[26]

In sum, to dismiss the claims, the *World Duty Free* tribunal relied on a combination of a contract-law doctrine, Latin maxims under the rubric of public policy, and international public policy or transnational public policy.

The second case is *Inceysa v. El Salvador*, in which the tribunal invoked an even wider array of concepts.[27] In its 2006 award, the tribunal dismissed the investor's claim for lack of jurisdiction on the basis of what the tribunal interpreted as an explicit legality requirement in the El Salvador-Spain BIT[28] and a finding of illegality at the time of the making of the investment.

But the tribunal did not stop there; it went on to analyze the legality of Inceysa's investment 'in light of the general principles of law' and, in that context, made significantly broader pronouncements.[29] The tribunal found the investment to be in violation of the principle of good faith,[30] the principle *nemo auditur propriam turpitudinem allegans* [no one can be heard to invoke his own turpitude],[31] international public policy,[32] and the prohibition of unjust enrichment.[33] The tribunal also referred to the maxim '[*e*]*x dolo malo non oritur actio*'.[34] It even invoked the 'meta-positive provision that prohibits attributing effects to an act done illegally'.[35] It further averred that '[n]o legal system based on rational grounds allows the party that committed a chain of clearly illegal acts to benefit from them'.[36]

In sum, as summarized in *Bank Melli* and illustrated by *World Duty Free* and *Inceysa*, tribunals have relied on a variety of theories to dismiss as inadmissible claims tainted by illegality. The common thread throughout the terminological and conceptual maze is the underlying suggestion that good faith prohibits a party from asserting claims themselves based on illegal acts.

25. *Ibid.*, para. 181 (quoting *Holman v. Johnson* (1775) 1 Cowp. 341, 343 (Lord Mansfield)).
26. *Ibid.*, paras 138-157 (quotation at para. 157).
27. *Inceysa Vallisoletana S.L. v. Republic of El Salvador*, ICSID Case No. ARB/03/26, Award, 2 August 2006.
28. *Ibid.*, paras 203, 207, 264.
29. *Ibid.*, para. 229.
30. *Ibid.*, paras 230-239.
31. *Ibid.*, paras 240-244.
32. *Ibid.*, paras 245-252.
33. *Ibid.*, paras 253-257.
34. *Ibid.*, para. 240.
35. *Inceysa*, ICSID Case No. ARB/03/26, Award, para. 248.
36. *Ibid.*, para. 244.

[B] Good Faith as a Form of 'Abuse' Defence

Tribunals have also relied with increasing frequency on the notions of abuse of rights and abuse of process to dismiss claims as inadmissible. They have done so in two distinct contexts: corporate restructurings whose sole or main purpose was to create international jurisdiction at a time when a dispute had already arisen or was already foreseeable and certain kinds of parallel overlapping claims. Each is addressed in turn below.

[1] Corporate Restructuring

In the first category of cases, tribunals have dismissed as inadmissible claims brought following corporate restructurings whose sole or main goal was to create investment treaty protection at a time when a dispute had already arisen or was already foreseeable.

The foundational case here is *Phoenix Action v. Czech Republic,*[37] the first decision in which an investment treaty tribunal dismissed claims in their entirety on the basis of a finding that the claimant had engaged in abusive conduct.

In that case, Phoenix, an Israeli company, brought a claim for denial of justice in February 2004 against the Czech Republic under the Czech-Israel BIT concerning the treatment of two Czech companies which it owned, BG and BP. Phoenix acquired its shareholding in BG and BP in December 2002 from two Czech companies owned by Czech nationals. At the time, in December 2002, both BG and BP were already involved in ongoing legal disputes that formed the basis for the denial of justice claim.[38]

The *Phoenix* tribunal dismissed the claims in their entirety, relying on a theory of abuse derived from the principle of good faith. In the words of the tribunal: 'The Tribunal is concerned here with *the international principle of good faith as applied to the international arbitration mechanism of ICSID*. The Tribunal has to prevent abuse of the system of international investment protection under the ICSID Convention, in ensuring that only investments that are made in compliance with the international principle of good faith and do not attempt to misuse the system are protected'.[39]

The *Phoenix* tribunal made a jurisdictional finding because it implied in the notion of investment a requirement that 'assets [be] invested *bona fide*'.[40] However, subsequent tribunals have tended to reframe the principle as a matter of admissibility of claims and not the jurisdictional definition of an investment.[41]

37. *Phoenix Action, Ltd v. The Czech Republic,* ICSID Case No. ARB/06/5, Award, 15 April. 2009.
38. *Ibid.*, paras 2-3.
39. *Ibid.*, para. 113 (emphasis in the original).
40. *Ibid.*, para. 114; *see also ibid.*, Dispositif (jurisdictional holding).
41. *See, e.g., Pac Rim Cayman LLC v. The Republic of El Salvador,* ICSID Case No. ARB/09/12, Decision on the Respondent's Jurisdictional Objections, 1 June 2012, para. 2.10 ('the Tribunal has noted that the Respondent's jurisdictional objection based on Abuse of Process by the Claimant does not, in legal theory, operate as a bar to the existence of the Tribunal's jurisdiction; but, rather, as a bar to the exercise of that jurisdiction, necessarily assuming jurisdiction to exist' but adding that '[f]or present purposes, the Tribunal considers this to be a distinction without a

This was the case, for instance, in the 2015 Award on Jurisdiction and Admissibility in *Philip Morris Asia Limited v. The Commonwealth of Australia.*[42]

Philip Morris Asia (incorporated in Hong Kong), on 27 June 2011, brought a claim under the Hong Kong-Australia BIT with regard to Australia's Plain Packaging laws.[43] Philip Morris Asia, the claimant, owned 100% of Philip Morris Australia (incorporated in Australia), which in turn owned 100% of PML (incorporated in Australia).[44] However, until February 2011, both Philip Morris Australia and PML were owned by Philip Morris Brands Sàrl (incorporated in Switzerland).[45] There is no Switzerland-Australia BIT.

In April 2010, Australia's Prime Minister and Health Minister jointly announced major tobacco control reforms, including the introduction of legislation to mandate plain packaging of tobacco products by July 2012.[46] The restructuring of the ownership of PM Australia and PML was completed in February 2011.[47] The plain packaging bill was introduced in parliament in April 2011 and became law in November 2011.[48]

The tribunal dismissed the claims as inadmissible on the ground that the commencement of the arbitration in June 2011, following the corporate restructuring of the Australian entities in February 2011, was an abuse of right:

> [T]he initiation of this arbitration constitutes an abuse of rights, as the corporate restructuring by which the Claimant acquired the Australian subsidiaries occurred at a time when there was a reasonable prospect that the dispute would materialise and as it was carried out for the principal, if not sole, purpose of gaining Treaty protection. Accordingly, the claims raised in this arbitration are inadmissible ....[49]

As to the foreseeability element, the tribunal found that 'there was no uncertainty about the Government's intention to introduce plain packaging' in April 2010, and that, therefore, there was 'at least a reasonable prospect that legislation equivalent to the

difference'); *Transglobal Green Energy, LLC and Transglobal Green Panama, S.A. v. The Republic of Panama*, ICSID Case No. ARB/13/28, Award, 2 June. 2016, para. 100 ('The Tribunal has chosen to consider this objection first, because the existence of abuse of process is a threshold issue that would bar the exercise of the Tribunal's jurisdiction even if jurisdiction existed.'); *But see Renée Rose Levy and Gremcitel S.A. v. Republic of Peru*, ICSID Case No. ARB/11/17, Award, 9 January 2015, para. 181 ('The Tribunal considers that the characterization of the abuse of process objection as a jurisdictional or as an admissibility issue can be left open in the present case.'). Relatedly, tribunals have emphasized the distinction between an abuse of process objection and a jurisdictional objection *ratione temporis*. *See, e.g., Hydro S.r.l., Costruzioni S.r.l., Francesco Becchetti, Mauro De Renzis, Stefania Grigolon, Liliana Condomitti v. Republic of Albania*, ICSID Case No. ARB/15/28, Award, 24 April 2019, para. 557 (emphasizing 'he conceptual difference between an abuse of process objection and a *ratione temporis* objection' and quoting the *Pac Rim* tribunal for the proposition that these are 'materially different' arguments).

42. *Philip Morris Asia Limited v. The Commonwealth of Australia*, PCA Case No. 2012-12, Award on Jurisdiction and Admissibility, 17 December 2015.
43. *Ibid.*, paras 5, 12.
44. *Ibid.*, para. 6.
45. *Ibid.*, para. 97.
46. *Ibid.*, para. 119.
47. *Ibid.*, paras 162-163.
48. *Ibid.*, paras 165, 176.
49. *Philip Morris*, PCA Case No. 2012-12, Award on Jurisdiction and Admissibility, para. 588.

Plain Packaging Measures would eventually be enacted, which would trigger a dispute'.[50] In other words, the dispute was foreseeable (and in fact actually foreseen).

The tribunal also carefully considered the parties' arguments concerning the rationale for the restructuring.[51] The claimant acknowledged that the dispute was done 'partly in order to obtain protection under the BIT'[52] but stressed that this was not the sole motive. The tribunal found that tax or other business reasons were not determinative for the restructuring,[53] and there were no 'contemporaneous corporate memoranda or other internal correspondence sufficiently explaining the business case for the restructuring in detail'.[54] It found that gaining treaty protection was the principal reason for the restructuring.

The tribunal founded its holding on the notions of abuse of rights and abuse of process:

> In view of the above considerations, the Tribunal concludes that the commencement of treaty-based investor-State arbitration constitutes an abuse of right (or abuse of process) when an investor has changed its corporate structure to gain the protection of an investment treaty at a point in time where a dispute was foreseeable.[55]

Other tribunals have likewise applied notions of abuse of rights and abuse of process – derived from the principle of good faith as identified in the seminal *Phoenix* decision – to dismiss, as inadmissible, claims commenced in the wake of a corporate restructuring whose principal purpose was to create international treaty protection when a dispute was already foreseeable. [56]

[2] Parallel Overlapping Claims

Unlike the application of the abuse doctrine to certain corporate restructurings – which has generated multiple decisions over many years – the application of the same doctrine to bar certain kinds of parallel overlapping claims is still relatively new and controversial.[57]

---

50. *Ibid.*, para. 566.
51. *See ibid.*, paras 570 et seq.
52. *Ibid.*, para. 580.
53. *Ibid.*, para. 582.
54. *Ibid.*
55. *Ibid.*, para. 554.
56. *See, e.g.*, *Renée Rose Levy*, ICSID Case No. ARB/11/17, Award; *ST-AD GmbH (Germany) v. The Republic of Bulgaria*, UNCITRAL, PCA Case No. 2011-06, Award on Jurisdiction, 18 July 2013; *Alapli Elektrik B.V. v. Republic of Turkey*, ICSID Case No. ARB/08/13, Award, 16 July. 2012.
57. *See Ampal-American Israel Corp., EGI-Fund (08-10) Investors LLC, EGI-Series Investments LLC, BSS-EMG Investors LLC and David Fischer v. Arab Republic of Egypt*, ICSID Case No. ARB/12/11, Decision on Jurisdiction, 1 February 2016, paras 328-339 (narrow application of the doctrine, forcing the same claimant to elect to pursue an ICSID claim or an UNCITRAL claim, once both tribunals affirmed jurisdiction; but denying more generally that four parallel proceedings are abusive: 'It is possible, as a jurisdictional matter, for different parties to pursue distinct claims in different for a seeking redress for loss allegedly suffered by each of them arising out of the same factual matrix.').

This new application of the abuse doctrine was prominently defended as counsel and in doctrinal writings by the late Professor Emmanuel Gaillard.[58] In a 2017 article, Professor Gaillard described new litigation strategies that he characterized as abusive, such as initiating multiple arbitral proceedings 'to resolve the same or related dispute in order to maximize ... chances of success' and 'initiating [arbitral] proceedings for purposes other than resolving genuine disputes'.[59] Professor Gaillard argued that the classic tools at the disposal of arbitrators were inadequate to address these new litigation strategies and thus advocated for 'more effective tools'.[60] After discarding the notions of *lis pendens* and the duty to concentrate a dispute as two potential such tools, he settled on the prohibition of abuse of rights and abuse of process. He wrote:

> Being principles common to many national legal systems and recognized under public international law, the prohibitions of abuse of rights and abuse of process may be recognized as general principles of law that may be applied by an arbitral tribunal, irrespective of the seat of the arbitration or the applicable law. Because abuse of rights looks beyond the literal application of the black letter law, it is perfectly suited to tackle circumstances in which parties to international arbitrations engage in tactics that do not violate any hard and fast rules, but which are nevertheless objectionable in the particular circumstances of the case.[61]

Professor Gaillard's position was adopted by the tribunal in the *Orascom TMT Investments v. Algeria* case, in which Professor Gaillard represented the Respondent.[62] Following the submission of a Notice of Dispute on 16 April 2012, on 24 October 2012, Orascom TMT Investments (OTMTI) submitted a Request for Arbitration to ICSID against Algeria under the ICSID Convention and the Agreement between the Belgo-Luxembourg Economic Union and the People's Democratic Republic of Algeria on the Reciprocal Promotion and Protection of Investments (the 'BLEU-Algeria BIT').[63]

Prior to bringing this claim, subsidiaries of OTMTI had already notified two separate claims against Algeria. On 2 November 2010, OTH notified Algeria of the existence of a dispute pursuant to the Egypt-Algeria BIT.[64] OTH subsequently filed a notice of arbitration under the UNCITRAL Arbitration Rules in a case administered by the Permanent Court of Arbitration (PCA).[65] OTH and Algeria eventually reached a settlement agreement, which the PCA tribunal recorded in a consent award.[66] On 8

58. Emmanuel Gaillard, *Abuse of Process in International Arbitration*, 32 ICSID Rev. 17 (2017) DOI: 10.1093/icsidreview/siw036.
59. Gaillard at 6-11.
60. Gaillard at 11.
61. Gaillard at 18.
62. *Orascom TMT Investments S.à r.l. v. People's Democratic Republic of Algeria*, ICSID Case No. ARB/12/35, Award, 31 May 2017, para. 587(a) ('The claims raised in this arbitration are inadmissible and the Tribunal is precluded from exercising jurisdiction over this dispute.').
63. *Ibid.*, paras 1, 18.
64. *Ibid.*, para. 485(c).
65. *Ibid.*, para. 485(f).
66. *See Orascom Telecom Holding S.A.E v. People's Democratic Republic of Algeria*, PCA Case No. 2012-20, Award on Agreed Terms, 12 March 2015.

November 2010, Weather Investments also submitted a Notice of Dispute to Algeria under the Italy-Algeria BIT.[67]

Although the three Notice of Disputes filed by OTMTI and its subsidiaries were brought under different BITs, they were signed by the same person and 'concerne[d] the same measures or events'.[68]

According to the *Orascom* tribunal, which heard the case brought by OTMTI:

> [A]n investor who controls several entities in a vertical chain of companies may commit an abuse if it seeks to impugn the same host state measures and claims for the same harm at various levels of the chain in reliance on several investment treaties concluded by the host state.[69]

On the facts before it, the *Orascom* tribunal found that such an abuse had occurred. In particular, the tribunal gave weight to the facts that OTMTI caused its subsidiaries OTH and Weather Investments to bring claims against Algeria and threaten Algeria with a different arbitration, respectively, while OTMTI itself also brought claims against Algeria 'for the same investment ... in relation to the same host state measures and the same harm'.[70] The tribunal considered this conduct 'an abuse of the system of investment protection, which constitutes a further ground for the inadmissibility of [OTMTI]'s claims'.[71]

OTMTI sought partial annulment of the ICSID award, specifically the portions of the award relating to admissibility and costs, relying on various annulment grounds.[72] On the admissibility holding in particular, the investor argued that 'the Tribunal seriously departed from a fundamental rule of procedure, the Tribunal manifestly exceeded its powers and failed to state the reasons on which the Award is based'.[73] An ICSID ad hoc committee chaired by Judge H. E. Peter Tomka of the International Court of Justice (ICJ) rejected the annulment application and upheld the award in full.[74] In reviewing the tribunal's analysis of the alleged abuse, the committee cited the ICJ's Judgment on Preliminary Objections in the *Immunities and Criminal Proceedings* case, analyzing the notions of abuse of process and abuse of rights, and the committee thus concluded: '[t]he Tribunal relied on an established legal concept under international law and it did not invent any new legal concept in this regard'.[75]

---

67. *Orascom*, ICSID Case No. ARB/12/35, Award, para. 485(d).
68. *Ibid.*, paras 485(d), 486.
69. *Ibid.*, para. 542.
70. *Ibid.*, paras 545, 546 ('conclusions on the inadmissibility of the claims are the result of the peculiar facts of the case, in which (i) the group of companies of which the Claimant was part was organized as a vertical chain; (ii) the entities in the chain were under the control of the same shareholder; (iii) the measures complained of by the various entities in the chain were the same and thus the dispute notified to Algeria by those entities was in essence identical; and (iv) the damage claimed by the various entities was, in its economic essence, the same.').
71. *Ibid.*, para. 545.
72. *Orascom TMT Investments S.à r.l. v. People's Democratic Republic of Algeria*, ICSID Case No. ARB/12/35, Decision on Annulment, 17 September. 2020, para. 94.
73. *Ibid.*, para. 130.
74. *Ibid.*, paras 66, 335.
75. *Ibid.*, paras 306, 315-316.

Notably, in the *Ampal v. Egypt* Decision on Jurisdiction,[76] rendered a year before the *Orascom* award and where Professor Gaillard also represented the Respondent, an ICSID tribunal took a similar but narrower approach, finding that it was acceptable 'to pursue distinct claims in different fora seeking redress for loss allegedly suffered by each [investor] arising out of the same factual matrix'.[77] The *Ampal* tribunal reasoned that 'contract claims are distinct from treaty claims' and that different treaty tribunals could consider treaty claims made by separate investors when those claims arise from distinct tranches of the same investment, especially absent a consolidation agreement.[78] However, it found that Ampal could not pursue claims in parallel arbitrations that are 'double pursuit of the same claim in respect to the same interest'.[79] According to the tribunal, although it is reasonable for a party to seek protection in multiple fora when the jurisdiction of each forum is unclear, continuing parallel pursuits of the same claims on the merits once the jurisdiction of a forum is confirmed would constitute an 'abuse of process'.[80] This is because once one of the tribunals seized has confirmed its jurisdiction to hear the claim, there is no longer a risk of 'a denial of justice occasioned by the absence of a tribunal competent to determine the ... claim'.[81]

On the facts, a PCA tribunal seized by the investor had confirmed it had jurisdiction to hear the same claim brought in the ICSID arbitration.[82] The *Ampal* tribunal dismissed Respondent's objection to its jurisdiction based on an alleged abuse of process by the investor, subject to the investor 'cur[ing] the abuse' by either submitting both claims to the ICSID tribunal, renouncing the claim before the ICSID tribunal in the PCA arbitration, or pursuing that claim at a later date.[83]

Illustrating the still controversial nature of the application of the abuse doctrine to parallel claims, Professor Jan Paulsson, in his book on '[t]he unruly notion of abuse of rights', has argued against it.[84] According to Professor Paulsson:

> It is common that international investments may involve more than one entity in the same corporate chain, and that each of them may have claims of different dimensions that arise from the same governmental acts. ... There is no reason to 'correct the law." In fact, it would be a usurpation of law-making authority. If states party to BITs wanted things to work this way, they would have so stipulated. They evidently either do not, or have not perceived it as something that needs to be excluded.[85]

76. *See Ampal*, ICSID Case No. ARB/12/11, Decision on Jurisdiction, 1 February 2016.
77. *Ibid.*, para. 329.
78. *Ibid.*
79. *Ibid.*, para. 331.
80. *Ibid.*
81. *Ibid.*, para. 333.
82. *Ibid.*, para. 332.
83. *Ibid.*, paras 334, 338-339, 345.
84. *See generally* Jan Paulsson, *The Unruly Notion of Abuse of Rights* (Cambridge Univ. Press 2020).
85. Paulsson at 94 (footnotes omitted); *see also Ronald S. Lauder v. Czech Republic*, UNCITRAL, Award, 3 September 2001, para. 174 ('Finally, there is no abuse of process in the multiplicity of proceedings initiated by Mr. Lauder and the entities he controls. Even assuming that the doctrine of abuse of process could find application here, the Arbitral Tribunal is the only forum with jurisdiction to hear Mr. Lauder's claims based on the Treaty. The existence of numerous parallel proceedings does in no way affect the Arbitral Tribunal's authority and effectiveness, and does

Going forward, it remains to be seen whether the decision in *Orascom* extending the abuse doctrine beyond corporate restructurings to certain kinds of parallel overlapping claims will be followed by other tribunals and initiate a trend in the decided cases or whether it will remain isolated.

§7.03 IDENTIFYING THE CONCEPTUAL UNDERPINNINGS OF THE GOOD FAITH ADMISSIBILITY DEFENCES

This section analyzes the conceptual underpinnings of these manifestations of the principle of good faith in the admissibility context. It first considers 'unclean hands' and 'transnational public policy', the two key concepts underlying the illegality defence in its admissibility guise, and then addresses 'abuse of rights' and 'abuse of process', the two distinct concepts that have been used, interchangeably to date, to justify the 'abuse' defence in its various forms.

[A] Unclean Hands and Transnational Public Policy

As shown in the previous section, tribunals dismissing claims as inadmissible on the grounds of illegality have mentioned many concepts to justify their decisions, including various Latin maxims, unclean hands, 'meta-positive provisions, transnational or international public policy, etc.[86] If they did not mention a single concept, it might be because they were not sure which concept was the operative one. So, which one is it? And, more fundamentally, does such a principle exist in the first place? In 2014, an eminent tribunal emphatically answered this question in the negative. When asked to consider the existence of the unclean hands doctrine at international law, the *Yukos* tribunal famously held: 'unclean hands" does not exist as a general principle of international law which would bar a claim by an investor'.[87] Significantly, the tribunal remained silent on transnational public policy.

The conclusion is remarkable for at least the following reasons: this was a central issue in the case, and the conclusion was reached in the light of a detailed briefing; the tribunal's reasoning was thorough; the stakes were high, and so was the compensation ultimately awarded; and the tribunal was eminent and unanimous, and included Judge Stephen Schwebel, who in his dissenting opinion in *Nicaragua v. United States* had

not undermine the Parties' rights. On the contrary, the present proceedings are the only place where the Parties' rights under the Treaty can be protected.'); *CME Czech Republic B.V. v. The Czech Republic*, UNCITRAL, Partial Award, 13 September 2001, para. 419 ('The inadmissibility argument is predominantly based on the fact that Mr. Lauder in parallel to the Claimant initiated other Treaty proceedings. However, the Claimant is free to initiate the Treaty proceedings, if there is an investment dispute in the meaning of Article 8 of the Treaty. The argument of abusive Treaty shopping is not convincing.'); Paulsson at 94 n. 25 (discussing *CME* and *Lauder* and emphasizing that the claimants 'offered to proceed in consolidated arbitrations but the state insisted on two distinct arbitrations.').

86. *Supra* n. 14.
87. *Yukos Universal Limited (Isle of Man) v. The Russian Federation*, PCA Case No. 2005-04/AA227, Final Award, 18 July 2014, para. 1363.

written one of the strongest statements supporting the existence of the unclean hands doctrine at international law.

Based on these remarkable features, at least one author, Dr Aloysius Llamzon, predicted shortly after the issuance of the award that *Yukos* was likely to be 'the leading case on the unclean hands doctrine that all succeeding international tribunals (investment treaty or not) will have to contend with'.[88] But that is not what has happened. Instead, distinguished tribunals engaging in detailed consideration of illegality defences, including as to admissibility, have felt comfortable not mentioning *Yukos* at all.

The *Churchill Mining and Planet Mining v. Indonesia*[89] award is illustrative. The tribunal in *Churchill* dismissed the claims on the basis of illegality post-dating the making of the investment. It referred to various concepts to justify this outcome, including the unclean hands principle, while noting that 'its status and exact contours are subject to debate and have been approached differently by international tribunals'.[90] A footnote refers to various cases but not *Yukos*.[91]

To be fair, this might have to do with the set-aside saga in the Dutch courts and the uncertain and changing status of the award at different points in time.[92] But, given the care with which the *Yukos* tribunal had approached the question, it might seem difficult to have a rigorous treatment of the topic without grappling with the *Yukos* panel's reasoning in one way or another.

Because *Yukos* did not address transnational public policy, one can rely on this concept without having to confront *Yukos*. However, transnational public policy comes with significant baggage. Instead of considering specific wrongs, the tribunal must consider entire categories of wrongs. That is, the issue is whether a particular kind of illegality is grave enough to violate transnational public policy. Eminent commentators, most famously Professor Reisman, have warned against a result-oriented expansion of the doctrine, cautioning that while 'public policy in domestic law is a legal concept with a verifiable judicial history', the same is not true of international law, where it could instead be invoked in an attempt to avoid doing the hard work and heavy lifting of establishing that the claimed norm is binding customary international law:

> [P]ublic policy in domestic law is a legal concept with a verifiable judicial history. Not so in international law. When an alleged international public policy is given the force of law by an international commercial arbitral tribunal, it is not subjected to the discipline of customary international law analysis which requires that the state practice justifying the inference that a customary rule has been produced must be shown to be wide and extensive and to be accompanied by *opinio juris*.

88. Aloysius Llamzon, *Case Comment: Yukos Universal Limited (Isle of Man) v. The Russian Federation – The State of the 'Unclean Hands' Doctrine in International Investment Law: Yukos as both Omega and Alpha*, 30(2) ICSID Rev. 315, 315-316 (2015) DOI: 10.1093/icsidreview/siv 014.
89. *Churchill Mining*, ICSID Cases Nos ARB/12/14 & ARB/12/40, Award.
90. *Ibid.*, para. 493.
91. *Ibid.*, n. 779.
92. *See generally* for an overview: Stan Putter, *What the Dutch Supreme Court Decided in the Yukos Case*, Global Arbitration Review (17 December 2021), https://globalarbitrationreview.com/what-the-dutch-supreme-court-decided-in-the-yukos-case.

> Without this discipline, the invocation of 'transnational public policy' becomes an easy way for those claiming to have an insight into the heart and the soul of international law to effect their own preferences without having to prove that they have become customary international law.[93]

The 2021 Final Award in *Littop v. Ukraine*[94] was the first in which a tribunal expressly disagreed with *Yukos* on the existence of the 'unclean hands' doctrine. After acknowledging the statement by the *Yukos* tribunal that Russia had 'had been unable to cite a single majority decision where an international court or arbitral tribunal has applied the principle of "unclean hands" in an inter-State or investor-State dispute' and '[thus] concluded that "unclean hands" does not exist as a general principle of international law', the *Littop* tribunal nonetheless held that it was not bound by the *Yukos* precedent, and found instead 'that the doctrine of clean hands, just like the concept of good faith, is now a principle of international law'.[95] Notably, the *Littop* tribunal included the Hon. L. Yves Fortier PC CC QC, the chairman of the *Yukos* tribunal.

Citing various authorities, the *Littop* tribunal stated it was 'clear that a party cannot come to investment arbitration with unclean hands'.[96] The tribunal further added that it had 'the authority and duty to uphold international public policy' which 'would allow and may in fact mandate that a tribunal decline jurisdiction or dismiss the claims of an investor if its investment was acquired, effected or somehow tainted/permeated by bribery and/or corruption, illegality or other internationally unacceptable behaviour'.[97]

Yet, despite confronting *Yukos* and finding that 'unclean hands' does exist as a principle of international law, in the *dispositif*, the *Littop* tribunal relied on international public policy to decline jurisdiction and not on 'unclean hands'.[98]

Where does that leave us? At this (late) stage in the development of the case law, it appears that good faith as a form of admissibility illegality defence may well be a theory – adorned by maxims – in search of a specific operative principle or rule of decision. But the lack of clarity about its precise content or operation has not prevented parties from arguing, and some tribunals from accepting, that claims should be barred on this basis.

[B] Abuse of Rights and Abuse of Process

The same conceptual uncertainties plague the 'abuse' defence as well.

93. W. Michael Reisman, *Law, International Public Policy (So-Called) and Arbitral Choice in International Commercial Arbitration*, in *International Arbitration 2006: Back to Basics?, ICCA Congress Series Vol. 13* 849, 855-856 (van den Berg ed. 2007).
94. *Littop Enterprises Limited, Bridgemont Ventures Limited and Bordo Management Limited v. Ukraine*, SCC Case No. V 2015/092, Final Award, 4 February 2021.
95. *Ibid.*, para. 438.
96. *Ibid.*, para. 439.
97. *Ibid.*, para. 442.
98. *Ibid.*, para. 654(i)(b).

Phoenix referred to 'the international principle of good faith', 'abuse of the system', and 'abuse of rights'.[99] *Orascom* speaks of 'the principle of abuse of rights (or abuse of process)' as if they were the same.[100] But they are not.

The issue was addressed in some detail in the *Orascom* annulment proceedings. As noted above, one of the grounds for annulment raised by the claimant was the tribunal's reliance on the 'abuse of rights' doctrine to dismiss the claims. The committee engaged in a detailed discussion of the concept and its pedigree under international law. '[W]ithout expressing an opinion on the application of the doctrine of abuse of rights by the Tribunal', the committee found that '[t]he Tribunal relied on an established legal concept under international law and it did not invent any new legal concept in this regard'.[101] But, in the course of its discussion, the committee underlined that the ICJ draws a distinction between 'abuse of right' and 'abuse of process'.

In the *Immunities and Criminal Proceedings* case, Equatorial Guinea instituted proceedings against France with regard to a dispute concerning the status of a building at 42 Avenue Foch, Paris, France, and alleged violation of the immunity from criminal jurisdiction of Second Vice-President Mr Teodoro Nguema Obiang Mangue.[102] The dispute arose when France searched the building at 42 Avenue Foch, seizing several luxury vehicles during the course of corruption investigations targeting Mr Mangue.[103] The Embassy of Equatorial Guinea sent a Note Verbale shortly thereafter to state that the building was used for the functions of its diplomatic mission. However, the French Ministry of Foreign Affairs refused to recognize the property as such.[104] Equatorial Guinea then made the building the official residence of its Permanent Delegate to UNESCO. Following additional searches and seizures, the Tribunal de grande instance found that the building had been purchased by Mr Mangue using the proceeds of alleged crimes. It 'ordered the attachment of the building (*saisie pénale immobilière*)'. Following this ruling, the Embassy of Equatorial Guinea then moved its offices to the building.[105]

Among France's preliminary objections was the argument that the case's referral to the ICJ was 'completely artificial' because 'Equatorial Guinea links its claims to conventional provisions which, given the facts of the case, cannot be regarded as a credible basis for the exercise of the Court's jurisdiction' and, as claimed in the oral proceedings, '*en l'absence manifeste de toute voie de droit*'.[106] France also contended

99. *Phoenix Action*, ICSID Case No. ARB/06/5, Award, para. 113.
100. *Orascom*, ICSID Case No. ARB/12/35, Award, para. 547.
101. *Orascom*, ICSID Case No. ARB/12/35, Decision on Annulment, paras 315-316.
102. *Immunities and Criminal Proceedings (Equatorial Guinea v. France)*, Preliminary Objections, Judgment, I.C.J. Reports 2018, p. 292, paras 1, 6.
103. *Ibid.*, paras 23-25.
104. *Ibid.*, para. 26.
105. *Ibid.*, paras 27-28.
106. *Immunities and Criminal Proceedings (Equatorial Guinea v. France)*, Preliminary Objections, Preliminary objections of France, 30 March 2017, paras 58-59.

that Equatorial Guinea's conduct constituted an abuse of rights, whereas the Application filed by Equatorial Guinea constituted an abuse of process and should, therefore, be dismissed.[107]

In its Judgment on Preliminary Objections, the Court stated: 'a distinction has been drawn between abuse of rights and abuse of process. Although the basic concepts of an abuse may be the same, the consequences of an abuse of rights or an abuse of process may be different'.[108] According to the Court, '[a]n abuse of process goes to the procedure before a court or tribunal and can be considered at the preliminary phase of these proceedings'. By contrast, 'abuse of rights cannot be invoked as a ground of inadmissibility when the establishment of the right in question is properly a matter for the merits'.[109]

This appears to suggest that the proper basis, if any, for the investor-State decisions dismissing claims as inadmissible on the ground of 'abuse' is the notion of 'abuse of process' and not that of 'abuse of right'. In that case, one would need precisely to explain which specific feature of the tribunal's procedure or of the dispute resolution mechanism is being abused, a requirement that could serve to constrain proposed further extensions of the doctrine going forward.

Professor Paulsson, in his recent book, also draws a distinction between abuse of rights and abuse of process. The thesis of his book is that 'the notion of abuse of right, whatever sympathy one may have for the idealistic impulses of its proponents, cannot be the foundation for a general principle of law or an acceptable rule of decision on the international plane'.[110] Abuse of process, on the other hand, 'should not be confused with abuse of right'.[111] It is 'the misuse of an institution; no one has the "right" to misuse the legal process'.[112]

In sum, like good faith as an illegality defence, good faith as an 'abuse' defence is a theory in search of a specific operative principle. As just explained above, it appears that 'abuse of process', and not 'abuse of right', ought to be the operative principle. But then one would need to explain precisely what procedure or process is being abused and how. Doing so may well lead to the re-conceptualization of the current applications of the doctrine and also affect its potential extensions.

§7.04 CONCLUSION

More discipline is needed in the invocation of 'good faith' as a defence in investor-State arbitration, and in particular in the admissibility context. It is a noble impulse to wish

107. *Immunities and Criminal Proceedings*, Preliminary Objections, Judgment, I.C.J. Reports 2018, paras 139-141.
108. *Ibid.*, para. 146.
109. *Ibid.*, paras 150-151 (quoted in *Orascom*, ICSID Case No. ARB/12/35, Decision on Annulment, para. 306).
110. Paulsson at x.
111. *Ibid.*, at 73.
112. *Ibid.*; *see also ibid.*, at 96 ('The expression "abuse of process", which does not, except in the most artificial sense, involve the misuse of any right, is probably the greatest source of incoherence.').

to condemn bad faith, illegality, and abuse, but it cannot replace rigorous legal analysis.

This is not to say that good faith has no role to play. On the contrary, good faith plays an important role in investor-State arbitration, as it informs specific rules and principles – its manifestations or emanations – that provide precise rules of decisions for tribunals. But that cannot be the end of the analysis. Just saying 'good faith' will not do. The precise rules of decisions for tribunals must be identified, elaborated, and justified.[113]

113. Gaillard at 21 ('Where certain types of conduct generate a sense of unease, they are first addressed through the application of general principles such as ... "good faith". Over time, new legal rules will emerge that are specifically designed to tackle particular types of procedural conduct.').

CHAPTER 8

Good Faith and Pre-arbitral Alternative Dispute Resolution Requirements*

Anya George

§8.01 INTRODUCTION

When a dispute arises, parties will often, in the first phase, seek to reach an amicable settlement and avoid formal proceedings. Parties do not necessarily consider this phase when drafting their contract, and in many cases, the dispute resolution clause will simply provide for arbitration.

However, when parties do consider this phase – which is increasingly the case – they regularly choose to provide for a staged resolution of their disputes in so-called escalation or multi-tier dispute resolution (MDR) clauses.[1] These clauses provide, in varying forms and combinations, that before resorting to arbitration, the parties must attempt other forms of alternative dispute resolution (ADR), for example, by conducting negotiations, mediation or conciliation or by abiding by a cooling-off period.[2]

This contribution will analyse the role of good faith in pre-arbitral ADR and specifically examine whether there is, in fact, an (implicit) duty for parties to act in good faith when they have agreed to specific ADR mechanisms (§8.02) and if so, the scope of such an obligation (§8.03), and whether and how it can be enforced (§8.04).

* The author would like to thank Sophia Deuchert for her valuable review and comments.

1. In the 2018 Queen Mary/White & Case International Arbitration Survey, it was reported that 60% of in-house counsel interviewees had expressed a preference for using international arbitration in combination with other forms of ADR and an overall majority of interviewees shared the view that escalation clauses are beneficial for the overall process of resolving a given dispute (*see* https://arbitration.qmul.ac.uk/media/arbitration/docs/2018-International-Arbitration-Survey-report.pdf).
2. *See*, for example, Gary B. Born, *International Commercial Arbitration*, Vol. I (Kluwer Law International 3d ed. 2021), pp. 973 et seq. for a detailed description of what multi-tier dispute resolution clauses are and why parties use them.

§8.02 EXISTENCE OF AN OVERARCHING DUTY TO ACT IN GOOD FAITH IN PRE-ARBITRAL ADR

In some cases, parties will make express reference in their MDR clause to a duty to act in good faith in the pre-arbitral ADR phase, for example, by providing that they must 'seek to resolve the dispute by consultations and negotiations in good faith'[3] or that if negotiations fail, they 'agree first to try in good faith to settle the matter by mediation'[4] before going to arbitration.

However, if the MDR clause does not include such an express reference, the question arises as to whether there is an *implicit or overarching duty to act in good faith* during negotiations, mediation or any other pre-arbitral ADR process that the parties have provided for. The answer to that question may vary depending on the law that governs the contractually agreed pre-arbitral ADR stage.[5]

The Swiss Supreme Court examined the issue of the applicable law in a case decided in 2014.[6] The parties' agreement incorporated the FIDIC conditions of contract, which require parties to submit their disputes to a dispute adjudication board prior to arbitration. The seat of the arbitration was Switzerland, but the contract was not governed by Swiss law.[7] The Supreme Court held that: 'It seems artificial to treat as distinct … the arbitration proceedings as such, on the one hand, and the mediation procedure (in the broader sense) that precedes them, on the other, all the more so if the issue to be determined is whether the latter is a pre-condition to the initiation of the

3. *Tulip Real Estate Investment and Development Netherlands B.V. v. Republic of Turkey*, ICSID Case No. ARB/11/28, Decision on bifurcated jurisdictional issue of 5 March 2013: Art. 8(2) of the Netherlands-Turkey BIT (1986): 'In the event of an investment dispute between a Contracting Party and an investor of the other Contracting Party, the parties to the dispute shall initially *seek to resolve the dispute by consultations and negotiations in good faith*. … If the dispute cannot be resolved through the foregoing procedures the investor concerned may choose to submit the dispute to the International Centre for the Settlement of Investment Disputes ("Centre") for settlement by arbitration, at any time after one year from the date upon which the dispute arose, provided that in case the investor concerned has brought the dispute before the courts of justice of the Contracting Country that is a party to the dispute, and there has not been rendered a final award.' (emphasis added) *See also United Group Rail Services Limited v. Rail Corporation New South Wales* [2009] NSWCA 177: '*[35.11] Negotiation* … [T]he dispute or difference is to be referred to a senior representative of each of the Principal and Contractor who must: (c) *meet and undertake genuine and good faith negotiations* with a view to resolving the dispute or difference; and (d) if they cannot resolve the dispute or difference within 14 days … the matter at issue will be referred to the Australian Dispute Centre for mediation. [35.12] Arbitration If the senior representatives referred to in Clause 35.11 cannot resolve the dispute or difference or, where the matter is referred to mediation under Clause 35.11(d), the matter is not settled within 42 days … or within such longer period of time as these representatives may agree in writing, the dispute or difference will be referred to arbitration.' (emphasis added).
4. Example taken from the author's own practice: 'If the parties fail to settle the dispute, controversy or claim through negotiation, the parties agree first to *try in good faith to settle the matter by Mediation*. If the parties are unable to settle the matter by Mediation, then the matter shall be settled by final and binding Arbitration' (emphasis added).
5. *See* on this issue: Christian Oetiker/Claudia Walz, *Non-compliance with Multi-tier Dispute Resolution Clauses in Switzerland*, ASA Bulletin Vol. 35 Issue 4 (2017), pp. 873 et seq. DOI: 10.54648/asab2017080.
6. Swiss Supreme Court, Decision 4A_124/2014 of 7 July 2014.
7. The decision does not indicate which law was the applicable *lex causae*.

former.'[8] On that basis, the Court concluded that Swiss law[9] could be applied to the question of whether the MDR clause was mandatory and whether it had been complied with,[10] and went on to hold that the principle of good faith 'govern[ed] the procedural conduct of the parties' in relation to the agreed pre-arbitral ADR procedure.[11] It, therefore, recognized an overarching duty to act in good faith during that phase.

Under English law, it is often said that there is no overarching duty to act in good faith[12] and in *Walford v. Miles*, the English House of Lords considered that a requirement for parties to negotiate in good faith would be 'inherently repugnant to the adversarial position of the parties when involved in negotiations'.[13] However, in that case, the parties were negotiating with a view to entering into a new contractual relationship, not to resolving a dispute. Requiring a party to negotiate in good faith when there is no contractual relationship is very different to requiring a party to make genuine efforts to take part in a process that it has contractually undertaken to abide by.

Recognizing this distinction, the English High Court held in *Emirates Trading v. Prime Mineral Exports*[14] that an implied duty of good faith does exist in pre-arbitral negotiations.[15] The MDR clause, in that case, required the parties to 'first seek to resolve the dispute or claim by friendly discussion'[16] without mentioning good faith. The Court nevertheless considered that '[t]he obligation to seek to resolve disputes by friendly discussions must import an obligation to seek to do so in good faith' and even considered that 'such an obligation goes without saying'.[17]

Most civil law jurisdictions recognize good faith as an overarching principle governing the parties' conduct at various stages of a dispute. Following the *Emirates*

---

8. Swiss Supreme Court, Decision 4A_124/2014 of 7 July 2014, para. 3.3 (unofficial translation).
9. Specifically, the Swiss Supreme Court considered that Art. 178(2) of the Swiss Private International Law Act (which provides that the arbitration agreement is valid if it conforms with the requirements of the law chosen by the parties to apply to the arbitration agreement, the *lex causae* or Swiss law) could apply *mutatis mutandis* to the agreement on a pre-arbitral ADR process.
10. Swiss Supreme Court, Decision 4A_124/2014 of 7 July 2014, paras 3.3-3.4.
11. Swiss Supreme Court, Decision 4A_124/2014 of 7 July 2014, para. 3.4.4.
12. *See* Oliver Krauss, *The Enforceability of Escalation Clauses Providing for Negotiations in Good Faith under English Law*, McGill Journal of Dispute Resolution, Vol. 2 (2015-2016) p. 153; Henry J. Brown/Arthur L. Marriott, *ADR Principles and Practice* (Sweet & Maxwell 2d ed. 1999), para. 6-061.
13. House of Lords, *Walford and others v. Miles and another* [1992] 2 AC 128.
14. High Court of Justice, *Emirates Trading Agency LLC v. Prime Mineral Exports Private Ltd.* [2014] EWHC 2014.
15. For an in-depth analysis of the *Emirates Trading* decision and of relevant prior case law, *see* Louis Flannery/Robert Merkin, *Emirates Trading, Good Faith, and Pre-arbitral ADR Clauses: A Jurisdictional Precondition?*, Arbitration International, Vol. 31 Issue 1 (2015), pp. 63-106 DOI: 10.1093/arbint/aiv005.
16. The entire clause read as follows: '11. Dispute Resolution and Arbitration 11.1 In case of any dispute or claim arising out of or in connection with or under this LTC including on account of a breaches/defaults mentioned in 9.2, 9.3, Clauses 10.1(d) and/or 10.1(e) above, the Parties shall *first seek to resolve the dispute or claim by friendly discussion*. Any party may notify the other Party of its desire to enter into consuLTCtion [sic] to resolve a dispute or claim. If no solution can be arrived at in between the Parties for a continuous period of 4 (four) weeks then the non-defaulting party can invoke the arbitration clause and refer the disputes to arbitration ...' (emphasis added).
17. High Court of Justice, *Emirates Trading Agency LLC v. Prime Mineral Exports Private Ltd.* [2014] EWHC 2104, para. 51.

Trading decision, it is fair to say that, at least in Europe, there is an emerging consensus that if parties have agreed to pre-arbitral ADR, their conduct during that phase is governed by the principle of good faith – even absent an express reference to good faith in the MDR clause.

The question remains, however, as to what the scope of good faith is in that context and whether/how an obligation to act in good faith can be enforced.

§8.03 SCOPE OF DUTY TO ACT IN GOOD FAITH IN PRE-ARBITRAL ADR

As highlighted in various other contributions to this publication, there is no universally accepted definition of good faith. When describing the principle of good faith, reference is often made to concepts of honesty, reasonableness and reliability. Other terms that are regularly used include genuineness, sincerity, playing fair, coming with clean hands and putting one's cards on the table.

However, when it comes to pre-arbitral ADR processes such as negotiation, mediation or conciliation, there is an inherent difficulty in defining good faith in those types of terms. Indeed, it would be unreasonable to consider that the principle of good faith requires parties to be fully transparent or to lay all their cards on the table.[18] Moreover, depending on the circumstances, it may be contrary to the principle of good faith for a party to rely on non-compliance with a pre-arbitral ADR requirement to resist arbitration.

This reflects the dual nature of good faith, which has both a positive (§8.03[A]) and a negative (§8.03[B]) function in relation to pre-arbitral ADR requirements.

[A] Positive Aspect of Good Faith

The positive aspect of good faith requires a party that has an obligation to perform that obligation in good faith. Therefore, the first question that must be answered is whether the parties are, in fact, under an obligation to comply with a pre-arbitral ADR requirement.[19] The answer to that question will depend on the specific circumstances of a given case, such as the wording of the MDR clause and the parties' intent.

Assuming that the parties are under such an obligation, the next question – and the one that is of interest for this contribution – is whether they are required to make a *'genuine' (good faith) effort* to engage with the other side in the pre-arbitral ADR process – and if so, how far that effort must go.

18. *See* New South Wales Court of Appeal, *United Group Rail Services Limited v. Rail Corporation New South Wales* [2009] NSWCA 177, para. 76: '[T]he obligation to undertake genuine and good faith negotiations does not require any step to advance the interests of the other party. The process is the self-interested one of negotiation.'
19. This question has been the focus of much debate in legal literature and has given rise to numerous court decisions, most of which focus on whether non-compliance with an MDR clause goes to jurisdiction or admissibility. The existence of a duty to act in good faith when complying with an MDR clause and the consequences of a failure to fulfil that duty do not materially impact this debate, which will therefore not be dealt with in this contribution.

Commenting on the *Emirates Trading*[20] decision, Flannery/Merkin highlight the issue in the following – somewhat colourful – terms:[21]

> [W]hat is meant by 'friendly'? What actually counts as a 'discussion'? Should the negotiators be trained in how to smile convincingly (or hug their counterparts)? And when is an attempt not made in good faith? Might a party whose negotiators sit grumpily at the settlement meetings (smiling through clenched teeth, staring at the ceiling, while mentally humming 'Rule Britannia') and refuse to accept anything less than 100 per cent of the claim, not still be acting in 'good faith', and even if the tribunal awards the claim in full? In other words, does acting 'in good faith' necessarily carry with it an implication that a party must be obliged to make (or at least ready to make) some material concession? If so, on what basis? And what if the court concludes that the discussions were unfriendly?

Although it is unlikely that the principle of good faith would require parties to make concessions, it would arguably require them to genuinely and actively engage with the pre-arbitral ADR process.[22] Whether or not a party has done so can only be assessed having regard to the specific circumstances of the case. At the very least, however, the parties may be required to abide by any contractually agreed parameters, such as taking part in meetings within a defined period of time, engaging in discussions to nominate a mediator, paying an advance on fees under agreed mediation rules, etc.

[B] Negative Aspect of Good Faith

Conversely, there are times when it would be contrary to good faith to require a party to comply with the contractually agreed pre-arbitral ADR process – and it may be abusive to rely on non-compliance.[23] This negative aspect of good faith is of relevance when a party seeks to challenge the jurisdiction of the arbitral tribunal (either at the outset or in later setting-aside proceedings) on the grounds that a pre-arbitral ADR requirement has not been fully complied with.[24]

---

20. *See* above; High Court of Justice, *Emirates Trading Agency LLC v. Prime Mineral Exports Private Ltd.* [2014] EWHC 2014.
21. *See* Louis Flannery/Robert Merkin, *Emirates Trading, Good Faith, and Pre-arbitral ADR Clauses: A Jurisdictional Precondition?*, Arbitration International, Vol. 31 Issue 1 (2015), p. 103 DOI: 10.1093/arbint/aiv005. The MDR clause in that case provided that the parties were to 'first seek to resolve the dispute or claim by friendly discussion'.
22. *See* Supreme Court of New South Wales, *Hooper Bailie Associated Ltd. v. Natcon Group Pty Ltd,* [1992] 28 NSWLR 194, para. 206: 'What is enforced is not co-operation and compromise but participation in a process from which co-operation and consent might come.'
23. *See* Christian Oetiker/Claudia Walz, *Non-compliance with Multi-tier Dispute Resolution Clauses in Switzerland,* ASA Bulletin Vol. 35 Issue 4 (2017), p. 878 DOI: 10.54648/asab2017080.
24. *See* Klaus Peter Berger, *Law and Practice of Escalation Clauses*, Arbitration International, Vol. 22 Issue 1 (2006), pp. 15 et seq. DOI: 10.1093/arbitration/22.1.1: 'The principle of good faith in the form of estoppel by conduct is ultimately of assistance in controlling dishonest behaviour of a party that seeks to rely on the apparent failure by the other party to comply with escalation levels before an arbitral tribunal. A party that has steadfastly boycotted the institution of ADR proceedings in the preliminary phase, such as by failing to pay an advance on fees as provided for in particular mediation rules, cannot then rely on this very same argument. Similarly, a party cannot impede the institution of arbitral proceedings if, in the preliminary phase, it continually gave the other party the impression that it would not attach any importance to the mandatory

The Swiss Supreme Court has dealt with the negative aspect of good faith in several decisions and considered that a party is acting abusively and is therefore precluded from relying on non-compliance with pre-arbitral ADR requirements to resist arbitration or challenge the award if:

- it did not itself make a good faith effort to engage in the pre-arbitral ADR process;[25]
- it did not raise an objection in the arbitration based on non-compliance with the pre-arbitral ADR requirement;[26]
- the negotiations, conciliation or mediation would, in any event, have been futile.[27]

This last condition is the most problematic, as parties may be quick to claim – and courts may be quick to accept – that the pre-arbitral ADR process is futile. If the standard for *futility* is set too low, the very purpose of the pre-arbitral ADR requirement is undermined: A party could bypass the agreed-upon process simply by claiming that there is no prospect of an amicable settlement because the parties' positions are too far apart, or because the other party is not interested in a genuine discussion.

However, even if negotiations, conciliation or mediation may appear futile, a party may be precluded from relying on that futility unless it has itself made a good faith effort to engage in the process.[28] Indeed, as highlighted by the ICSID tribunal in

requirement of initiating preliminary ADR proceedings as provided for in the escalation clause, but then seeks to rely on the plea of failure to comply with these escalation levels with respect to the action before the state court or arbitral tribunal. In both cases, the party is acting in blatant contradiction to its previous behaviour.'

25. Swiss Supreme Court, Decision 4A_18/2007 of 6 June 2007, para. 4.3.3.1., referring to an unpublished para. 4 of DSC 129 III 675; *see also*, Swiss Supreme Court, Decision 4A_628/2015 of 16 March 2016, para. 2.4.3.1.; Christian Oetiker/Claudia Walz, *Non-compliance with Multi-tier Dispute Resolution Clauses in Switzerland*, ASA Bulletin Vol. 35 Issue 4 (2017), p. 878 DOI: 10.54648/asab2017080: '[E]nforcing an MDR-clause – i.e. inhibiting arbitral proceedings – will not be possible if this amounts to an abuse of rights. The party invoking the non-compliance with an MDR-clause must act in good faith. This requires that this party has indeed proposed to the other party to hold the pre-arbitral tier before the arbitration. If it did not, it commits an abuse of rights by invoking the non-compliance in the arbitral proceedings. If the other party initiated the pre-arbitral tier, the party invoking non-compliance with an MDR-clause must actually have participated, or at least offered to participate, in such pre-arbitral tier.'
26. Swiss Supreme Court, Decision 4A_18/2007 of 6 June 2007, para. 4.3.3.1. (informal translation): '[T]he applicant chose to participate in the arbitration whilst keeping the opportunity to rely on the failure to comply with the preliminary concilation in reserve.'
27. Swiss Supreme Court, Decision 4A_46/2011 of 16 May 2011, para. 3.5.2; *see also* Gary B. Born, *International Commercial Arbitration*, Vol. I (Kluwer Law International 3d ed. 2021), pp. 995 et seq.
28. Appearing to concur, Bernhard Berger/Franz Kellerhals, *International and Domestic Arbitration in Switzerland* (Stämpfli Publishers 4th ed. 2021), para. 583a: 'In our view, this case law should not be considered as establishing a precedent. A general assumption that a party's breach of the dispute resolution clause is simply "cured" if the other party fails to react does not seem justified. In our view, generally the party commencing the arbitration should still have to prove that it had requested the other party to conciliate or mediate.'

Murphy v. Ecuador,[29] a process that may initially seem futile may nevertheless end up yielding positive results:

> [The cooling off period] is not about a mere formality, which allows for the submission of a request for arbitration although the six-month waiting period requirement has not been met, and if the other party objects to it, withdraws and resubmits it. It amounts to something much more serious: an essential mechanism enshrined in many bilateral investment treaties, which compels the parties to make a genuine effort to engage in good faith negotiations before resorting to arbitration. Of course, this Tribunal does not ignore the fact that if both parties cling obstinately to their positions, the possibilities for having a successful negotiation become null. However, there have been many cases in which parties with seemingly irreconcilable points of view at first, manage to reach amicable solutions. To find out if this is possible, they must first try it.

It is therefore not unreasonable to require the party relying on futility to explain on what basis it has concluded that there is no prospect of reaching an amicable settlement, for example, by demonstrating that it made genuine efforts to engage with the other party, that it carried out the steps required under the pre-arbitral ADR process, but that the other party remained passive and/or uncooperative.

§8.04 ENFORCEMENT OF DUTY TO ACT IN GOOD FAITH IN PRE-ARBITRAL ADR

[A] Framework

Whereas legal authorities in civil law jurisdictions tend to focus on whether there is an obligation, and not merely an option,[30] to take part in a pre-arbitral ADR process in good faith, authorities in common law jurisdictions tend to focus on the issue of whether the requirement to take part in the pre-arbitral ADR process in good faith is enforceable.[31]

---

29. ICSID Tribunal:, *Murphy Exploration and Production Company International v. Republic of Ecuador*, ICSID Case No. ARB/08/4, Award on Jurisdiction of 15 December 2010, paras 154 et seqq.
30. *See* Swiss Supreme Court, Decision 4A_124/2014 of 7 July 2014; Domitille Baizeau, Chapter 18, Part XVI: *Multi-tiered and Hybrid Arbitration Clauses* (Manuel Arroyo ed., Arbitration in Switzerland: The Practitioner's Guide, Kluwer International Law 2d ed. 2018), p. 2788; Christian Oetiker/Claudia Walz, *Non-compliance with Multi-tier Dispute Resolution Clauses in Switzerland*, ASA Bulletin Vol. 35 Issue 4 (2017), p. 876 DOI: 10.54648/asab2017080; Craig Tevendale /Hannah Ambrose/Vanessa Naish, *Multi-Tier Dispute Resolution Clauses and Arbitration*, The Turkish Commercial Law Review Vol. 1 Issue 1 (February 2015), p. 40 DOI: 10.5040/9781509 910441.ch-004.
31. *See* Gary B. Born, *International Commercial Arbitration*, Volume I (Kluwer Law International 3d ed. 2021), pp. 976-980; Louis Flannery/Robert Merkin, *Emirates Trading, Good Faith, and Pre-arbitral ADR Clauses: A Jurisdictional Precondition?*, Arbitration International, Vol. 31 Issue 1 (2015), pp. 67 et seqq. DOI: 10.1093/arbint/aiv005; Craig Tevendale/Hannah Ambrose/ Vanessa Naish, *Multi-tier Dispute Resolution Clauses and Arbitration*, The Turkish Commercial Law Review Vol. 1 Issue 1 (February 2015), pp. 35 et seqq. DOI: 10.5040/9781509910441.ch-004.

In either case, one of the key questions is whether the parties have agreed on a *framework* for the pre-arbitral ADR process that is sufficiently *specific or certain*. Indeed, tribunals and courts struggle with the concept that a 'bare' undertaking to negotiate or mediate (in good faith), without framework or limitations, is mandatory and/or enforceable.

For example, the Swiss Supreme Court examined a clause which provided that the matter could only be referred to arbitration 'after an attempt at conciliation has failed'.[32] The clause did not provide for a time limit for the initiation of conciliation proceedings, indicate whether a mediator should be appointed, or establish any kind of procedural framework. According to the Supreme Court, this lack of specificity 'certainly does not speak in favour of the mandatory character of the conciliation that is to be attempted', and it found that the parties had not agreed to a mandatory pre-arbitral step – despite the fact that the contract also provided that the parties 'will' first seek an amicable resolution of the dispute.[33]

Similarly, in *Cable & Wireless v. IBM*, the English High Court held that there is an obvious lack of certainty in a mere undertaking to negotiate in good faith because a court would have insufficient objective criteria to decide whether one or both parties were in compliance or breach of such an undertaking.[34]

By contrast, in the more recent *Emirates Trading* decision mentioned above, the English High Court held that an obligation to seek to resolve a dispute by friendly discussions in good faith has an identifiable standard, namely, 'fair, honest and genuine discussions aimed at resolving a dispute'.[35] It further held that:

> Difficulty of proving a breach in some cases should not be confused with a suggestion that the clause lacks certainty. In the context of a dispute resolution clause pursuant to which the parties have voluntarily accepted a restriction upon their freedom not to negotiate it is not appropriate to suggest that the obligation is inconsistent with the position of a negotiating party. Enforcement of such an agreement when found as part of a dispute resolution clause is in the public interest, first, because commercial men expect the court to enforce obligations which they have freely undertaken and, second, because the object of the

32. Swiss Supreme Court, Decision 4A_46/2011 of 16 May 2011, para. 3.1.1: 'En cas de litige à l'occasion de l'interprétation ou de l'exécution des présents, un accord à l'amiable sera d'abord recherché par les parties. Les litiges éventuels qui viendraient à naître du fait de l'interprétation ou de l'exécution des dispositions du présent MARCHE seront soumis, après échec d'une tentative de conciliation, à un tribunal arbitral, sans aucun recours aux tribunaux judiciaires.' Informal translation: 'In case of dispute as to the interpretation or performance of the present [Contract], the parties will first seek an amicable resolution. Any disputes that may arise due to the interpretation or performance of the provisions of the present [Contract] will be referred, after an attempt at conciliation has failed, to an arbitral tribunal.'
33. Swiss Supreme Court, Decision 4A_46/2011 of 16 May 2011, para. 3.5.2: 'Ce manque de précision ne plaide sans doute pas en faveur du caractère obligatoire de la conciliation à tenter.'; *see also* Domitille Baizeau, Chapter 18, Part XVI: *Multi-tiered and Hybrid Arbitration Clauses*, Manuel Arroyo ed., Arbitration in Switzerland: The Practitioner's Guide, 2d ed. (2018), p. 2790.
34. High Court of Justice, *Cable & Wireless PLC v. IBM United Kingdom Limited* [2002] EWHC 2059.
35. High Court of Justice, *Emirates Trading Agency LLC v. Prime Mineral Exports Private Ltd.* [2014] EWHC 2104, para. 64: 'The agreement is not incomplete; no term is missing. Nor is it uncertain; an obligation to seek to resolve a dispute by friendly discussions in good faith has an identifiable standard, namely, fair, honest and genuine discussions aimed at resolving a dispute.'

agreement is to avoid what might otherwise be an expensive and time-consuming arbitration.[36]

However, it is worth noting that in the *Emirates Trading* case, the MDR clause did include a time limitation on the obligation to conduct friendly discussions[37] and was, therefore, not a 'bare' obligation.

In other words, even though a 'bare' obligation to conduct negotiations or mediation in good faith may be enforceable in theory, courts and tribunals are much more likely to give effect to an undertaking to negotiate, conciliate or mediate in good faith that is placed within a framework,[38] e.g., where the MDR clause includes a time limit for any steps to be taken,[39] refers to specific rules (of mediation)[40] or sets out a clear process for discussions, defining when one step has failed and the next has begun, how the next step can be started and by whom.[41]

[B] Proof of Good Faith

Even if an MDR clause is considered mandatory and sufficiently certain to be enforced, it will often be extremely difficult in practice to prove that a party acted or failed to act in good faith in the pre-arbitral ADR phase.

While it is possible to prove that a party took part in a meeting or initiated mediation as an objective fact, it is by definition more difficult to determine whether that party did so 'in good faith'. Indeed, although compliance with a defined framework for pre-arbitral ADR may be indicative of good faith, it is not necessarily conclusive proof of such. That being said, while non-compliance with a measurable step is not necessarily proof that a party failed to act in good faith, it does tend to shift

36. High Court of Justice: *Emirates Trading Agency LLC v. Prime Mineral Exports Private Ltd.* [2014] EWHC 2104, para. 64.
37. The clause is reproduced in *supra* n. 16.
38. *See* Gary B. Born, *International Commercial Arbitration*, Vol. I (Kluwer Law International 3d ed. 2021), p. 976: 'Most courts uphold the validity of agreements to negotiate only where there is a reasonably clear set of substantive and procedural requirements against which a party's negotiating efforts can be meaningfully measured. Absent such guidelines, courts from both civil law and common law jurisdictions have frequently held that particular agreements to negotiate the resolution of disputes are inherently uncertain and indefinite, and therefore invalid or unenforceable.'
39. *See* Christian Oetiker/Claudia Walz, *Non-compliance with Multi-tier Dispute Resolution Clauses in Switzerland*, ASA Bulletin Vol. 35 Issue 4 (2017), p. 877 DOI: 10.54648/asab2017080; Craig Tevendale/Hannah Ambrose/Vanessa Naish, *Multi-tier Dispute Resolution Clauses and Arbitration*, The Turkish Commercial Law Review Vol. 1 Issue 1 (February 2015), p. 40 DOI: 10.5040/9781509910441.ch-004: 'In order to sufficiently certain, there should be clear, ascertainable time limits for each step, such that it is unambiguous when one step ends and the next begins.'
40. *See* Swiss Supreme Court, Decision 4A_628/2015 of 16 March 2016: MDR clause provided for conciliation pursuant to the ADR Rules of the ICC; Craig Tevendale/Hannah Ambrose/Vanessa Naish, *Multi-tier Dispute Resolution Clauses and Arbitration*, The Turkish Commercial Law Review Vol. 1 Issue 1 (February 2015), p. 40 DOI: 10.5040/9781509910441.ch-004.
41. *See* Craig Tevendale/Hannah Ambrose/Vanessa Naish, *Multi-tier Dispute Resolution Clauses and Arbitration*, The Turkish Commercial Law Review Vol. 1 Issue 1 (February 2015), p. 40 DOI: 10.5040/9781509910441.ch-004.

the burden onto the non-complying party. And if a party has complied with a measurable step, there will often be a presumption (in fact, if not in law) that it did so in good faith.

One issue that can arise in this context is what evidence the parties may rely on to demonstrate their good faith. Elements such as a claim letter proposing negotiations or a request for the appointment of a mediator can usually be introduced as evidence. However, the settlement discussions or mediation themselves are invariably conducted 'without prejudice', meaning that the parties are effectively barred from relying on them in subsequent proceedings. This can pose substantial problems for a party that needs to demonstrate that the other side did not carry out the pre-arbitral steps in good faith or that the process was futile (and could, therefore, legitimately be terminated prematurely), as it may neither rely on the content of the pre-arbitral discussions nor on the subjective elements of the other side's conduct during that phase.[42]

[C] Consequences of Failure to Act in Good Faith

The consequences of a failure to act in good faith in the pre-arbitral ADR phase will usually be the same as the consequences for not complying with the objective elements of an MDR clause, such as a required negotiation period or the initiation of mediation, namely: the tribunal will consider that it lacks jurisdiction – i.e., the authority to make a decision affecting the merits of the case – or that the claim is inadmissible – i.e., the claim may not be decided at that point in time, due to a temporary or permanent defect or bar.[43]

However, the parties could agree to other consequences, such as an impact on costs. In an example taken from this author's practice, the parties agreed to mediation as a mandatory pre-arbitral step. The MDR clause provided that if mediation terminated following a notification by the mediator that mediation was not likely to produce a settlement or following a party's election to withdraw from mediation not less than thirty days after commencing mediation, the mediator was, at the request of any party, to state in a report to the arbitral tribunal whether each party participated in the mediation in good faith. The arbitral tribunal could, in its sole discretion, upon a report that a party failed to act in good faith during mediation, apportion all costs and expenses of both the mediation and arbitration, including legal fees, against that party.

---

42. *See* Christopher Boog/James Menz, *Landmark Swiss Decision on Failure to Comply with a Mandatory Pre-arbitral Tier*, Kluwer Arbitration Blog (4 May 2016); Louis Flannery/Robert Merkin, *Emirates Trading, Good Faith, and Pre-arbitral ADR Clauses: A Jurisdictional Precondition?*, Arbitration International, Vol. 31 Issue 1 (2015), pp. 103 et seq. DOI: 10.1093/arbint/aiv005.
43. As mentioned above (*supra* n. 19), there is a heated debate as to whether non-compliance with an MDR clause is to be viewed as an issue of jurisdiction or admissibility. This debate is beyond the scope of this contribution and in any event, not directly relevant to the issue of good faith as such. In other words, whether a party acted in good faith or not in the pre-arbitral ADR phase will, in principle, not change whether non-compliance with the MDR clause is viewed as an issue of jurisdiction or admissibility. *See*, amongst others, Milivoje Mitrovic, *Dealing with the Consequences of Non-compliance with Mandatory Pre-arbitral Requirements in Multi-tiered Dispute Resolution Clauses: The Swiss Approach and a Look Across the Border*, ASA Bulletin Vol. 37 Issue 3 (2019), pp. 574 et seqq.

This approach allows the parties to avoid having to (re-)start discussions or mediation in a situation where it is highly unlikely that an amicable settlement can be reached. At the same time, it provides a suitable incentive to the parties to properly engage with the pre-arbitral ADR process, as they otherwise face a significant cost risk. This solution does, however, place a great burden on the mediator, and there could be difficulties in applying it in practice.

§8.05 CONCLUSION

Good faith plays an important role in pre-arbitral ADR. It acts as an overarching principle governing this phase, even absent an express reference in the MDR clause. While its scope – in this as in other areas – is not clearly defined, there appears to be a degree of consensus that it requires parties to genuinely and actively engage with the contractually agreed-upon pre-arbitral ADR process. It also bars parties from abusively relying on non-compliance with a pre-arbitral ADR requirement to challenge the jurisdiction of the tribunal or the admissibility of a claim.

In that context, courts and tribunals should not be too quick to accept a non-complying party's claim that settlement discussions or mediation would have been futile, as this could undermine the very purpose of the pre-arbitral ADR process, which is to attempt to find an amicable solution to a situation where the parties may at first have seemingly irreconcilable views.

While in theory, a 'bare' undertaking to negotiate or mediate in good faith may be enforceable, in practice, courts and tribunals in both civil and common law jurisdictions are more willing to enforce an MDR clause that contains measurable steps or a defined framework. Even when a clause is considered enforceable, and it can be demonstrated that a party complied (or failed to comply) with those measurable steps or framework, there is an inherent difficulty in proving that the party did so in good (or bad) faith, which is exacerbated by the fact that settlement discussions and mediation are generally conducted on confidential/without prejudice basis.

Although the enforcement of the parties' duty to act in good faith in the pre-arbitral ADR phase remains fraught with difficulty, it would be wrong to discount the importance of this principle in practice. Even if it is not enforced as a stand-alone obligation, courts and tribunals will judge the parties' conduct by the standard of good faith.

CHAPTER 9

The Parties' Procedural Good Faith Obligations in Arbitration*

Flavio Peter

§9.01 INTRODUCTION

The duty to act in good faith is a universally recognized principle of law.[1] In Switzerland, the good faith principle forms part of both substantive and procedural public policy[2] and equally applies in the framework of arbitral proceedings.[3] Accordingly, many sets of institutional arbitration rules refer to the parties' duty to act in good

* This chapter is based on the presentation given at the ASA Annual Conference held on 4 February 2022 in Geneva. However, the content of this chapter may slightly deviate from the original presentation, be it because I elaborated on certain thoughts or omitted other aspects for the purposes of this written contribution. Throughout this chapter, masculine forms (he/his/him) or feminine forms (she/her) are to be understood as referring to all genders, except when referring to a particular person. I am grateful to Konstantin Christie, Partner at Peter&Kim, Geneva, for his review of this chapter and his valuable comments.

1. Pierre Mayer, *Le principe de bonne foi devant les arbitres du commerce international*, in *Etudes de droit international en honneur de Pierre Lalive*, 547 et seq. (Christian Dominicé et al., eds, 1993); many Civil law jurisdictions have codified the principle of good faith, such as Switzerland (Art. 2 Swiss Civil Code), France (Art. 1104 French Civil Code, and *see also* Art. 1464 French Code of Civil Procedure), Germany (§ 242 German Civil Code, BGB), Italy (Art. 1175 Italian Civil Code); *see* Duarte Henriques, *The Role of Good Faith in Arbitration: Are Arbitrators and Arbitral Institutions Bound to Act in Good Faith?* 33 ASA Bull. 515 (2015) DOI: 10.54648/asab2015043; Bernardo Cremades, *Good Faith in International Arbitration*, 27(4) American University International Law Review (hereinafter 'Am. U. Int'l L. Rev.') 768 (2012).
2. Cf. Manuel Arroyo, Art. 190 of the Swiss Private International Law Act ('SPILA') in *Arbitration in Switzerland – the Practitioner's Guide* (Manuel Arroyo ed., 2d ed. 2018) paras 104 and 163.
3. Decision of the Swiss Federal Supreme Court ('DSFSC') 4A_600/2010, reas. 4.2; DSFSC 4P_196/2003, reas. 5.2; *see* Felix Dasser & Danielle Gauthey, *La bonne foi dans l'arbitrage* 33 ASA Bull, 239-273 (2015) DOI: 10.54648/asab2015021 (hereinafter 'Dasser & Gauthey'), 243 et seq., 250; *see also* Simon Weber & Julie Martinez, *Good Faith in International Arbitration: Comparative Approaches in ICC Awards*, ICC Disp Res Bull 120 (2020) (hereinafter 'Weber & Martinez') with further references.

faith in arbitration,[4] such as, for instance, Article 16(1) of the Swiss Rules of International Arbitration 2021 (hereinafter 'Swiss Rules 2021').[5]

Yet, the respective provisions provide little guidance or clarity on the definition and/or scope of the parties' procedural good faith obligations in an arbitration.

Often, the obligation to act in good faith is mentioned in the same breath as the prohibition of an abuse of rights. For instance, Article 22(2) of the Arbitration Rules 2021 of the Russian Arbitration Center states that 'the Parties and their representatives shall exercise their procedural rights in good faith and without abuse'.[6] This raises the question of whether the duty of good faith in the procedural context of an arbitration sets forth specific precepts or whether it only works as a corrective.[7]

In the book 'The Unruly Notion of Abuse of Rights', Prof. Jan Paulsson writes that:

> We all know that 'abuse of process' is not to be tolerated, but the phrase itself leads nowhere until it is given some specificity ....[8]

The same concern may be raised in relation to the obligation to act in good faith. The parties' procedural good faith obligations will depend on the individual circumstances of the case and, absent any further specifications, will be difficult to pinpoint.

§9.02 PRELIMINARY CONSIDERATIONS

Before addressing different possible manifestations of good faith obligations in the procedural context, this section will set out a few preliminary considerations shaping one possible understanding of the parties' procedural good faith obligations.

It should be noted at this juncture that this chapter focuses on the good faith obligations of the parties in a procedural context; it does not address the question of the

---

4. Cf. Art. 16(1) Swiss Rules 2021, Art. 24(1) of the Arbitration Rules of the Belgian Centre for Arbitration and Mediation 2023 (hereinafter 'CEPANI Rules 2023'), Art. 26(3) of the Arbitration Rules of the Finland Chamber of Commerce 2020 (hereinafter 'FAI Rules 2020'), Art. 9 of the China International Economic and Trade Arbitration Commission Arbitration Rules 2015 (hereinafter 'CIETAC Rules 2015'), Art. 9 of the Arbitration Rules of the Milan Chamber of Arbitration 2020 (hereinafter 'CAM Rules 2020') or Art. 22(2) Arbitration Rules 2021 of the Russian Arbitration Center.
5. Article 16(1) Swiss Rules 2021 states as follows: '1. All participants in the arbitration proceedings shall act in good faith and make every effort to contribute to the efficient conduct of the proceedings and to avoid unnecessary costs and delays. The parties undertake to comply with any award or order made by the arbitral tribunal or emergency arbitrator without delay.'
6. *See also* Art. 24(1) CEPANI Rules 2023, which requires the parties to 'act in a rapid manner and in good faith' and to 'abstain from any dilatory act as well as from any other action having the object or effect of delaying the proceedings'.
7. Also from a general Swiss law perspective it is not entirely clear to what extent Art. 2(1) and (2) of the Swiss Civil Code (ZGB) are merely 'mirror images' (*Spiegelbildtheorie*), respectively, to what extent they serve different but complementary functions; *see, e.g.*, CHK- Patrick Middendorf & Beatrice Grob, ZGB, note 1 ad Art. 2 ZGB, with further references; *see also* BK- Heinz Hausheer & Regina Aebi-Müller, Einleitung, Art. 1-9 ZGB (2012), note 58 and Art. 2 ZGB, with detailed elaborations on the different views.
8. Jan Paulsson, *The Unruly Notion of Abuse of Rights*, Cambridge University Press, July 2020, 1, 5.

parties' substantive good faith obligations. Neither does this chapter discuss the arbitrator's or the arbitral institutions' potential procedural good faith obligations, nor will this chapter touch upon any rules of professional conduct and the ethical duties of party representatives.[9]

[A] Protecting the Parties' 'Legitimate Expectations' Regarding the Procedure

One may seek to determine the content of procedural good faith obligations by seeking to identify the purpose and rights protected by the good faith principle. From this perspective, the principle of good faith can be said to protect the 'legitimate expectations' of the parties.[10] Procedural good faith is, thus, infringed if a party's legitimate expectations with respect to the procedure are violated.

The following points should, however, be borne in mind:

- First, what may constitute 'good faith' conduct and what may constitute 'legitimate expectations' respectively, may vary over the course of time. Thus, 'good faith' conduct is a fluid concept, understood differently depending on the cultural and legal backgrounds of the parties, their counsel and the arbitrators.[11]
- Second, it is the legitimate expectations of the parties that are decisive in determining what procedural good faith obligations the parties agreed to follow. Whilst the experience and expertise of external counsel (or more generally of the arbitration practitioners) and their own separate expectations will undoubtedly shape their understanding of how an arbitration procedure should evolve, neither the experience nor the expectations of the practitioners have any bearing on the determination of the parties' expectations at the relevant point in time of concluding an arbitration agreement (or a contract containing an arbitration clause), as the latter often occurs years before the dispute arises and most likely without the involvement of such external counsel.

It has been suggested that when the parties conclude an arbitration agreement, they are obliged to act in good faith and, thus, 'to assist in the initiation of the

9. In relation to the expected conduct of party representatives, *see, e.g., IBA Guidelines on Party Representation in International Arbitration* (25 May 2013), https://www.ibanet.org/MediaHandler?id=6F0C57D7-E7A0-43AF-B76E-714D9FE74D7F.
10. *See* Dasser & Gauthey, 243; for Switzerland *see, e.g.*, BK- Heinz Hausheer & Regina Aebi-Müller, Einleitung, Art. 1-9 ZGB (2012), note 4 et seq. ad Art. 2 Swiss Civil Code.
11. *See* Weber & Martinez, 114: 'Good Faith Is Therefore a Dynamic, Moving, Ever-Changing Concept'; Patrick Taylor & Shreya Aren et al., Harmonising Cultural Differences in International Arbitration: The Role of Parties' Reasonable Expectations and Counsel's Ethical Rules, in *Stockholm Arbitration Yearbook 2020* (Axel Calissendorff & Patrik Schöldström eds) Ch. 4, 43-64, §4.05 53 et seq. (Kluwer Law International 2020); Dasser & Gauthey, 239, 246.

proceedings, further the proceedings and to refrain from all actions that might frustrate them'.[12]

Yet, it is submitted that legitimate expectations arise from a specific factual and legal context. Parties with a particular background are faced with a particular dispute that is subject to a specific *lex causae* and governed by a *lex arbitri*. Very often, the parties make specific procedural rules (arbitration rules) applicable by reference. Thus, any procedural good faith obligations do not exist in a legal or factual vacuum. Rather, procedural obligations emanate from the *lex arbitri* and the rules of arbitration designated by the parties. However, such rules may themselves have evolved over time.

Therefore, the applicable procedural rules primarily shape 'expectations' of what the arbitration procedure should look like,[13] whereas the relevant circumstances of each specific case will demonstrate the 'legitimacy' of such expectations.[14]

Consequently, the parties' procedural good faith obligations are sculpted by the applicable legal framework and the factual setting of the individual case; they do not, in principle, exist by nature of the mere fact that the parties concluded an arbitration agreement.

[B] Considering the Adversarial Nature of Arbitration

It has also been argued that the good faith principle inherent in the arbitration agreement requires the parties 'to do all things necessary as to cooperate in achieving the contractual aim', including, presumably, its arbitration clause.[15] This could be read in line with Article 14.2 of the LCIA Arbitration Rules 2020, which states that the 'parties *shall do everything necessary in good faith* for the fair, efficient and expeditious conduct' of the arbitration.

However, the aspiration that the parties 'co-operate in achieving the contractual aim' of an arbitration agreement may take insufficient account of the adversarial

12. Anna-Maria Tamminen, *Chapter II: The Arbitrator and the Arbitration Procedure – The Obligation to Pay the Advance on Costs under the Vienna Rules and Austrian Law*, in Austrian Arbitration Yearbook 281-300 (Christian Klausegger & Peter Klein et al., eds, 2009) (hereinafter 'Tamminen').
13. In DSFSC 126 III 249, reas. 3.b., the Swiss Federal Supreme Court held that procedural public policy (including procedural good faith) cannot serve as a basis to deduce a 'procedural code of arbitration' which the parties' freely determined procedure has to satisfy (in the original German: 'Namentlich kann aus dem verfahrensrechtlichen Ordre public nicht ein 'code de procédure arbitrale' abgeleitet werden, dem das von den Parteien frei gewählte Verfahren genügen müsste'). This corroborates the conclusion that the good faith principle may not by itself determine the 'code de procédure arbitrale' expected by the other party and/or other actors in the arbitration.
14. *See also* Dasser & Gauthey, 269.
15. *See* online publication of Squire Patton Boggs: Tim O'Shannassy, *Procedural Good Faith in International Arbitration* (August 2018), https://www.squirepattonboggs.com/en/insights/publications/2018/08/procedural-good-faith-in-international-arbitration; Weber & Martinez, referring to *Suad A. Niazi And Another v. St. Paul Mercury Insurance Company*, 119, 265 Minn. 222 (1963), where it was held that: 'The parties to an arbitration agreement are under a duty to act in good faith – each owes to the other the obligation to make a fair effort to carry out the provisions of the arbitration agreement and to accomplish the real object of the contract.'

nature[16] of the arbitration proceedings. Often, parties only initiate an arbitration after having attempted to negotiate and settle the dispute. Once such endeavours fail, the parties knowingly and willingly enter the arbitration battlefield with different rules of the game: [17]

> Le contentieux judiciaire est un combat régi par des règles de 'fair-play'. Mais, comme dans le sport, être fair-play ne signifie pas être accommodant et candide, être fair-play signifie être ferme, mais correct.[18]

By concluding an arbitration agreement, the parties do not conclude a simple partnership (in the sense of a joint venture).[19] There is neither an *affectio societatis* nor are the parties' interests necessarily aligned.[20] Therefore, the parties are entitled to make and implement a strategy and seek a procedural and/or substantive advantage over the opposing party in order to win the case.

Certainly, just because the parties' positions are opposed in an adversarial proceeding, a party should not resort to dilatory tactics to disrupt the proceedings. But it may be too much to ask from a party in general (and regardless of the individual circumstances of the case) to take all the steps necessary to cooperate in order to further the proceedings in all aspects instead of primarily pursuing its own legitimate interests.

[C] Institutional Arbitration Versus Ad Hoc Arbitration

The foregoing may require some specification:

> Given that the procedural framework agreed on will shape the parties' expectations as to their procedural good faith obligations, the parties' expectations in an institutional arbitration may well vary from those in an ad-hoc arbitration, particularly where the parties have not made reference to any set of arbitration rules (such as, for example, the UNCITRAL Arbitration Rules).

On the one hand, one may argue that absent any agreement on a specific set of procedural rules, the conclusion of an ad hoc arbitration agreement suggests that the parties may have higher expectations as to the opposing parties' duty to cooperate and, thus, to its duty to contribute to the commencement and furtherance of the arbitration. The rationale for such position would be that considering the absence of detailed

16. In this context the term 'adversarial nature' is used as a contrast to the non-contentious nature of e.g., the procedure of amicable settlement discussions. The term is not to be understood as the opposite of the inquisitorial system – in relation to such context, *see* David Price, *Must Arbitration Always Be 'Adversarial' in Nature? A Breeze of Change*, 59 Arbitration: The International Journal of Arbitration, Mediation and Dispute Management 7-13 (1993).
17. Dasser & Gauthey, 246 et seq., but *see* relativization at 265 et seq.
18. In English: 'Litigation is a fight governed by rules of "fair play". But, as in sport, fair play does not mean being accommodating and candid, fair play means being firm, but correct.'
19. *See* Flavio Peter & Urs Weber-Stecher, *The Myth of Partial Awards on Advances on Costs in International Commercial Arbitration in Switzerland under the Swiss Rules*, 39 ASA Bull. 545-569, with further references (2021) DOI: 10.54648/asab2021051 (hereinafter 'Peter & Weber-Stecher').
20. Peter & Weber-Stecher, 560.

procedural rules, the parties have an increased obligation to contribute and further the arbitration in order to give effect to such arbitration agreement.

On the other hand, one could argue the opposite, namely that when parties opt for institutional arbitration proceedings, they may seek heightened protection from the administering institution, whereas the parties opting for an ad hoc arbitration might deliberately have sought more flexibility and only the bare 'minimum' of procedural protection as very often safeguarded by the *lex arbitri* (e.g., providing for State court intervention in specific cases).[21]

§9.03 POSSIBLE MANIFESTATIONS OF PROCEDURAL GOOD FAITH OBLIGATIONS

The above considerations already provide a flavour of the difficulties encountered when attempting to define the potential procedural good faith obligations of the parties in an arbitration.

In an attempt to provide further specification, case law and legal doctrine, as well as different sets of arbitration rules, indicate that the procedural duty to act in good faith may have different manifestations.[22]

[A] Duty to Contribute to the Efficient Conduct of the Arbitration

One of the most important and common manifestations may be the parties' duty to conduct an arbitration efficiently.[23]

Accordingly, many sets of rules not only refer to the parties' general duty of good faith but also the specification of this general duty, namely the duty to conduct the arbitration efficiently (as set out in Table 9.1).[24] Some sets of rules refer only to good faith or efficiency, whereas some arbitration rules do not contain any explicit reference to either obligation.[25]

---

21. *See, e.g.*, with respect to Switzerland, Arts 179(2), 180a(2), 180b(2), 183(2), 184(2) and 185 SPILA, providing for the assistance of the local state courts (*'juge d'appui'*).
22. *See* further examples in Dasser & Gauthey, 247 et seq.
23. DSFSC 111 Ia 259, reas. 2a : 'en effet, l'un des buts de l'arbitrage est de permettre une solution rapide des litiges, de sorte que les parties sont tenues par les règles de la bonne foi d'éviter tout ce qui pourrait retarder sans nécessité absolue le déroulement normal de la procédure arbitrale'; Menalco Solis, *Adverse Inferences in Defense of Good Faith*, Kluwer Arbitration Blog, 1 (23 April 2018).
24. *See*, for instance, Art. 16(1) Swiss Rules 2021, which states that 'All participants in the arbitration proceedings shall act in good faith *and* make every effort to contribute to the efficient conduct of the proceedings *and* to avoid unnecessary costs and delays' (emphasis added).
25. However, other provisions in those sets of rules clarify that the good faith principle and the requirement of an efficient conduct are enshrined: *see* for examples, Art. 17(1) of the UNCITRAL Arbitration Rules 2013 which provides that 'The arbitral tribunal, in exercising its discretion, shall conduct the proceedings so as to avoid unnecessary delay and expense and to provide a fair and efficient process for resolving the parties' dispute.'; Art. 19.1 of the SIAC Rules 2016 which provides that 'The Tribunal shall conduct the arbitration in such manner as it considers appropriate, after consulting with the parties, to ensure the fair, expeditious, economical and final resolution of the dispute.'; Art. 28(1) of the VIAC Rules of Arbitration and Mediation 2021,

Table 9.1 Summary Chart of Arbitration Rules References to the Parties‘ Duties

Arbitration Rules Explicitly Referring to the Parties' Duty	*To Act in Good Faith*	*To an Efficient Conduct*
Swiss Rules 2021	Article 16(1)	Article 16(1)
CEPANI Rules 2023	Article 24(1)	Article 24(1)
FAI Rules 2020	Article 26(3)	Article 26(3)
LCIA Rules 2020	Article 14.2/32.2	Article 14.2
CIETAC Rules 2015	Article 9	–
Arbitration Rules 2021 of the Russian Arbitration Center	Article 22(2)	–
CAM Rules 2020	Article 9	–
ICC Rules 2021	–	Article 22(1)
SCC Rules 2023	–	Article 2
Hong Kong International Arbitration Centre (HKIAC) Administered Arbitration Rules 2018	–	Article 13.5
German Arbitration Institute (DIS) Rules 2018	–	Article 27(1)
UNCITRAL Arbitration Rules 2013	–	–
Singapore International Arbitration Centre (SIAC) Rules 2016	–	–
VIAC Rules of Arbitration and Mediation 2021	–	–
American Arbitration Association (AAA)/ International Centre for Dispute Resolution (ICDR) Rules 2021	–	–
Netherlands Arbitration Institute (NAI) Arbitration Rules 2015	–	–

which state that 'The arbitral tribunal shall conduct the arbitration in accordance with the Vienna Rules and the agreement of the parties in an efficient and cost-effective manner, but otherwise at its own discretion. The arbitral tribunal shall treat the parties fairly. [...]'; or Art. 13.1 of the AIAC Arbitration Rules 2021 which provide that 'The Arbitral Tribunal shall, after consulting the Parties, conduct the arbitration in such manner as it deems appropriate to ensure the fair, expeditious, economical and final resolution of the dispute, provided always that the Parties are treated with equality and are given a reasonable opportunity to present their case.'

Arbitration Rules Explicitly Referring to the Parties' Duty	*To Act in Good Faith*	*To an Efficient Conduct*
Asian International Arbitration Centre (AIAC) Arbitration Rules 2021	–	–

The duty to contribute to the efficient conduct of the proceedings – as one manifestation of the good faith principle as well as of its 'reverse image', i.e., of the prohibition of abuse of rights – is certainly very important in arbitration practice. Indeed, one of the main reasons for choosing arbitration is that the parties seek a swift and efficient resolution of their dispute, particularly when they have their domicile in a jurisdiction with a slow and/or an overburdened court system. Thus, it may well be that the parties legitimately expect that the arbitration will proceed in an efficient manner.

The respective provisions also warn 'the parties that not everything is admissible on the arbitral battlefield'.[26]

Yet, it is not entirely clear what 'contributions' to the efficient conduct of the proceedings may or may not legitimately be expected. This question shall be discussed in relation to a few examples below.

[B] The Respondent Party's Duty to Submit an Answer/Response

From the very beginning of the arbitration, various sets of rules require the respondent party to submit an answer to the notice of arbitration[27] (respectively, depending on the set of rules, also referred to as answer to the request[28] or the response[29]). The respective provisions state that the respondent party 'shall' submit such an answer/response and, thereby, indicate that the respondent party has an obligation to do so.

Therefore, one may reasonably argue that the claimant party may legitimately expect the respondent party to submit an answer/response and that a respondent party violates the legitimate expectations (and, thus, procedural good faith obligations) if it does not submit an answer/response.

Yet, the question arises whether a different conclusion is to be drawn where the applicable arbitration rules provide for the scenario of a defaulting party. For instance, Article 30 of the Swiss Rules 2021 provides that even if the respondent party fails to

26. Wolfgang Peter, *Some Observations on the Swiss Rules of International Arbitration*, in ASA Special Series No. 22, May 2014, 8.
27. *See, e.g.*, Art. 4(1) Swiss Rules 2021: '1. Within 30 days from the date of receipt of the Notice of Arbitration, the Respondent shall submit to the Secretariat an Answer to the Notice of Arbitration. ...'.
28. *See, e.g.*, Art. 5 of the International Chamber of Commerce Arbitration Rules 2021 (hereinafter 'ICC Rules 2021').
29. *See, e.g.*, Art. 2 of the London Court of International Arbitration Rules 2020 (hereinafter 'LCIA Rules 2020').

submit its 'defence', the arbitration continues unless the respondent party can show sufficient cause for its failure.

Given that the Swiss Rules 2021 provide for a rule governing this default scenario, one may argue that 'defaulting' may become a procedural option. After all, the parties' expectations are shaped by the applicable arbitration rules – and in the case of the Swiss Rules 2021, they govern the scenario of a defaulting party.

Thus, since the respondent party's failure to submit the answer/response does, in principle, not have a bearing on the continuation of the arbitration, may one infer that there is no violation of any procedural good faith obligation?

[C] The Parties' Duty to Nominate an Arbitrator

In the case of a three-member tribunal, many sets of arbitration rules foresee that each party 'shall' nominate or designate an arbitrator, failing which a default mechanism applies. Most commonly, the arbitration rules state that where a party fails to designate an arbitrator, a specific body of the arbitral institution will make the appointment instead.[30]

Would it be fair to say that a party failing to nominate an arbitrator violated its procedural duty of good faith because it did not further the proceedings?

On the one hand, we note that most sets of arbitration rules govern the scenario of a party failing to designate an arbitrator and provide for a default mechanism. Therefore, when concluding an arbitration agreement (referring to such a set of arbitration rules), one may reasonably have to account for the fact that such a scenario may occur. Hence, one may conclude that a party's legitimate expectations are not frustrated if a scenario arises that is explicitly foreseen by the applicable rules.

On the other hand, however, we may distinguish (a) the breach of duty from (b) the procedural consequence set forth in the rules. In other words, just because the applicable rules of arbitration govern the procedural consequences of a default, this does not mean that the primary duty (i.e., to nominate an arbitrator) has not been infringed.

The above example illustrates the various areas of tension and the difficulty of determining procedural good faith obligations, which also becomes apparent in the context of the discussion regarding a party's failure to pay its share of the advances on costs.

[D] Regarding the Parties' Payment of their Respective Shares of the Advances on Costs

In arbitration practice, the question of whether the parties have an obligation to pay their respective shares of the advances on costs has been somewhat controversial. The

30. *See* Art. 11(1) and (2) Swiss Rules 2021; Art. 12(4) ICC Rules 2021.

question has been the subject of different articles[31] and will not be addressed in further detail in this contribution. Suffice it to note that the question of whether the parties have a (good faith) obligation to pay their respective advances on costs is answered differently in the various rules of arbitration:

- For instance, Article 41(1) of the Swiss Rules 2021 states that '*The Arbitral Tribunal, once constituted, and after consulting with the Court, shall request each party to deposit an equal amount as an advance for the costs* … .' Thus, the provision may be understood to be directed at the arbitral tribunal only, entitling the arbitral tribunal to request deposits. Arguably, the provision does not establish a direct duty of the parties to pay advances in the first place.[32]

  But even if it does, Article 41(4) of the Swiss Rules 2021 sets forth the default mechanism: The other party may substitute for the required payment instead, and if such substitute payment is not made, the arbitral tribunal may order the suspension or termination of the arbitration proceedings.
- Article 41 of the Swiss Rules 2021 is different from, e.g., Article 24 of the LCIA Rules 2020. Under Article 24(1) of the LCIA Rules 2020, the LCIA Court asks the Parties to pay advances of costs. If such advance is not paid, the other party will be asked to effect payment of the advance (Article 24.6), and such party is, in turn, entitled to ask the arbitral tribunal to make an order or award to recover the amount paid on behalf of the defaulting party.[33]

In view of the different wording of the rules and the different remedies available to the substituting party, it is submitted that the parties' procedural duties under the above-referenced rules may have to be qualified differently.[34]

Moreover, even if we were to assume more generally that the parties are under a duty to pay the advances on costs, would it not be considered a breach of a good faith obligation if the respondent party refused to make payment, even if, for instance, the claimant party has filed spurious and/or non-arbitrable claims against the respondent party? Would it not be possible to accept the argument that one cannot legitimately

---

31. For a more recent article, *see, e.g.*, Flavio Peter & Urs Weber-Stecher, *The Myth of Partial Awards on Advances on Costs in International Commercial Arbitration in Switzerland under the Swiss Rules*, 39 ASA Bull 545-569 (2021); on this issue *see also* Thomas Rohner & Michael Lazopoulos, *Respondent's Refusal to Pay Its Share of the Advance on Costs*, 29 ASA Bull. 549-573 (2011); Anne Carole Cremades & Alexandre Mazuranic, *Costs in Arbitration*, in *International Arbitration in Switzerland: A Handbook for Practitioners* (Elliott Geisinger & Nathalie Voser, eds, 2013) Ch. 9, subsection D, 185 et seqq. (2013); Tamminen, 281-300; and for an overview of the ICC practice cf. e.g., Nadia Darwazeh & Simon Greenberg, *No One's Credit Is as Good as Cash: Awards and Orders for the Payment of the ICC Advance on Costs*, 31 J. Intl Arb. 557-574 (2014).
32. Peter & Weber-Stecher, 549 et seq.
33. A rule similar to Art. 24 LCIA Rules 2020 is contained in Art. 51(3) and (5) of the Stockholm Chamber of Commerce Arbitration Rules 2023 (hereinafter 'SCC Rules 2023'). In relation to Art. 36 of the 2012 ICC Rules, the French *Cour de cassation*, n° 21-11.253 (9 February 2022) held that under Art. 36 of the 2012 ICC Rules the parties to an ICC arbitration had a clear obligation to pay their share of the advance on costs.
34. *See* Peter & Weber-Stecher, 548 et seq.

expect the respondent party to pay advances on costs if the respondent party has legitimate reasons not to do so?[35]

If we answer in the affirmative, we have to accept that there is no unconditional good faith obligation to pay the share of the advances on costs.

[E] The Parties' Duties in Relation to the Submission of and the Taking of Evidence

Legal authority and different provisions of arbitration rules suggest that the parties may have different procedural duties arising in the context of the submission of evidence or in relation to the taking of evidence. For instance, one author points to the parties' duty not to use illegally obtained evidence, their duty not to withhold evidence, as well as their duty not to submit superfluous documentary evidence or witness evidence and not to request unnecessarily costly hearings.[36]

Regarding the latter purported duty (not to submit superfluous documentary evidence), I submit it will be difficult to define the point in time when a party's submission of evidence exceeds the requisite standard of proof to the extent that it has entered the realm of 'superfluous' evidence. It is each party's prerogative and fundamental right to introduce the evidence deemed relevant to present its case. Unless a party files an avalanche of documents that have no bearing on the matter whatsoever, it will be tricky for an arbitral tribunal to find a violation of any procedural good faith obligation, given that it risks violating the submitting party's fundamental right to present its case.[37]

The situation with the production of documents in response to the document production requests of the other party is a bit different and is often the subject of more specifically defined rules. For instance, Article 30(3) of the Swiss Rules 2021 states that where a party is 'duly invited to *produce documentary or other evidence*, fails to do so within the time limit set by the arbitral tribunal, without showing sufficient cause for such failure, the arbitral tribunal may make the award on the basis of the evidence before it'.

Thus, where a party fails to produce evidence, the provision above seems to envisage that the arbitral tribunal will decide on the basis of the evidence otherwise available to it. One may, therefore, conclude that under the Swiss Rules 2021, the non-production of evidence may be considered simply as a procedural issue of the rules of evidence: the non-production may not constitute a violation of a procedural good

35. *See also* Peter & Weber-Stecher, 553 et seq.
36. Bernando Cremades, *Good Faith in International Arbitration*, Am. U. Int'l L. Rev. 27 no. 4 (2012), 787 et seq.
37. Such conduct, however, is often discouraged and may be taken into account by the arbitral tribunal when allocating the costs of the arbitration, allowing the arbitral tribunal to penalize a party for submitting excessive amounts of irrelevant evidence.

faith obligation but is merely an aspect considered in the allocation of the burden of proof and the assessment of the evidence.[38]

In contrast, certain arbitral tribunals have held that the parties' general good faith obligations entail a duty to cooperate with the arbitral tribunal in its fact-finding mandate, from which it has been derived that the arbitral tribunal has the authority to order disclosure of documents.[39]

Different from the Swiss Rules 2021, the IBA Rules on the Taking of Evidence 2020 (hereinafter 'IBA Rules') foresee in Articles 9(7) and 9(8) that:

> (7) If a Party *fails without satisfactory explanation to make available any other relevant evidence*, including testimony, sought by one Party to which the Party to whom the request was addressed has not objected in due time or *fails to make available any evidence, including testimony, ordered by the Arbitral Tribunal to be produced*, the Arbitral Tribunal *may infer that such evidence would be adverse to the interests of that Party.*
>
> (8) If the Arbitral Tribunal determines that a *Party has failed to conduct itself in good faith in the taking of evidence*, the Arbitral Tribunal may, in addition to any other measures available under these Rules, take such failure into account in its *assignment of the costs of the arbitration*, including costs arising out of or in connection with the taking of evidence.

The IBA Rules attach different consequences to the default in the production of evidence, including that the arbitral tribunal may draw adverse inferences or even consider the defaulting parties' conduct in the allocation of the costs. This may indicate that where the arbitral tribunal may apply (or take guidance from) the IBA Rules, such default may have to be treated differently from a case where the default is merely subject to the Swiss Rules 2021, corroborating the above thesis that the content and scope of procedural good faith obligations depends on the content, scope and nature of the legal framework chosen by the parties.

Yet, others may argue that the mere absence of the mentioning of the arbitral tribunal's power to draw adverse inference does not necessarily mean that the arbitral tribunal could not resort to such remedy.[40] But if that were true, introducing a remedy or consequence that was not originally foreseen by the rules may alter the nature and qualification of the procedural duty. In addition, the amended character of a procedural rule may no longer be covered by the parties' legitimate expectations when they first concluded the arbitration agreement.[41]

---

38. *See* Noradèle Radjai & Christian Oetiker, Art. 30 Swiss Rules 2021, in: *Swiss Rules of International Arbitration, Commentary* (Tobias Zuberbühler, Christoph Müller & Philipp Habegger, eds, 3rd ed. 2023) (hereinafter 'Radjai & Oetiker') paras 58 et seq.
39. Gary Born, *International Commercial Arbitration* 2507 et seq. (3d ed. 2021) (hereinafter 'Born'), with further references; *see*, for instance, Rule 37 of the US Federal Rules of Civil Procedure, which makes clear that the parties have a duty to cooperate in US discovery and, if in breach of such duty, can be sanctioned according to the sub-sections of Rule 37.
40. Born, 2488, and *see* 2489 et seq., referring to a more general practice that arbitral tribunals may occasionally impose monetary sanctions for refusals to obey disclosure orders, respectively ordering such party to pay a counter-party's legal costs; Radjai & Oetiker, paras 58 et seq.
41. Thus, for an arbitration governed by the Swiss Rules 2021 it is suggested that, since the Swiss Rules 2021 do not mention the possibility of drawing adverse inferences, such remedy/consequence should be included in the arbitral tribunal's procedural order. no. 1; *see*,

A party's failure to produce documentary or other evidence touches upon an additional issue, namely a situation where a party fails to follow the arbitral tribunal's 'invitation', i.e., it fails to comply with an arbitral tribunal's procedural order to produce certain documents (requested by the opposing party or by the arbitral tribunal itself). This issue will be addressed in the following section.

[F] The Parties' Duty to Comply with Procedural Orders and Awards

Among legal authors and practitioners, it is widely acknowledged that the parties to an arbitration have a duty to comply with procedural orders and awards rendered by the arbitral tribunal. Such duty is considered to be an aspect of the parties' more general obligation to participate in arbitral proceedings in good faith.[42]

Accordingly, different sets of arbitration rules, such as Article 16(1) of the Swiss Rules 2021, Article 2 of the SCC Rules 2023 or Article 22(5) and Article 35(6) of the ICC Rules 2021, explicitly refer to such duty alongside the general duty to arbitrate in good faith.

In principle, this author concurs with the view that a party failing to abide by the arbitral tribunal's orders may breach its procedural good faith obligations. It is the basic 'rules of the game' that an arbitral tribunal (just as much as a State court) may issue procedural orders to further the proceedings, and the same is explicitly set out in the arbitration rules. The parties may, therefore, legitimately expect that any procedural orders issued by the arbitral tribunal must be complied with.

Yet again, it is submitted that such duty to comply with procedural orders is not unconditional. The question similarly arises whether it would be against the good faith duty of a party to refuse to comply with an order if the arbitral tribunal clearly had no jurisdiction (for instance, if there was no arbitration agreement in the first place) or if the arbitral tribunal has, for example, ordered measures that are not possible under the *lex arbitri* (or *lex fori*).

Thus, once more, the individual circumstances of the case will be decisive in determining whether or not a party breaches a procedural good faith obligation if such party fails to comply with a procedural order.

Regarding the parties' duty to comply with any award made by the arbitral tribunal without delay, the following should be noted:

- First, depending on the chosen seat of arbitration, the parties have the possibility to challenge the arbitral award within a certain period of time. For instance, when choosing Switzerland as the seat of arbitration, the parties may challenge an arbitral award before the Swiss Federal Supreme Court within a deadline of thirty days from the issuance of the award.[43]

---

e.g., Anna Masser, Art. 28 Swiss Rules, in *Arbitration in Switzerland – The Practitioner's Guide* (Manuel Arroyo ed., 2d ed. 2018), para. 54.

42. *See* Born, 2396 and fn. 629.

43. *See, e.g.*, for Germany, § 1059 (3) ZPO, providing for a three-month deadline for filing the challenge to the arbitral award; for England *see* section 70(3) of the English Arbitration Act 1996, providing for a twenty-eight-day deadline.

Under Article 192 SPILA, a general clause in the arbitration rules stating that the award is final and binding on the parties or needs to be complied with 'without delay' would not constitute a valid waiver of a party's right to challenge the award.

Therefore, one can reasonably argue that when agreeing on arbitration in Switzerland, a party may expect that the opposing (losing) party may not comply with the award – at least not 'without delay'.

- Second, in this author's view, the formal and substantive legal force (i.e., the *res judicata* effects) of an arbitral award is not subject to the parties' autonomy and, thus, not dependent on any wording within any sets of arbitration rules. In more concrete terms, whether or not the arbitration rules state that an award is final and binding is not of primary relevance in the first place. It is the *lex loci arbitri* that governs the question as to what point in time and under which conditions an arbitral award deploys res judicata effects and is, thus, enforceable.

  From a Swiss legal perspective, the majority view is that an arbitral award becomes final and binding with the valid notification of the arbitral award to the parties.[44] Thus, in this case, the legal norms (as per which the award is enforceable as of its issuance to the parties) do not necessarily coincide with the parties' conduct and expectations (and their right to challenge an award).
- Third, whilst it is certainly preferable that parties voluntarily comply with an arbitral award, it is submitted that a party cannot necessarily account for the opposing party's cooperation in the implementation of the award. Not only may the opposing (losing) party have legitimate grounds to resist enforcement, e.g., under the grounds listed in Article V of the New York Convention, but more generally, it is questionable whether any alleged duty of the parties to 'further' the proceedings would also extend to the post-arbitration phase. After all, by agreeing to arbitration, the parties do not agree to opt out of any State court proceedings at the enforcement stage. Thus, the New York Convention cannot be seen as a guarantee of voluntary compliance with an award but rather promotes and facilitates the enforcement of an arbitral award amongst the member states of the New York Convention.

These legal considerations call into question to what extent the parties to an arbitration have a duty to comply with an award made by the arbitral tribunal.

§9.04 CONCLUSION

The parties' procedural good faith obligations are shaped by the applicable procedural framework chosen, i.e., the specific chosen rules of arbitration and the applicable *lex*

44. *See* Manuel Arroyo, Art. 190 SPILA, in *Arbitration in Switzerland – The Practitioner's Guide* (Manuel Arroyo ed., 2d ed. 2018) paras 8 et seq.

arbitri. The mere fact that a party concluded an arbitration agreement cannot on its own constitute a sufficient basis to identify specific procedural good faith obligations, as they do not exist in a legal or factual vacuum. Thus, when determining the parties' expectations of the arbitration process, due consideration must be given to the clear wording of the applicable arbitration rules or the absence of the same.

The parties' 'legitimate' expectations of the arbitration process are further defined by the adversarial nature of the arbitration process. Any obligation of the parties to cooperate in and/or further the proceedings should, therefore, not be overestimated. Whereas the parties certainly must not resort to any dilatory tactics, in the author's opinion, they are entitled to seek a procedural and/or substantive advantage over their opponent. After all, they have knowingly and willingly applied to eventually settle their dispute on a 'battlefield' with high stakes and an expectation to prevail, not an 'exhibition game' where there is no loser.

The quest for specificity of the parties' procedural good faith obligations is a very difficult task. Any attempt to pinpoint procedural good faith obligations may fail in view of the relevance of the individual circumstances of the case and, thus, the numerous factual variables that speak against any general and unconditional procedural good faith obligations.

However, these challenges should not discourage the various stakeholders from attempting to identify and set out such good faith obligations in relevant laws and arbitration rules. Identifying with precision the good faith obligations can be a useful tool for the promotion of efficiency and fairness in arbitration proceedings.

CHAPTER 10

Procedural Implications of Good Faith and the Duty of Arbitrators and Arbitral Institutions

Duarte Henriques & Adetola Adebesin

§10.01 INTRODUCTION

> The principle of good faith comprises many different aspects of substantive and procedural nature. As a result, there is, as such, no precise or widely accepted definition of the concept of 'good faith' in a contractual context. It is a vague standard. Its meaning and effect are, therefore, likely to vary considerably depending on the context. Generally, one can only say that an obligation to behave in good faith is likely to require that the parties observe a reasonable commercial standard of fair dealing, be faithful to the agreed purpose of the agreement, and act consistently with the legitimate expectations of the other party. –
> *Gephar LLC v. Danstar Ferment AG* – ICC Case No. 19890/EMT.[1]

The notion of good faith is a widely known, studied and relied upon principle of both substantive and procedural law. Yet, despite its very wide reach, a comprehensive definition for this concept remains elusive, and the above passage aptly illustrates the difficulty in understanding the principle with real precision. Indeed, good faith is like an elephant; it is easier to recognize than to define. It has been noted that its lack of

1. Available at: https://jusmundi.com/en/document/decision/en-gephar-llc-v-danstar-ferment-ag-final-award-wednesday-5th-august-2015#decision_8462.

precision is a defining feature of the duty of good faith, providing the flexibility required for balancing the rights of parties.[2]

The tendency of international arbitrators to resort to the principle of good faith is well known. It is difficult to find an international award that is not based on or at least does not mention 'good faith'.[3] While this approach is debatable, based on its potential to 'kill or shortcut' the legal reasoning in an award,[4] the reliance on the principle is largely based on the tenets of equity and fairness that underpin its application. Admittedly, the resort to good faith and its corollaries by arbitrators typically relate to the substance of the dispute when arbitrators determine the parties' rights and obligations as to the underlying legal relationship. However, this chapter focuses on questions concerning the procedural implications of the principle of good faith in international arbitration and the duty of the arbitrators and arbitral institutions to act in good faith. Specifically, what options are open to a party where one or more arbitrators show a lack of good faith in the conduct of proceedings? Will such remedy be different where an award has been rendered? How can parties and their counsel identify arbitrators with potential bad faith behavior in view of the sacred confidentiality in commercial arbitration? How does a party prove that an arbitrator's conduct amounts to a violation of the principle of good faith? What is the role of arbitral institutions in ensuring good faith in arbitral proceedings?

The objective of this chapter is three-fold. First, we examine whether the principle of good faith exists as a general principle of law under various legal systems and the duty of arbitrators and arbitral institutions in this respect. Second, we examine the possibility of procuring evidence of bad faith in light of the duty of confidentiality that often applies in commercial arbitration through the lens of the increasingly innovative research tools in international arbitration. Third and finally, we turn to the remedies available to parties for the violation of procedural good faith in international arbitration. We pursue this endeavor using a case law analysis of reported instances where supervising and enforcing courts have been called upon to determine the implications of the 'bad faith' conduct of arbitrators and arbitral institutions.

§10.02 THE NOTION OF GOOD FAITH AS A GENERAL PRINCIPLE OF LAW

The notion of good faith has already been the subject of extensive legal literature[5]. As already indicated, an endeavor to find an exhaustive definition for the good faith principle is likely to be futile. One could refer to it as a set of values shared by all condign, fair and conscious persons, such as loyalty, honesty, sincerity, cooperation,

2. John Carter and Wayne Courtney, Good Faith in Contracts: Is There an Implied Promise to Act Honestly? 75 The Cambridge Law Journal 608-619 (2016) DOI: 10.1017/s0008197316000507.
3. Bernardo Cremades, *Good Faith in International Arbitration*, 27 American University International Law Review, 761 (2012).
4. *See* Francesco Galgano, *Diritto Civile e Commerciale Vol. 2 Tome 1* 630 (2004).
5. *See*, for example, Lorena Carvajal Arenas, *Good Faith in Lex Mercatoria: An Analysis of Arbitral Practice and Major Western Legal Systems*, PhD Thesis, University of Portsmouth School of Law (2011).

diligence, integrity and belief. Its application in practice evinces a polymorphic and polyvalent notion, filled in by a multitude of values intrinsic to human nature when oriented towards the 'good'.[6]

As Prof. Emily Sipiorski has stated: 'There is no fixed mode of application. Any attempt to codify or define the term would be counterintuitive to its value as a principle in international law and undermine the integral purpose and usefulness of the term. The principle must have flexibility to be effective in its role and usage'.[7]

At its core, the concept of 'good faith' builds upon fundamental notions to act reasonably and fairly. While this has substantive and procedural consequences, its implications are wide-reaching in the context of international arbitration. This rather obvious proposition is bolstered by the appearance of good faith in almost every legal regime. As we shall see, although a fluid concept evasive of a concrete definition, good faith is indeed a notion of universal application. The question of whether a definition is even necessary comes to mind. Alternatively, is it sufficient to say that we can recognize good faith or the lack of it when we see it? This brings to mind the quote of Justice Stewart of the U.S. Supreme Court, who stated in relation to good faith: 'I shall not today attempt to define [it] ... But I know it when I see it.'[8]

[A] Public International Law

The principle of good faith can be said to be at the heart of the idea of the pacific settlement of disputes by States under public international law. With the coming into force of the Charter of the United Nations (hereinafter 'UN Charter') in 1945, there was a broad international consensus to replace the force of war with the rule of law. As such, Article 2(2) of the UN Charter provides that 'All members, in order to ensure to all of them the rights and benefits resulting from membership, shall fulfil in good faith the obligations assumed by them in accordance with the present Charter'. This good faith obligation guides the conduct of States on the international plane.

Article 26 of the Vienna Convention on the Law of Treaties 1969 (hereinafter 'VCLT') provides for the cardinal rule of treaty interpretation (hereinafter '*pacta sunt servanda*'), according to which every treaty in force is binding upon the parties to it and must be performed by them in good faith. This provision mandates a duty of honesty, loyalty and reasonableness in international relations, guarantees the prohibition of the abuse of power and abuse of rights, and provides equitable solutions in legal relationships between sovereigns and private actors.[9]

6. Duarte Henriques, *The Role of Good Faith in Arbitration: Are Arbitrators and Arbitral Institutions Bound to Act in Good Faith?* 33 ASA Bull. 515 (2015).
7. Emily Sipiorski, *Interpretation in Good Faith and Its Relevance in International Investment Law: Additions to Justice or Ensuring Justice?* 23 International Community Law Review 57-78 https://doi.org/10.1163/18719732-12341458 (2021) DOI: 10.1163/18719732-12341458.
8. *Jacobellis v. State of Ohio 378 US 184, 197 (1964)* (Supreme Court, per J Stewart), referring to obscene material.
9. Talya Ucaryilmaz, *The Principle of Good Faith in Public International Law,* 43 Estudios de Deusto, Vol. 68/1, (2020). Art. 31 of the VCLT also provides that 'a treaty shall be interpreted in *good faith*

The concept of good faith also appears many times in the International Law Commission's draft articles on the Responsibility of States for Internationally Wrongful Acts (2001),[10] which reflects the customary international law rules for attribution and damages under international law. Notably, Article 52(4) includes an exception to the obligation of a State legally implementing countermeasures to suspend such measures in certain circumstances where the responsible state fails to engage in the dispute resolution mechanism in good faith.[11] The case law of international courts and tribunals also reflects the application of the principle of good faith. In the *Nuclear Test Case*, the International Court of Justice (ICJ) held as follows:

> One of the basic principles governing the creation and performance of legal obligations... is good faith. Trust and confidence are inherent in international cooperation, in particular in an age when this cooperation in many fields is becoming increasingly essential. Just as the very rule of pacta sunt servanda in the law of treaties is based on good faith, so also is the binding character of an international obligation. Thus, interested States may take cognisance of unilateral declarations and place confidence in them, and are entitled to require that the obligation thus created be respected.[12]

Again, in the *Temple of Preah Vihear Case (Thailand v. Cambodia)*,[13] the ICJ relied on principles of acquiescence and estoppel to reject Thailand's claims and held that 'the good faith that must prevail in international relations, inasmuch as consistency of conduct or opinion on the part of the State to the prejudice of another is incompatible with good faith'.[14]

[B] Private International Law

Article 7(1) of the United Nations Convention on Contracts for the International Sale of Goods (CISG) provides that 'in the interpretation of this Convention, regard is to be had to its international character and to the need to promote uniformity in its application and the observance of *good faith* in international trade.'[15]

---

in accordance with the ordinary meaning to be given to the terms of the treaty in their context and in the light of its object and purpose'. (Emphasis added).

10. Text adopted by the International Law Commission at its fifty-third session, in 2001, and submitted to the General Assembly as a part of the Commission's report covering the work of that session (A/56/10).
11. Article 52 (4) provides: 'paragraph 3 does not apply if the responsible State fails to implement the dispute settlement procedures in good faith'.
12. *Nuclear Tests Case (Australia v. France) (Merits)* [1974] ICJ Rep 253.
13. Case concerning the *Temple of Preah Vihear (Cambodia v. Thailand) (Merits)* [1962] ICJ.
14. *Ibid.* Separate Opinion of Judge Alfaro.
15. This provision appears to circumscribe the relevance of the principle of good faith to a mere tool of interpretation as opposed to one creating substantive obligations. *See generally*, Onni Rostila and Justi Lampinen, *Application of the Good Faith Principle under the CISG: A Mere Tool for Interpretation or Something More*? Available at https://merkuriuslaw.fi/en/application-good-faith-principle-cisg/.

In the context of investment arbitration, the principle of good faith has governed the arbitrator's conduct since its inception.[16] Article 14 of the ICSID Convention 1966 requires that arbitrators shall be of high moral character. Implicit in this rule is the obligation for arbitrators to act honestly, fairly and in a manner consistent with the justice of each case. In other words, this treaty language implies a real formulation of a duty to act in good faith. Indeed, being of a 'high moral character' is a facet of being and acting in good faith. The case law of investment tribunals has also firmly established the principle of good faith.

In *Inceysa Vallisoletana S.L. v. Republic of El Salvador*, the arbitral tribunal clearly stated that 'good faith is a supreme principle, which governs legal relations in all of their aspects and content'.[17] More recently, in *Vattenfall AB & Others v. Germany*,[18] it was held that 'good faith requires the terms of a multilateral treaty have a single and consistent meaning for all parties. The need for coherence in interpretation is embedded in the text of Article 31 of the VCLT'.

[C] Transnational Principles and *Lex Mercatoria*

The principle of good faith also features significantly in transnational principles of law and *lex mercatoria*. Generally, good faith in international contracts was present from 1880 onwards, the period known as collectivism,[19] as a compulsory cooperation since it was applied under the aegis of international private law and fulfilled its role in cross-border agreements guided by the strictness of municipal systems of law. This generational evolution of its application is reflected in attempts at its codification in transnational principles.

Article 1.7 of the UNIDROIT Principles of International Commercial Contracts 2016 (hereinafter 'UNIDROIT Principles') provides that parties must act in accordance with good faith and fair dealing in international trade. This obligation is considered to be the cornerstone of international commerce, and the parties are not allowed to exclude or limit its application.[20] It should be further noted that there are a number of provisions throughout the UNIDROIT Principles which provide for a direct or indirect application of the principle of good faith and fair dealing. Suffice it to say, therefore, that good faith and fair dealing may be considered to be one of the fundamental ideas underlying the UNIDROIT Principles.[21]

In the same vein, the Principles of European Contract Law (PECL), which are framed in the context of the European harmonization of law, provide for a good faith obligation. Article 1:201 PECL reflects the core norm and provides that 'Each party

---

16. *See Lanco Int'l v. The Argentine Republic ICSID Case no. ARB/97/6*, Jurisdiction of the Arbitral Tribunal (8 December 1998), 40 I.L.M. 457 (2001).
17. ICSID Case No. ARB/03/26, Award, ¶ 230 (2 August 2006), 28 ICSID Rep. 311 (2008).
18. ICSID Case No. ARB/12/12, Award on Jurisdiction, ¶ 153 (31 August 2018).
19. Clarence Carson, *The Fateful Turn. From Individual Liberty to Collectivism 1880-1960* (The Foundation for Economic Education, New York 1963) pp. 71.
20. *See* Art. 1.7 (2) of the UNIDROIT Principles.
21. *See* Art. 1.7, UNIDROIT Principles commentary. Available at: https://www.unidroit.org/english/principles/contracts/principles2016/principles2016-e.pdf.

must act in accordance with good faith and fair dealing; and the parties may not exclude or limit this duty'. Indeed, this principle is a significant philosophy sustaining international commercial contracts.

[D] National Law

The tendency of a legal system to embrace good faith or explicitly require its application is typically related to a number of historical, cultural and institutional factors.[22] As such, the usual divergence between Common law and Civil law jurisdictions exists in this respect.

Under common law, good faith, as a general principle, is accepted by the law of the United States,[23] whereas English law has traditionally refused to develop the principle as one of general application. As is widely known, English law has hitherto declined to adopt a general principle of good faith. One author notes that 'the predictability of the legal outcome of a case is more important than absolute justice'.[24]

As Lord Bingham stated in *Interfoto Picture Library Ltd. v. Stiletto Visual Programmes Ltd:*[25] 'English Law has, characteristically, committed itself to no such overriding principle but has developed piecemeal solutions in response to demonstrated problems of unfairness'. This line of reasoning is consistent with the pronouncement of Lord Ackner in *Walford v. Miles,* who considered 'good faith inherently repugnant to the adversarial position of the parties when involved in negotiations'.[26] The foregoing notwithstanding, good faith's force is also at work in Common law legal systems through the use of concepts such as estoppel and other steadily anchored doctrines that may find their roots in the concept of good faith or at least in a manifestation of that concept.

Indeed, the concept of good faith has surfaced in several legal provisions, such as section 17 of the Marine Insurance Act 1906, Regulation 4 of the Commercial Agents Regulations 1993, and the Unfair Terms in Consumer Contracts Regulations 1994, SI 1994/3159. Similarly, English courts have progressively changed their approach in accepting this doctrine. In *Director General of Fair Trading v First National Bank plc,*[27] the Court noted that: 'good faith was not an artificial or technical concept but connoted fair and open dealing, which required terms to be expressed fully and clearly, without hidden pitfalls and with appropriate prominence being given to matters which might operate disadvantageously to the customer, and required the supplier not to take

22. E. Sipiorski, *Good Faith in International Investment Arbitration*, p. 23, 2021 – Oxford International Arbitration Series.
23. In the US, the notion of good faith can be traced back to as early as 1890: in *Armstrong v. Agricultural Ins. Co. insurers* [1890] 29 N. E. 991 (NY) were considered to be under an obligation of good faith when demanding proof of loss.
24. Roy Goode, *The Concept of 'Good Faith' in English Law* (Centro di Studi e Ricerca di Diritto Comparato e Straniero, Roma 1992) 9.
25. [1989] QB 433, 439, CA.
26. [1992] 2 A.C. 128 (H.L.) 138 (U.K.).
27. [2002] 1 AC 481, [2001] 1 All ER 97 (HL).

advantage, deliberately or unconsciously, of factors indicative of the consumer's weaker bargaining position'.

Conversely, however, there is no doubt that good faith is a key and typically Civil law concept and is accepted as a general principle of contract law in continental jurisdictions. To see this most clearly, the Swiss,[28] French,[29] Chinese[30] and Egyptian[31] Civil Codes, as well as the German BGB,[32] are cases in point. Indeed, the German Federal Supreme Court has stated: 'that the notion of good faith is a supra-national legal principle that is inherent in all legal systems,[33] and the obligations of good faith extend to both contract negotiation and performance.'[34] Suffice it to say, therefore, that the reach of the concept has expanded in Civil law systems.

[E] Institutional Rules

One of the most relevant considerations for present purposes are the institutional rules under which arbitrations are conducted. As it is well known, these rules provide the broad institutional framework pursuant to which procedural standards are set and are agreed on by the parties.

It should be noted at the outset that several sets of arbitration rules explicitly refer to the parties' duty of good faith and/or the parties' duty to contribute to the efficient conduct of the arbitration. Notably, Article 16 (1) of the Swiss Arbitration Rules 2021 (hereinafter 'Swiss Rules') provides that 'All participants in the arbitration proceedings shall act in good faith and make every effort to contribute to the efficient conduct of the proceedings and to avoid unnecessary costs and delays. The parties undertake to comply with any award or order made by the arbitral tribunal or emergency arbitrator without delay'.

The rule articulated above relates to the conduct of all the players in arbitrations governed by the Swiss Rules. Other rules provide guidance with respect to the conduct of arbitrators and arbitral institutions.

A classic example of this is found in Article 9 of the 2020 Milan Rules, which provides as follows: 'The Chamber of Arbitration, the arbitrators, the experts, the parties and their counsel shall act in good faith along any phase of the proceedings ... The Arbitral Tribunal may sanction any breach of its decisions and any unlawful

28. Article 2 of the Swiss Civil Code provides that 'Every person must act in good faith in the exercise of his or her rights and in the performance of his or her obligations.'
29. Article 1104 of the French Civil Code provides that 'Contracts must be negotiated, formed and performed in good faith. (2) This provision is a matter of public policy'.
30. Article 7 of the Chinese Civil Code provides as follows: 'When conducting a civil activity, a person of the civil law shall, in compliance with the principle of good faith, uphold honesty and honour commitments.'
31. Article 148 of the Egyptian Civil Code provides as follows: 'A contract must be performed in accordance with its contents and in compliance with the requirements of good faith.'
32. § 242 of the BGB provides as follows: 'An obligor has a duty to perform according to the requirements of good faith, taking customary practice into consideration.'
33. German Federal Supreme Court, NJW 1993, at 259, 263.
34. Klein and Bachechi, Precontractual Liability and the Duty of Good Faith Negotiation in International Transactions (1994) 17 (1) Houston Journal of International Law 1, 17.

conduct that is contrary to *good faith.*'[35] Similarly, Article 32.2 of the LCIA Rules 2020 states that 'For all matters not expressly provided in the Arbitration Agreement, the LCIA, *the LCIA Court*, the Registrar, *the Arbitral Tribunal*, any tribunal secretary and each of the parties *shall act at all times in good faith*, respecting the spirit of the Arbitration Agreement, and shall make every reasonable effort to ensure that any award is legally recognised and enforceable at the arbitral seat'.[36]

As indicated above, Article 14 of the ICSID Convention 1966 also requires that persons designated to sit on the ICSID panel of arbitrators shall, among other things, be of 'high moral character'. This requirement – in the authors' view – is a manifestation of what must be understood as 'good faith' on the panel of ICSID arbitrators. The inclusion of the obligation of good faith, either expressly or implicitly, in the foregoing arbitral institutional rules demonstrates its existence not only as a substantive principle of law but also as a procedural requirement.

§10.03 LACK OF EVIDENCE OF BREACH OF GOOD FAITH BY ARBITRATORS AND ARBITRAL INSTITUTIONS

Having established the existence of a procedural rule of good faith according to which arbitrators, arbitral institutions, and all players in arbitration, more generally, are required to conduct the business of private dispute resolution in a fair, impartial and reasonable manner, the question arises as to how a breach of this duty can be identified.

It should be noted that the lack of good faith can be broadly identified in two ways in arbitration proceedings: first, where an arbitrator accepts an arbitral appointment with full knowledge of a conflict of interest or other impediment (such as lack of relevant experience or expertise) that could preclude the exercise of his effective adjudicatory discretion, without full disclosure; second, in the making of orders, decisions and the conduct of the proceedings. However, it necessarily follows that other than the parties and their counsel who are involved in these specific cases and cases that eventually go before the courts (either through the challenge of arbitrators, fixation of fees, annulment or enforcement proceedings), the details of such international arbitration proceedings are largely unknown.

The reasons for this are obvious. First, confidentiality is usually a critical obligation for commercial parties and is one of the factors that make commercial arbitration thrive.[37] Thus, in the commercial context, anecdotal evidence is the only way that the international arbitration community can be aware of arbitrators with bad faith tendencies. Additionally, social politeness and the risk of being involved in futile

35. *See* Art. 9(3). Emphasis added.
36. Emphasis added. This is consistent with Art. 14(1) and (2) of the LCIA Rules which imposes a good faith duty on arbitrators in the conduct of arbitral proceedings.
37. *See* Queen Mary University – White & Case LLP International Arbitration Survey (2021) – Adapting arbitration to a changing world, https://www.whitecase.com/publications/insight/2021-international-arbitration-survey.

and seemingly frivolous allegations against the very arbitrators who are tasked with deciding a party's dispute could account for the lack of evidence in this area.

In investment arbitration, the proceedings are partly accessible, and awards are usually publicly available. Accordingly, the lack of evidence could be less visible. Notwithstanding, the landscape is not much different from the commercial arbitration setting, with a notable exception.

In *Landesbank Baden-Württemberg and others v. Kingdom of Spain*,[38] the respondent contended that the arbitral tribunal lacked the *high moral character* required under the ICSID Convention and sought to disqualify all members of the arbitral tribunal pursuant to Article 57 of the ICSID Convention.[39] Spain argued that 'the Tribunal's decision in procedural order No. 20 to hold the hearing virtually was grounded on "*serious misrepresentations and misleading statements*", and "speculative [...] arguments"; "*all of which qualify as* 'dishonest *behavior*'".[40] This shows, Spain argued, that the Tribunal lacks the "high moral character" required by the ICSID Convention, and the World Bank's policies and regulations'.

Spain further argued that the arbitrators made dishonest statements in an attempt to trick the parties, which demonstrated that the arbitral tribunal 'prioritized their private interest' at the cost of 'basic procedural rights, such as efficiency, equal and fair treatment'.[41]

Although some arbitral institutions currently publish sanitized digests of decisions on challenges and some awards, in the authors' view, this has been insufficient to identify bad faith procedures and recognize the arbitrators concerned. Thus, the reliance on anecdotal evidence is grossly inadequate, and the importance of procedural fairness in international arbitration calls for a more scientific and empirical approach. In any event, this endeavour currently faces significant psychological, cultural, sociological, strategic, and procedural constraints.

As we see it, a more scientific and empirical approach could be largely based on existing tools of reporting in international arbitration. Platforms such as Global Arbitration Review (GAR),[42] Kluwer Arbitration,[43] Investment Arbitrator Reporter,[44] Jus Mundi,[45] Transnational Dispute Management,[46] Arbitrator Intelligence,[47] and Italaw,[48] which are dedicated to providing a comprehensive caselaw database should be explored to achieve this objective.

Worthy of note is the work of Arbitrator Intelligence in this regard. This platform is a data-driven tool which provides an analysis of arbitrators based on their caseload.

---

38. ICSID Case No. ARB/15/45.
39. It should be noted however, that the proposal to disqualify all the members of the arbitral tribunal in this case was rejected by the Chair of ICSID's Administrative Council.
40. *Ibid.*, ¶ 43.
41. *Ibid.*, ¶ 46.
42. Global Arbitration Review.
43. Kluwer Arbitration.
44. Investment Arbitration Reporter.
45. Jus Mundi.
46. Transnational Dispute Management.
47. Arbitrator Intelligence.
48. italaw.

It also plans to publish periodic reports which show feedback on arbitrators with a view to harnessing the collective intelligence of the international arbitration community and systematic responses.

These platforms will no doubt contribute to procedural efficiency in international arbitration and harness the collective intelligence of the international arbitration community. At the outset, counsel can easily identify arbitrators with pre-existing conflicts. Coupled with the adoption of artificial intelligence, these platforms have the potential of bringing to light – for useful purposes (such as avoiding arbitrators who act in bad faith) – information which would otherwise remain confidential and unknown.

Notwithstanding the existence of these tools, reports on the arbitrators and/or arbitral institutions' lack of good faith are rare, if they exist at all, with very few exceptions.[49]

§10.04 CONSEQUENCES OF A VIOLATION OF GOOD FAITH BY ARBITRATORS AND ARBITRAL INSTITUTIONS

Although different sides of the same coin, a clear distinction must be made between procedural bad faith by arbitrators on the one hand and arbitral institutions on the other. While arbitrators are charged with the overall conduct of the arbitration, arbitral institutions may also be the subject of bad faith allegations in their administrative functions and general administration of the proceedings, including appointment of arbitrators (where applicable), deciding challenges, and fixing fees. Accordingly, the crux of this chapter is to discuss the consequences of a violation of good faith in international arbitration. From a purely 'marketing' and reputational perspective, and in view of the private nature of international arbitration, the first immediate consequence is the loss of reputation of the arbitrators and the arbitral institution.

Second, there is the potential to invoke the disciplinary procedures which exist in certain institutional frameworks. For instance, under the 2014 Regulations of the Chartered Institute of Arbitrators (hereinafter 'CIArb Regulations'), in egregious cases,[50] should the arbitrator(s) in question be subject to such regulation? Indeed, Article 10 of the CIArb Regulations empowers CIArb's professional conduct committee to suspend or expel a member, withdraw his chartered status or make an order for costs against him if a complaint is made out.

While these two kinds of broad remedies may be useful as deterrents, they do not, in fact, redress the injustice or malfeasance that may have been caused by the conduct of the arbitrator or arbitral institution, which is reflected in an award or in the proceedings themselves. In the succeeding paragraphs, we shall discuss, in turn,

49. *See* the *Landesbank Baden-Württemberg and others v. Kingdom of Spain* case above cited. Another example may be found in Duarte Henriques, *The Role of Good Faith in Arbitration: Are Arbitrators and Arbitral Institutions Bound to Act in Good Faith?* 33 ASA Bull. 515 (2015) DOI: 10.54648/asab2015043, where the Portuguese Commercial Arbitration Center acted in a way incompatible with the protection of legitimate expectations of the parties.

50. Available at: https://www.ciarb.org/media/1559/regulations.pdf. This is only applicable: (a) where the arbitrator(s) in question is a Member of the Chartered Institute of Arbitrators; and (b) where a complaint is made and the same is well founded.

specific remedies that the parties may adopt during the arbitration and *ex post factum* to redress a breach of good faith.

[A] Challenging the Arbitrator(s)

The possibility to challenge the appointment of an arbitrator is a critical safeguard of the integrity of arbitration and is intrinsic to the notion of arbitral justice. Indeed, the legitimacy of the outcome of an arbitration is premised on the valid appointment of and the procedural good faith exhibited by arbitrators. Most national laws and arbitration rules provide for the challenge of an arbitrator where 'circumstances exist that give rise to justifiable doubts as to the arbitrator's impartiality or independence'.[51]

Could one of such circumstances be a procedural breach of good faith? In *C Ltd v D and X*,[52] the claimant brought challenge proceedings before the LCIA, alleging that the sole arbitrator had failed to treat the parties fairly (a manifestation of bad faith) and impartially in the interim measures decision and the procedure leading up to it. Although the challenge was rejected on the facts, it does show that where such a claim of procedural bad faith is well founded, a party could successfully remove an arbitrator and possibly recover the costs of the application to remove him/her.[53]

Be that as it may, while a show of bad faith by an arbitrator does not necessarily imply a lack of independence and impartiality, a lack of independence and impartiality could manifest itself in procedural bad faith. Further, it should be noted that under the 2022 American Arbitration Association Commercial Arbitration Rules and Mediation Procedures (hereinafter 'AAA-CARMR'), a breach of the performance of their duties in good faith is intertwined with the duty of independence and impartiality and constitutes a specific ground for the disqualification of the arbitrator concerned. It provides that 'Any arbitrator shall be impartial and independent and shall perform his or her duties with diligence and in good faith, and shall be subject to disqualification for inter alia inability or refusal to perform his or her duties with diligence and in good faith.'[54]

In the authors' view, the showing of bad faith from the arbitrators can amount to a situation where a challenge can be brought against them and, thus, can present a separate and distinct ground to challenge an arbitrator even if the applicable institutional rules do not expressly require the 'high moral character' of the arbitrator (such as it is provided in Article 14 of the ICSID Convention) or do not expressly allow his/her disqualification, as the AAA-CARMR do.

[B] Annulment of the Award

The setting aside of arbitral awards is generally governed by the national law of the seat of arbitration. At the international level, the principles of judicial supervision of

51. Article 12 of the UNCITRAL Model Law on International Commercial Arbitration (UNCITRAL Model Law).
52. [2020] EWHC 1283 (Comm).
53. *See Cofely Ltd v. Bingham and another* [2016] EWHC 240 (Comm).
54. Rule 1 9 – AAA-CARMR.

arbitration contained in the UNCITRAL Model Law represent a general consensus on the proper balance between finality and legitimacy.[55] As such, an ever-increasing number of jurisdictions have adopted the UNCITRAL Model Law as the basis for their regulation of arbitration. This brings about global convergence in many aspects, notably, a uniform list of the grounds on which an arbitral award may be annulled.

Specifically, Article 34 of the UNCITRAL Model Law allows a party to apply to set aside an award on certain grounds. These include where 'the composition of the arbitral tribunal, or the arbitral procedure was not in accordance with the agreement of the parties, unless such agreement was in conflict with a provision of this law from which the parties cannot derogate, or, failing such agreement, was not in accordance with this law'.[56] This ground is targeted at procedural irregularity and may be employed where there is an alleged breach of a good faith obligation contained in the applicable procedural rules or law of the seat. Admittedly, however, given the elastic and flexible nature of the good faith principle, the same must be applied with circumspection so as not to undermine the outcome of an otherwise legitimate arbitral process.

[C] Resisting Recognition and Enforcement of the Award

Recognition and enforcement of international arbitration awards are generally governed by the Convention on the Recognition and Enforcement of Foreign Arbitral Awards, 1958 (hereinafter 'New York Convention'). The New York Convention is one of the essential components for the global acceptance of international arbitration and has been described as 'the mortar in the edifice of international commercial arbitration'.[57] It provides the legal framework for the recognition and enforcement of international arbitral awards and has universal application.

Article V provides specific grounds upon which the recognition and enforcement of an international arbitration award may be challenged. These include (a) invalidity of the arbitration agreement, (b) violation of due process, (c) excess of authority, (d) irregular constitution of the arbitral tribunal, (e) irregular procedure, (f) arbitrability, and (g) public policy.

While the grounds in Article V of the New York Convention do not expressly relate to a breach of good faith in the underlying proceedings, the author's view is that the ground of procedural irregularity contained in Article V(d) can be pursued. Article V(d) provides that the recognition and enforcement of an arbitral award may be resisted where 'the composition of the arbitral authority, or the procedure was not in

55. Pavic, Vladimir, Annulment of Arbitral Awards In International Commercial Arbitration (2010). Investment and Commercial Arbitration – Similarities and Divergencies, Christina Knahr, Christian Koller, Walter Rechberger and August Reinisch, eds, pp. 131-152, Eleven International Publishing, 2010, pp. 133.
56. Article 34 (iv), UNCITRAL Model Law.
57. Richard J. Graving, *Status of the New York Arbitration Convention: Some Gaps in Coverage but New Acceptances Confirms its Vitality*, 10 ICSID Review (1995) DOI: 10.1093/icsidreview/10.1.1.

accordance with the agreement of the parties, or, failing such agreement, was not in accordance with the law of the country where the arbitration took place.'

This provision lays down the rule that recognition and enforcement of the award can be refused if the respondent can prove procedural irregularity and is generally understood to be the broad ground to challenge awards based on the arbitrators' failure to comply with arbitral procedure agreed by the parties, or, in the absence of an agreement on these matters, the law of the seat.[58] Since the duty to act in good faith can be understood as a principle underpinning the performance under any agreement (such as the arbitration agreement), the violation of such obligation amounts to a situation where the 'procedure was not in accordance with the agreement of the parties', thus paving the way to a refusal of recognition or enforcement of an arbitral award under Article V(d) of the New York Convention.

It should be noted, however, as it relates to the annulment and the resistance to the enforcement of an award, it is doubtful whether courts seized of such applications will be prepared to refuse the recognition or the enforcement of an arbitral award where the alleged breach of good faith has not been raised by the aggrieved party during the proceedings. Indeed, the Swiss Federal Supreme Court has held that a party cannot keep a procedural violation 'in reserve' in case it loses .... It is inconsistent with procedural good faith not to raise an objection immediately.[59]

[D] Liability of the Arbitrator(s) and Arbitral Institutions

The liability of arbitral institutions and, to a larger extent, arbitrators have been the subject of cautious controversy in international arbitrations. With the continued emergence of arbitral institutions as powerful actors with new functions in and outside of the arbitration proceedings, the debate on liability has remained evergreen and national arbitration laws are increasingly legislating on these questions despite the exclusion of liability typically included in arbitral rules and terms of reference.

The liability of arbitrators and arbitral institutions is ultimately a function of the legal relationship they have with the parties. In Common law jurisdictions, arbitral institutions are perceived as an integral administrative element of the arbitral process and exalted to a quasi-judicial status.[60] As such, this perceived notion of the institution's quasi-judicial function and the need to preserve the independence of this function, US courts project onto arbitral institutions acting in arbitral proceedings the near-absolute immunity from liability given to federal judges in judicial proceedings.[61] The continental approach is to characterize the legal relationship between arbitrating

58. Albert Jan van den Berg, *The New York Arbitration Convention of 1985, Annotated List of Topics*; 2013, 49.
59. Decision of the Swiss Federal Supreme Court of 24 May 2013, Case No. 4A_476/2012.
60. Luigi Fumagalli, *Liability of Arbitral Institutions for the Administration of Arbitration Proceedings*, 14 Croat Arbit YB 61, 64 (2007) DOI: 10.1093/law/9780198783206.003.0002 (hereinafter 'Fumagalli').
61. Susan Franck, The Liability of International Arbitrators: A Comparative Analysis and Proposal for Qualified Immunity, 20 NY L Sch J Int'l & Comp L 1, 16-18 (2000) DOI: 10.59022/ijlp.46 (hereinafter 'Franck').

parties and the institution as being of a contractual nature, based on the notion that arbitration is the product of a mutual agreement between the disputing parties.[62]

Notwithstanding the immunity generally understood to apply to arbitrators in respect of their adjudicative function, there is scope to pursue liability for outright bad faith. More relevant for present purposes, the English Arbitration Act 1996 qualifies immunity for arbitral institutions so as to give parties a remedy in cases of 'bad faith'.[63] Section 74(1) of the 1996 Act is a mandatory provision which exempts an arbitral institution from liability in tort, contract or otherwise, for anything done in its function of appointing an arbitrator, unless it involves bad faith.

In the same vein, section 29 of the English Arbitration Act 1996 provides that: 'An arbitrator is not liable for anything done or omitted in the discharge or purported discharge of his functions as arbitrator unless the act or omission is shown to have been in bad faith.'

In 2011, Hong Kong adopted a new Arbitration Ordinance[64] which expressly confers immunity on an arbitral appointing or administering authority unless it is proved that, in relation to the exercise or performance of its function, an act is done or omitted to be done 'dishonestly'.[65] Dishonesty, in this context, has been described as 'a lack of probity, deception, fraud or unlawful acquisition of an advantage or personal gain'.[66] In other words, it equates to 'bad faith'.

Article 31 of the LCIA Rules 2020 (Limitation of Liability) provides for two exceptions, including where the act or omission is shown to constitute conscious and deliberate wrongdoing; again, in other words, bad faith. This is consistent with the general principle that liability cannot be excluded where bad faith, wilful misconduct, or gross negligence exists.[67] As such, limitation and exclusion of liability clauses are likely to be inoperative if an arbitrator or arbitral institution is acting in bad faith.[68]

In 2009, the Paris Court of Appeal held in *SNF S.A.S. v. CCI*[69] that, in principle, the International Chamber of Commerce (ICC) could face a claim for damages if it were to fail in the performance of its core duties when administering arbitration cases, despite

62. Fumagalli.
63. Franck, at p. 35.
64. Cap 609, which took effect on 1 July 2011.
65. Arbitration Ordinance (Cap 609), section 105.
66. Neil Kaplan & Robert Morgan, National Report – Hong Kong (1999), in Jan Paulsson (ed.), ICCA International Handbook on Commercial Arbitration, 38. Editorial note: This chapter discusses 2GN of the previous legislation, the Arbitration Ordinance (Cap 341).
67. *See Airfreight Express, Ltd. v. Evergreen Air Center, Inc., (215 Ariz. 103, 158 P.3d 232)*, where the Arizona Court of Appeal held that '[a]s a matter of public policy, a party should not benefit from a bargain it performed in bad faith.' Examples of bad faith include 'evasion of the spirit of the bargain, lack of diligence and slacking off, wilful rendering of imperfect performance, abuse of a power to specify terms and interference with or failure to cooperate in the other party's performance.' Again, in *NEP Canada ULC v. Mec OP LLC*, 2021 ABQB 180, the Court of the Queen's Bench of Alberta held that the duty of good faith was indeed breached by a party who tried to escape its own fraudulent deception in a contract by hiding behind a limited liability clause in the same agreement.
68. It follows that the duty of good faith is an overriding principle of law that will negate limitation clauses and the doctrine of *culpa lata* may be available in this regard.
69. Court of Appeal of Paris, 22 January 2009.

the wording of Article 34 of the ICC Rules,[70] although in the case at hand the ICC was not found liable.

More recently, the French courts have had the opportunity to clarify the type of misconduct that may give rise to civil liability of arbitral institutions. Ruling on 23 March 2021[71] on claims that the ICC had failed to manage properly the transition between two panels of arbitrators (the constitution of the first one having been found to be irregular), the Paris Court of Appeal confirmed that only the most serious misconduct was excluded from the scope of the limitation clauses stipulated in their rules.[72]

In relation to the liability of arbitrators, the February 2017 decision of the Spanish Supreme Court is instructive. The Court declared that two of the three arbitrators in a sports brand dispute were professionally liable and ordered them to reimburse part of their fees. In a landmark judgment, the Court upheld judgments of a first instance court and the Court of Appeal of Madrid, holding two Spanish arbitrators liable for the setting aside of the award and ordering them to reimburse EUR 750,000 in fees each plus interest and costs.[73]

Relevant for present purposes is the reasoning of the court in coming to this determination. It held that the two arbitrators had 'palpably violated the arbitration rules' by excluding the third arbitrator in the case from deliberations, leading to the setting aside of the award and the need for a second arbitration. The court found the exclusion of the third arbitrator from the case, at the very least, grossly negligent.

The basis of the liability imposed upon the arbitrators was Article 21.1 of the 2003 Spanish Arbitration Act, which says that arbitrators must 'faithfully discharge their functions' or they will be 'liable for damages caused in bad faith, wilful disregard or fraud.' Indeed, this case underscores the fact that although arbitrators cannot be held liable for the use of their adjudication powers, they have a contractual duty towards the parties, and in the event that they recklessly violate these obligations, which the Supreme Court unanimously found in this case, they must compensate them.[74]

§10.05 CONCLUSION

As we have seen above, the principle of good faith imposes a moral behavioral standard on arbitrators and arbitral institutions. This important procedural safeguard is essential for many reasons, not least of which is to maintain the legitimacy of international arbitration. The current state of play of using anecdotal evidence in

70. The applicable version of the ICC Rules of Arbitration was the 1998 version, Article 34 of which stated: 'Neither the arbitrators, nor the Court and its members, nor the ICC and its employees, nor the ICC National Committees shall be liable to any person for any act or omission in connection with the arbitration'.
71. CA Paris, 23 March 2021, n°18/14817. It confirms the judgment rendered on 12 February 2018 by the TGI of Paris in the same case (n°16/08752).
72. The applicable version of the ICC Rules of Arbitration was the 1998 version.
73. Judgment of the Spanish Supreme Court – Judgment No. 102/2017 – 15 February 2017.
74. As it has been noted above, limitation of liability clauses are likely to be inoperative where bad faith is shown.

identifying bad faith conduct presents a significant lacuna in practice. This chapter thus attempts to identify ready and workable solutions based on existing international arbitration tools. The remedies available to a party who alleges the breach of a procedural good faith obligation at different stages of the proceedings have also been identified.

The authors also advance the proposition that being a general principle of both substantive and procedural law, good faith or a lack of it presents a basis to challenge an arbitrator or award as part of the independence and impartiality criteria but should also be considered as a distinct and separate ground.

It is hoped that this contribution adds to the existing literature on the subject and makes the practice more international based on general principles of law, such as 'good faith'.

CHAPTER 11

Use and Misuse of 'Good Faith' in Actions to Set Aside

Philippe Pinsolle

Good faith in actions to set aside. Many would view this as an empty set. The lack of good faith of one party is not, per se, a ground to set aside an arbitral award, and this proposition holds true in many, if not all, jurisdictions. The same is true for the lack of good faith of the arbitral tribunal or even the institution organizing the arbitration when there is one. Actions to set aside are based on precise grounds, not on general principles, some would say. In some jurisdictions, like France and Switzerland, these grounds are exhaustively defined, and the lack of good faith is not one of them. The discussion could, therefore, stop there. But is it so, really?

The reality, of course, is very different and far more nuanced. Good faith does play an important role in actions to set aside, but a distinction is to be made. A comparative study between France and Switzerland, two jurisdictions which are unquestionably arbitration-friendly, shows that good faith is actually a filter, a gatekeeper, a pre-condition to making a request to set aside an award. Most of the time, a request not made in good faith will be held inadmissible (§11.01). By contrast, the role of good faith is more limited when it comes to the merits of the action to set aside, but it is not altogether absent (§11.02).

§11.01 GOOD FAITH AS A PRE-CONDITION TO RAISING A GROUND FOR ANNULMENT

It would be an understatement to say that good faith plays an important role in annulment proceedings. In reality, good faith operates as a gatekeeper in these proceedings. Whether or not any given ground of annulment will be admissible, with the exception of substantive international public policy, is regulated by a principle deeply rooted in good faith. That principle is the principle according to which any irregularity that could give rise to an annulment ground must be raised immediately before the arbitral tribunal each time it is possible, failing which the annulment ground will be held inadmissible by the court.

This principle has developed in parallel in France and Switzerland. Through a comparative analysis, we will examine first its genesis (§11.01[A]), followed by its broad scope of application (§11.01[B]) and the limited exceptions to it (§11.01[C]).

[A] The Genesis of the Principle According to Which an Irregularity Must Be Raised Before the Arbitral Tribunal Each Time It Is Possible

Both France and Switzerland have long recognized the principle according to which a party is not entitled to keep an annulment ground up its sleeve as a poison pill against the award should the award prove unfavourable. In both jurisdictions, the principle was initially judge-made. Interestingly, both countries ended up codifying this principle with the most recent revisions of their respective arbitration acts.

In France, this principle was affirmed in a series of decisions that initially characterized the situation as waiver:

> Et attendu que la Cour d'appel a relevé que la société Beugnet avait participé activement à l'arbitrage; qu'elle doit donc être réputée avoir renoncé à se prévaloir ultérieurement des irrégularités qu'elle s'est, en connaissance de cause, abstenue d'invoquer devant l'arbitre.'[1]
>
> Mais attendu que l'arrêt constate que l'acte de mission, établi après un premier échange de mémoires, ne reproduit que partiellement la clause litigieuse, que cet acte n'a jamais été signé par la société Sagua et qu'au contraire celle-ci a, dès le mois de mars 2001 et à plusieurs reprises, contesté la privation du recours aux tribunaux étatiques envisagée par l'acte de mission en dépit des termes explicites de la clause; que, dès lors que *la renonciation d'une partie à soulever une irrégularité doit s'apprécier au vu de son comportement au cours de la procédure d'arbitrage,* la cour d'appel, qualifiant la clause figurant au contrat du 8 octobre 1996 comme instituant une procédure de conciliation préalable à la saisine de la juridiction étatique, a pu juger que les arbitres s'étaient attribué une mission d'arbitre sans l'accord des parties; qu'elle a ainsi légalement justifié sa décision au regard des textes susvisés.'[2]

Subsequently, the French courts have also used the concept of estoppel:

1. Civ. 2ème, 11 juill. 2002, *Rev. Arb.* 2004.283.
2. Civ. 1ère, 11 juill. 2006, n° 03-20.802: 'And whereas the Court of Appeal noted that the company Beugnet had actively participated in the arbitration; that it must therefore be deemed to have waived its right to subsequently invoke the irregularities which it knowingly refrained from invoking before the arbitrator. But whereas the judgment notes that the terms of reference, drawn up after an initial exchange of briefs, only partially reproduces the disputed clause, that these terms of reference were never signed by Sagua and that, on the contrary, Sagua has, since March 2001 and on several occasions, contested the deprivation of recourse to State courts envisaged by the terms of reference, despite the explicit terms of the clause; since a party's waiver of its right to raise an irregularity must be assessed in the light of its conduct during the arbitration proceedings, the Court of Appeal, qualifying the clause in the contract of October 8, 1996 as instituting a conciliation procedure prior to referral to the State courts, was able to rule that the

> Mais attendu que, dans ses écritures devant la cour d'appel, la société Income faisait grief au liquidateur de s'être volontairement abstenu de participer à la procédure après en avoir été pleinement informé et avoir été mis en cause, ce qui lui interdisait de s'en plaindre en appel, et en tirait la conclusion qu'il était censé avoir renoncé à se prévaloir des éventuelles irrégularités de la procédure; que la société ajoutait que le liquidateur avait agi sciemment, par collusion frauduleuse et dans le but de se réserver un moyen de recours contre la sentence; que, dès lors que les domaines d'application respectifs de la *règle de l'estoppel* et du principe de la renonciation peuvent, dans certains cas, être identiques et qu'il appartient au juge de l'annulation de faire respecter la loyauté procédurale des parties à l'arbitrage, c'est sans violer le principe de la contradiction que la cour d'appel a qualifié d'estoppel l'attitude procédurale du liquidateur.[3]

Eventually, however, the fact that the principle was an autonomous principle based on good faith was clearly affirmed when France reformed its arbitration law:

> L'article 1466 consacre le principe de l'estoppel, déjà reconnu par la jurisprudence. Cette notion, empruntée au droit anglo-saxon, constitue une exception procédurale destinée à sanctionner, *au nom de la bonne foi*, les contradictions dans les comportements d'une partie, celle-ci étant liée par son comportement antérieur et, dès lors, empêchée à faire valoir une prétention nouvelle.[4]

The principle was subsequently codified as Article 1466 of the French *Code de procédure civile* (CPC) when France enacted its new arbitration decree in 2011:

> La partie qui, en connaissance de cause et sans motif légitime, s'abstient d'invoquer en temps utile une irrégularité devant le tribunal arbitral est réputée avoir renoncé à s'en prévaloir.
>
> A party who, with full knowledge of the facts and without legitimate reason, refrains from invoking an irregularity in good time before the arbitral tribunal shall be deemed to have waived the right to invoke it.

---

arbitrators had taken on the role of arbitrator without the agreement of the parties; it thus legally justified its decision in the light of the aforementioned texts.' (informal English translation of the French original).

3. Civ. 1ère, 6 mai 2009, n° 08-10.281: 'But whereas, in its pleadings before the Court of Appeal, the company Income complained that the liquidator had voluntarily refrained from participating in the proceedings after having been fully informed and accused, which precluded him from complaining on appeal, and drew the conclusion that he was deemed to have waived his right to rely on any irregularities in the proceedings; the company added that the liquidator had acted knowingly, by fraudulent collusion and with the aim of reserving a means of appeal against the award; given that the respective fields of application of the estoppel rule and the principle of waiver may, in certain cases, be identical, and that it is the role of the annulment judge to ensure that the procedural fairness of the parties to the arbitration is respected, it was without violating the adversarial principle that the Court of Appeal qualified the liquidator's procedural attitude as estoppel.' (informal English translation of the French original).
4. Rapport au Premier ministre relatif au décret n° 2011-48 du 13 janvier 2011 portant réforme de l'arbitrage, JORF n° 0011 du 14 janvier 2011: 'Article 1466 enshrines the principle of estoppel, already recognized by case law. This concept, borrowed from Anglo-Saxon law, constitutes a procedural defence designed to sanction, in the name of good faith, contradictions in the conduct of a party, the latter being bound by its previous conduct and therefore prevented from asserting a new claim.' (informal English translation of the French original).

Article 1466 of the French CPC is applicable to international arbitration through a cross-reference in Article 1526 CPC.

The situation in Switzerland is almost the same, although it was always clear that the principle that objections should be first raised in front of the arbitral tribunal was derived directly from good faith.

The principle itself has long been recognized by the Swiss Federal Tribunal:

> a) La partie qui s'estime victime d'une violation de son droit d'être entendue ou d'un autre vice de procédure doit l'invoquer d'emblée dans la procédure arbitrale. A défaut, elle n'est plus habilitée à s'en plaindre dans un recours contre la sentence (Lalive/Poudret/Reymond, n. 4d ad art. 36 CIA, n. 12 ad art. 182 LDIP et n. 5d ad art. 190 LDIP avec les réf.). En effet, le comportement consistant à invoquer un vice de procédure seulement dans le cadre du recours dirigé contre une décision - parce que celle-ci se révèle en définitive défavorable -, alors que ledit vice aurait déjà pu être signalé en cours de procédure, constitue une violation du principe de la bonne foi (ATF 113 Ia 67; dans le même ordre d'idées, ATF 111 Ia 161 consid. 1b, 116 Ia 135 consid. 4, 387 consid. 1 pp. 389, 485 consid. 2c; cf., également, Imboden/Rhinow, Schweizerische Verwaltungsrechtsprechung, t. 1, 6ème éd., pp. 489 s., no 79 III et Rhinow/Krähenmann, t. complémentaire, p. 254, no 79 III).[5]

The fact that the principle is directly grounded in good faith has also always been very clear from the beginning:

> En tout état de cause, le défendeur ne peut pas se prévaloir de la violation de son droit d'être entendu, faute de l'avoir invoquée d'emblée. La partie qui s'estime victime d'une telle violation ou d'un autre vice de procédure doit en effet s'en plaindre sur-le-champ dans la procédure arbitrale. A ce défaut, elle n'est plus habilitée à le faire dans un recours contre la sentence. Le comportement consistant à n'invoquer un vice de procédure que dans le cadre du recours dirigé contre une décision, - parce que celle-ci se révèle en définitive défavorable - alors que ledit vice aurait déjà pu être signalé en cours de procédure, constitue une violation du *principe de la bonne foi* (ATF 119 II 386, consid. 1a et les références).[6]
>
> Le principe de la bonne foi s'oppose à ce qu'une partie qui constate un prétendu vice de procédure ne le signale pas immédiatement, à un moment où il pourrait encore être le cas échéant corrigé, mais attende l'issue de la procédure pour l'invoquer ultérieurement si celle-ci lui a été défavorable.[7]
>
> En outre, le *principe de la bonne foi* s'oppose à ce qu'une partie qui constate un prétendu vice de procédure ne le signale pas immédiatement, à un moment où

5. Decision of the Swiss Federal Tribunal (DSFT) 119 II 386 of 7 September 1993: 'a) A party who considers himself to be the victim of a violation of his right to be heard or of another procedural defect must invoke it from the outset in the arbitration proceedings. Otherwise, he or she is no longer entitled to complain about it in an appeal against the award (Lalive/Poudret/Reymond, n. 4d ad art. 36 CIA, n. 12 ad art. 182 LDIP and n. 5d ad art. 190 LDIP with references). Indeed, to invoke a procedural defect only in the context of an appeal against a decision - because the latter ultimately turns out to be unfavorable - when the defect could already have been pointed out in the course of the proceedings, constitutes a violation of the principle of good faith (ATF 113 Ia 67; in the same vein, ATF 111 Ia 161 consid. 1b, 116 Ia 135 consid. 4, 387 consid. 1 pp. 389, 485 consid. 2c; cf, also, Imboden/Rhinow, Schweizerische Verwaltungsrechtsprechung, t. 1, 6th ed., pp. 489 f., no. 79 III and Rhinow/Krähenmann, supplementary t., p. 254, no. 79 III).' (Informal English translation of the French original).
6. DSFT of 27 July 1997, 18 ASA Bull 96 (2000).
7. DSFT 4A_18/2007 of 6 June 2007.

> il pourrait encore être le cas échéant corrigé, mais attende l'issue de la procédure pour l'invoquer ultérieurement si celle-ci lui a été défavorable. Agit, dès lors, de manière abusive la partie qui invoque le non-épuisement du préalable obligatoire de conciliation dans son recours contre la sentence, alors qu'elle ne l'avait pas proposé à l'autre partie avant l'arbitrage (arrêt 4A_18/2007, précité, consid. 4.3.3.1 et les références).[8]

In 2021, the Swiss legislator codified the principle, at least insofar as procedural objections are concerned, as the new Article 182 (4) of the Swiss Private International Law Act (SPILA):

> Une partie qui poursuit la procédure d'arbitrage sans faire valoir immédiatement une violation des règles de procédure qu'elle a constatée ou qu'elle aurait pu constater en faisant preuve de la diligence requise ne peut plus se prévaloir de cette violation ultérieurement.
>
> A party who continues the arbitration proceedings without immediately asserting a breach of the rules of procedure which it has discovered or could have discovered by exercising due diligence may not subsequently assert such breach.

As we shall see, in both countries, this principle has, in fact, a pretty broad scope of application.

[B] The Broad Scope of Application of This Principle

Initially, the principle developed in both countries in two distinct types of situations: due process irregularities and issues going to the constitution of the arbitral tribunal, primarily an alleged lack of independence of an arbitrator or alleged lack of disclosure. The most recent case law in France made it very clear, however, that the principle is of general application with only one exception: substantive international public policy.

Starting with Switzerland, the Swiss Federal Tribunal made clear in its case law that the principle applied to what it referred to as 'procedural irregularities':

8. DSFT 4A_18/2007 of 6 June 2007: 'In any event, the defendant cannot claim that his right to be heard has been violated, as he has not invoked it from the outset. A party who considers himself to be the victim of such a violation or of another procedural defect must immediately raise a complaint in the arbitration proceedings. Failing this, they are no longer entitled to lodge an appeal against the award. It is an infringement of the principle of good faith to invoke a procedural defect only in the context of an appeal against a decision - because the decision is ultimately unfavorable - when the defect could already have been pointed out in the course of the proceedings (ATF 119 II 386, recital 1a and references). The principle of good faith precludes a party who notices an alleged procedural defect from not immediately pointing it out, at a time when it could still be corrected if necessary, but waiting until the end of the proceedings to invoke it at a later date if the outcome was unfavourable. Furthermore, the principle of good faith precludes a party who notices an alleged procedural defect from not immediately reporting it, at a time when it could still be corrected if necessary, but waiting until the end of the proceedings to invoke it at a later date if the proceedings have been unfavorable. A party is therefore acting improperly if it invokes the non-exhaustion of the mandatory conciliation prerequisite in its appeal against the award, even though it had not proposed this to the other party prior to the arbitration (judgment 4A_18/2007, cited above, recital 4.3.3.1 and references).' (Informal English translation of the French original).

En tout état de cause, s'il est vrai que le principe de la bonne foi, applicable également dans le domaine de la procédure (ATF 123 III 220 consid. 4d p. 228), commande au plaideur de se prévaloir de ses moyens sans tarder (arrêt 4C. 347/2000 du 6 avril 2001, consid. 2a), et si l'on admet par hypothèse que l'intimée n'a pas respecté cette injonction – ce qu'elle conteste et qui reste à démontrer – il ne s'ensuit pas pour autant que le Tribunal arbitral aurait dû écarter le moyen de défense soulevé par elle, sous peine de violer l'ordre public. C'est le lieu de rappeler que si *l'inobservation de l'obligation de signaler à temps les vices de procédure est sanctionnée, en général, par la péremption*, une exception doit être faite pour les vices particulièrement graves qui doivent être redressés d'office et qui peuvent être invoqués jusqu'en fin de cause (cf. Jean-François Egli, La protection de la bonne foi dans le procès, in Juridiction constitutionnelle et juridiction administrative, Zurich 1992, p. 225 ss, 239 let. B).[9]

Il principio della buona fede obbliga infatti la parte che constata un vizio di procedura a segnalarlo subito, in un momento ove sia ancora possibile rimediarvi, e le vieta di attendere passivamente l'esito della causa, allo scopo di prevalersene – se del caso – successivamente dinanzi all'autorità di ricorso (DTF 119 II 386 *consid. 1a*). ... *Trattandosi di una questione procedurale, essa va fatta valere immediatamente (cfr. quanto già esposto al consid. 4.2). Il Tribunale federale ha tuttavia già ammesso la possibilità di fare un'eccezione in caso di vizi particolarmente gravi, cui è necessario porre rimedio d'ufficio e in ogni stadio della causa. Fra questi il difetto di personalità giuridica e della capacità di essere parte in un procedimento giudiziario, perché altrimenti ci si troverebbe nella situazione di dover riconoscere la qualità di parte a un'entità giuridicamente inesistente* (DTF 128 III 191 *consid. 8 non pubblicato*). *Anche se presentata per la prima volta in questa sede, la censura è pertanto ammissibile. Essa è però destinata all'insuccesso.*[10]

Procedural irregularities encompass such situations as the alleged violation of a party's right to be heard:

9. DSFT 4P.282/2001 of 3 April 2002, 20 ASA Bull 358 (2002): 'In any case, while it is true that the principle of good faith, which is also applicable in procedural matters (ATF 123 III 220 consid. 4d p. 228), requires the litigant to put forward his case without delay (decision 4C. 347/2000 of April 6, 2001, consid. 2a), and if we accept that the respondent did not comply with this injunction – which it disputes and which remains to be proven – it does not follow that the Arbitral Tribunal should have set aside the defence raised by it, on pain of violating public policy. It should be remembered that, while failure to comply with the obligation to report procedural defects in good time is generally punishable by waiver, an exception must be made for particularly serious defects which must be remedied ex officio and which can be invoked right up to the end of the case (cf. Jean-François Egli, La protection de la bonne foi dans le procès, in Juridiction constitutionnelle et juridiction administrative, Zurich 1992, pp. 225 ff., 239 let. B.' (Informal English translation of the French original).
10. DSFT 4P.146/2005 of 10 October 2005: 'In fact, the principle of good faith obliges the party who notices a procedural defect to report it immediately, at a time when it can still be remedied, and prohibits it from passively awaiting the outcome of the case, with the aim of prevailing - if necessary - later before the appeals authority (BGE 119 II 386 consid. 1a) ... Since this is a procedural issue, it must be asserted immediately (see above in consid. 4.2). However, the Federal Supreme Court has already admitted the possibility of making an exception in the case of particularly serious defects, which need to be remedied ex officio and at any stage of the case. These include the lack of legal personality and of the capacity to be a party to judicial proceedings, because otherwise one would find oneself in the situation of having to recognize the status of party to a legally nonexistent entity (BGE 128 III 191 consid. 8 unpublished).' (Informal English translation of the Italian original).

> En tout état de cause, *le défendeur ne peut pas se prévaloir de la violation de son droit d'être entendu, faute de l'avoir invoquée d'emblée.* La partie qui s'estime victime d'une telle violation ou d'un autre vice de procédure doit en effet s'en plaindre sur-le-champ dans la procédure arbitrale. A ce défaut, elle n'est plus habilitée à le faire dans un recours contre la sentence. Le comportement consistant à n'invoquer un vice de procédure que dans le cadre du recours dirigé contre une décision - parce que celle-ci se révèle en définitive défavorable - alors que ledit vice aurait déjà pu être signalé en cours de procédure, constitue une violation du principe de la bonne foi (ATF 119 II 386, consid. 1a et les références).[11]

The Swiss Federal Tribunal made clear, however, that procedural irregularities were not limited to due process issues but also covered the improper constitution of the arbitral tribunal:

> Aux termes de l'art. 20 CIA, *la récusation doit être demandée d'entrée de cause, ou dès que la partie requérante a connaissance des motifs de récusation.* Bien que cette disposition ne prévoie pas une durée ferme du délai, elle oblige les parties à faire preuve de diligence. Il leur appartient donc de faire valoir leurs moyens de récusation sans tarder. Si elles s'en abstiennent, elles sont déchues de la possibilité d'invoquer ultérieurement la cause de récusation (cf. TF in SJ 1980, p. 75 et 1983 p. 541 ss), sauf si celle-ci se rapporte à un vice irréparable (cf. par ex. ATF 107 Ia 161/162); en effet, l'un des buts de l'arbitrage est de permettre une solution rapide des litiges, de sorte que les parties sont tenues par les règles de la bonne foi d'éviter tout ce qui pourrait retarder sans nécessité absolue le déroulement normal de la procédure arbitrale (ATF 109 Ia 83 consid. 2a, ATF 108 Ia 201).[12]

As such, in a situation where the contract provided for a mandatory preliminary conciliation, which the parties ultimately did not carry out, and where one of the parties did not object at the time, a subsequent annulment request based on the same circumstances was held inadmissible:

> En outre, le principe de la bonne foi s'oppose à ce qu'une partie qui constate un prétendu vice de procédure ne le signale pas immédiatement, à un moment où il pourrait encore être le cas échéant corrigé, mais attende l'issue de la procédure

11. DSFT of 27 July 1997, 18 ASA Bull 96 (2000): 'In any event, the defendant cannot claim that his right to be heard has been violated, as he has not invoked it from the outset. A party who considers himself to be the victim of such a violation or of another procedural defect must immediately lodge a complaint in the arbitration proceedings. Failing this, they are no longer entitled to lodge an appeal against the award. It is a violation of the principle of good faith to invoke a procedural defect only in the context of an appeal against a decision - because the decision is ultimately unfavorable - when the defect could already have been pointed out in the course of the proceedings (ATF 119 II 386, recital 1a and references).' (Informal English translation of the French original).
12. DSFT 111 Ia 259 of 8 November 1985: 'Under art. 20 CIA, challenge must be requested from the outset, or as soon as the requesting party is aware of the grounds for the challengel. Although this provision does not stipulate a fixed time limit, it does oblige the parties to act with diligence. It is therefore incumbent on them to put forward their grounds for challenge without delay. If they fail to do so, they are deprived of the possibility of subsequently invoking the ground for challenge (cf. TF in SJ 1980, p. 75 and 1983 pp. 541 ff), unless it relates to an irreparable defect (cf. eg. ATF 107 Ia 161 /162); in fact, one of the aims of arbitration is to enable disputes to be settled rapidly, so that the parties are bound by the rules of good faith to avoid anything that could delay the normal course of the arbitration proceedings without absolute necessity (ATF 109 Ia 83 consid. 2a, ATF 108 Ia 201).' (Informal English translation of the French original).

> pour l'invoquer ultérieurement si celle-ci lui a été défavorable. Agit, dès lors, de manière abusive la partie qui invoque le non-épuisement du préalable obligatoire de conciliation dans son recours contre la sentence, alors qu'elle ne l'avait pas proposé à l'autre partie avant l'arbitrage (arrêt 4A_18/2007, précité, consid. 4.3.3.1 et les références).[13]

The recent codification of the principle does not seem to have altered its scope of application.

By contrast, in France, the principle was broadened by case law following its codification. Initially, like in Switzerland, the principle was applied in situations where there was an alleged breach of due process. For example, it was applied to a situation where one of the parties did not challenge the arbitral tribunal's jurisdiction until after the award on jurisdiction. In such a case, the ground for annulment was declared inadmissible by the Paris Court of Appeal:

> Considérant, en troisième lieu, qu'aux termes de l'article 1466 du code de procédure civile, applicable en matière internationale par renvoi de l'article 1506: 'La partie qui, en connaissance de cause et sans motif légitime, s'abstient d'invoquer en temps utile une irrégularité devant le tribunal arbitral est réputée avoir renoncé à s'en prévaloir; ...
>
> Considérant que ce n'est que par un mémoire déposé le 15 mars 2012 auprès du tribunal arbitral, que DIPCO a contesté la compétence de celui-ci, en faisant valoir que toutes les parties étant égyptiennes, les différends devaient, en vertu de l'article 20.6 (d) du contrat, être soumis à un arbitrage conduit conformément au droit égyptien, et non à un arbitrage international administré par la Cour de la C.C.I;
>
> Mais considérant que DIPCO, qui connaissait cette circonstance dès la signature de l'acte de mission et qui s'est abstenue de l'invoquer préalablement à la sentence sur la compétence, ne s'est pas conformée à l'obligation de relever les irrégularités en temps utile, en s'en prévalant un an plus tard lors des débats sur le fond;
>
> Qu'ainsi, le moyen qui manque en fait en sa première branche est irrecevable en ses deux autres branches.[14]

13. DSFT 4A_628/2015 of 16 March 2016: 'Furthermore, the principle of good faith precludes a party who notices an alleged procedural defect from not immediately pointing it out, at a time when it could still be corrected if necessary, but waiting until the end of the proceedings to invoke it at a later date if the outcome was unfavorable. A party is therefore acting improperly if it invokes the non-exhaustion of the mandatory conciliation prerequisite in its appeal against the award, even though it had not proposed this to the other party prior to the arbitration (judgment 4A_18/2007, cited above, recital 4.3.3.1 and references).' (Informal English translation of the French original).
14. C.A. Paris, 25 avril 2017, n° 15/07642: 'Thirdly, under the terms of article 1466 of the French Code of Civil Procedure, applicable in international matters by reference to article 1506: "A party who, with full knowledge of the facts and without legitimate reason, refrains from invoking an irregularity in due time before the arbitral tribunal shall be deemed to have waived its right to invoke it"'; 'Considering that it was only in a brief filed with the arbitral tribunal on March 15, 2012 that DIPCO challenged the tribunal's jurisdiction, arguing that since all the parties were Egyptian, the disputes should, under article 20.6 (d) of the contract, be submitted to arbitration conducted in accordance with Egyptian law, and not to international arbitration administered by the ICC Court. But considering that DIPCO, which was aware of this circumstance from the signing of the terms of reference and which refrained from invoking it prior to the award on

It is, however, in the field of the constitution of the arbitral tribunal that the principle developed in the most spectacular fashion, in particular, in the Tecnimont saga.[15] To cut a long story short, in this matter that lasted almost twenty years from start to finish, the French *Cour de cassation* eventually held that the failure by a party to challenge an arbitrator before the ICC within the prescribed 30-day period of the ICC rules resulted in a subsequent request for annulment, based on the lack of independence of the arbitrator, being inadmissible:

> Mais attendu, d'abord, que l'arrêt constate que, dans sa requête en récusation, la société Avax ne faisait aucune allusion à la révélation qu'aurait constitué pour elle l'information publiée dans une revue le 20 août 2007 selon laquelle Sofregaz et Tecnimont étaient des filiales de Maire Tecnimont, ce qui n'aurait pas été cohérent avec les déclarations de l'arbitre et l'aurait conduite à des investigations complémentaires, révélant que Sofregaz était une filiale à 100 % de Tecnimont, mais se bornait à évoquer des recherches complémentaires qu'elle aurait faites au mois d'août 2007; qu'il relève que les recherches alléguées, qui, tirées du site internet de Sofregaz, sont publiques et aisément accessibles, auraient pu être menées le jour même de la réception du courriel de l'arbitre du 26 juillet 2007; que, de ces énonciations et constatations, la cour d'appel, qui n'était pas tenue d'effectuer les recherches prétendument omises que celles-ci rendaient inopérantes, a exactement déduit, sans inverser la charge de l'obligation de révélation, que la requête en récusation était tardive pour avoir été introduite plus d'un mois après que la société Avax eut reçu les renseignements qui auraient altéré sa confiance dans le président du tribunal arbitral, et sans qu'aucune information complémentaire, qui fût notoire, ait été entre-temps découverte de sorte que cette société n'était plus recevable à invoquer à l'appui du recours en annulation de la sentence les faits sur lesquels cette requête se fondait.[16]

The rule is, therefore, extremely strict in France. If the rules of the institution supervising the arbitration provide for a deadline to file a challenge (and they always

jurisdiction, did not comply with the obligation to point out the irregularities in good time, by invoking them a year later during the debates on the merits.' (Informal English translation of the French original).

15. The author wishes to disclose that he was counsel to Tecnimont in the first annulment decision of the Paris Court of appeal.
16. Civ. 1ère, 19 déc. 2018, n° 16-18.349: 'But whereas, first of all, the judgment notes that, in its challenge, Avax made no reference to the revelation that would have constituted for it the information published in a magazine on August 20, 2007 to the effect that Sofregaz and Tecnimont were subsidiaries of Maire Tecnimont, this would not have been consistent with the arbitrator's statements and would have led her to carry out further investigations, revealing that Sofregaz was a 100% subsidiary of Tecnimont, but merely referring to additional research she had carried out in August 2007; that the alleged research, which was taken from Sofregaz's website and is public and easily accessible, could have been carried out on the same day as the arbitrator's e-mail of July 26, 2007; that, from these statements and observations, the Court of Appeal, which was not required to carry out the allegedly omitted research which they rendered inoperative, correctly deduced, without reversing the burden of disclosure, that the application for challenge was untimely in that it was lodged more than a month after Avax had received the information which would have altered its confidence in the Chairman of the Arbitral Tribunal, and without any additional information, which was not widely known, having been discovered in the meantime, so that the company was no longer entitled to invoke the facts on which the application was based in support of its claim for annulment of the award.' (Informal English translation of the French original).

do), a challenge must be filed within this time period in order to preserve the ability subsequently to bring the matter before French courts in annulment proceedings. Similarly, if the challenge before the institution fails, the requesting party would be well advised to reserve its rights in an express fashion following an unfavourable decision by the institution. Otherwise, there would be a very strong argument that the requesting party has acquiesced to the decision, rejecting its challenge by failing to reserve its rights.

Not only is the rule strict, but it is also quite broad. By a series of recent decisions, the Paris Court of Appeal decided that Article 1466 of the French CPC, which codifies the rule, applies to all annulment grounds with the exception of substantive international public policy:

> Aux termes de l'article 1466 du code de procédure civile, la partie qui, en connaissance de cause et sans motif légitime, s'abstient d'invoquer en temps utile une irrégularité devant le tribunal arbitral est réputée avoir renoncé à s'en prévaloir.
>
> Ce texte ne vise pas les seules irrégularités procédurales mais tous les griefs qui constituent des cas d'ouverture du recours en annulation des sentences, en ce compris le principe d'égalité des armes qui relève de l'ordre public international de protection, à l'exception des moyens tirés de ce que la reconnaissance ou l'exécution de la sentence violerait l'ordre public international de fond.[17]

This formulation has been systematically used by the Paris Court of Appeal since 2019, including in very recent decisions.[18]

Given its broad scope of application, especially in France, it is legitimate to consider the exceptions to the principle.

[C] The Exceptions to the Principle

As is the case for every rule, the rule according to which objections not raised before the arbitral tribunal will be inadmissible in a subsequent action to set aside does have exceptions. In France, the exceptions are relatively circumscribed. By contrast, the Swiss Federal Tribunal takes a broader view of the exceptions.

Starting with France, the clearest exception is substantive international public policy. The Paris Court of Appeal has expressly excluded it from the scope of the rule:

> Aux termes de l'article 1466 du code de procédure civile, la partie qui, en connaissance de cause et sans motif légitime, s'abstient d'invoquer en temps utile

17. C.A. Paris, 19 oct. 2021, n° 19/23071, *Heliotrop*: 'Under the terms of article 1466 of the French Code of Civil Procedure, a party who, with full knowledge of the facts and without a legitimate reason, refrains from invoking an irregularity in due time before the arbitral tribunal is deemed to have waived the right to invoke it. This text does not refer only to procedural irregularities, but to all the grievances that constitute grounds for an action to set aside an award, including the principle of equality of arms, which falls within the scope of international public policy, with the exception of grounds alleging that recognition or enforcement of the award would violate substantive international public policy.'
18. C.A. Paris, 17 mai 2022, n° 20/15162, *Saudi Tumpane*.

> une irrégularité devant le tribunal arbitral est réputée avoir renoncé à s'en prévaloir.
>
> Ce texte ne vise pas les seules irrégularités procédurales mais tous les griefs qui constituent des cas d'ouverture du recours en annulation des sentences, en ce compris le principe d'égalité des armes qui relève de l'ordre public international de protection, à l'exception des moyens tirés de ce que la reconnaissance ou l'exécution de la sentence violerait l'ordre public international de fond.[19]

This means that when there is an alleged breach of substantive public policy, it is permissible to raise the corresponding ground in an action to set aside for the first time. It is also permissible for the court to reexamine the issue afresh, if necessary, on the basis of new evidence that was not presented to the arbitral tribunal. Corruption allegations are the best example of how this exception works. This was the case, in particular, in the *Belokon* matter, where new evidence was considered by the Paris Court of Appeal that subsequently annulled the award.[20] This decision was then confirmed by the French *Cour de cassation*.[21] This was also the case in the *Alstom* matter.[22]

If the exception concerning substantive public policy goes to the scope of the rule according to which a ground must first be raised before the arbitral tribunal each time it is possible, there is another exception that goes to the regime of any objection based on the lack of jurisdiction.

In summary, it is sufficient that a jurisdictional objection is raised before the arbitral tribunal even though the precise ground for which jurisdiction is said to be lacking may have been modified between the arbitral tribunal and the court of appeal. For example, with the exception as it stands today, in a treaty case, a State party may rely on the lack of protected investment before the arbitral tribunal and subsequently raise a different jurisdictional ground before the court of appeal, for example, denying the characterization of protected investor to the claimant. This new ground will, in principle, be admissible.

The fact that a general jurisdictional objection is sufficient was clearly affirmed in the *Schooner* case, where Poland, the Respondent, invoked an entirely new jurisdictional objection before the Court of Appeal. According to the French *Cour de cassation*, this new ground was nonetheless admissible before the Court of Appeal because a jurisdictional objection had already been articulated, albeit in different terms, before the Arbitral Tribunal:

---

19. C.A. Paris, 19 oct. 2021, n° 19/23071, *Heliotrop*: 'Under the terms of article 1466 of the French Code of Civil Procedure, a party who, with full knowledge of the facts and without a legitimate reason, refrains from invoking an irregularity in due time before the arbitral tribunal is deemed to have waived the right to invoke it. This text does not refer only to procedural irregularities, but to all the grievances that constitute grounds for an action to set aside an award, including the principle of equality of arms, which falls within the scope of international public policy, with the exception of grounds alleging that recognition or enforcement of the award would violate substantive international public policy.' (Informal English translation of the French original).
20. C.A. Paris, 21 fév. 2017, n° 15/01650.
21. Civ. 1ère, 23 mars 2022, n° 17-17.981.
22. Civ. 1ère, 23 mars 2022, n° 17-17.981.

> [L]orsque la compétence a été débattue devant les arbitres, les parties ne sont pas privées du droit d'invoquer sur cette question, devant le juge de l'annulation, de nouveaux moyens et arguments et à faire état, à cet effet, de nouveaux éléments de preuve.
>
> Pour déclarer irrecevables les moyens fondant la compétence du tribunal arbitral tirés, d'une part, de l'usage abusif par la République de Pologne de l'exclusion des questions fiscales par l'article VI du Traité, d'autre part, du bénéfice de la clause de la nation la plus favorisée stipulée à l'article I du Traité, l'arrêt retient que, ceux-ci n'ayant pas été plaidés devant le tribunal arbitral, les investisseurs ne sont pas recevables à développer devant le juge de l'annulation un argumentaire différent en droit et en fait de celui qu'ils avaient soumis aux arbitres, auquel ils sont présumés avoir renoncé.
>
> En statuant ainsi, la cour d'appel a violé les textes susvisés.[23]

By contrast to the French *Cour de Cassation*, the Swiss Federal Tribunal relies on a more abstract formula to neutralize the mechanical effect of the rule, rendering inadmissible a ground that was not relied upon first before the arbitral tribunal. This abstract formula makes reference to very serious irregularities (in French, '*vices particulièrement graves*').

An example of the former is the absolute lack of standing to sue:

> [S]i l'inobservation de l'obligation de signaler à temps les vices de procédure est sanctionnée, en général, par la péremption, *une exception doit être faite pour les vices particulièrement graves* qui doivent être redressés d'office et qui peuvent être invoqués jusqu'en fin de cause (cf. Jean-François Egli, La protection de la bonne foi dans le procès, in Juridiction constitutionnelle et juridiction administrative, Zurich 1992, p. 225 ss, 239 let. B). *Or,* le défaut de capacité d'être partie et d'ester en justice entre de toute évidence dans cette catégorie de vices.[24]

This was repeated in another case:

> Trattandosi di una questione procedurale, essa va fatta valere immediatamente (cfr. quanto già esposto al consid. 4.2). Il Tribunale federale ha tuttavia già ammesso la possibilità di fare un'eccezione in caso di vizi particolarmente gravi, cui è necessario porre rimedio d'ufficio e in ogni stadio della causa. Fra questi il

23. Civ. 1ère, 2 déc. 2020, n° 19-15.396: '[W]hen jurisdiction has been debated before the arbitrators, the parties are not deprived of the right to raise new pleas and arguments on this issue before the judge responsible for the annulment, and to adduce new evidence to this effect. In order to declare inadmissible the grounds on which the jurisdiction of the arbitral tribunal is based: firstly, the improper use by the Republic of Poland of the exclusion of tax matters by Article VI of the Treaty, and secondly, the benefit of the most-favoured-nation clause stipulated in Article I of the Treaty, the ruling held that, as these issues had not been argued before the arbitral tribunal, the investors were not entitled to develop before the annulment judge an argument that differed in law and in fact from the one they had submitted to the arbitrators, which they were presumed to have renounced. In so ruling, the Court of Appeal violated the aforementioned texts.' (Informal English translation of the French original).
24. DSFT 4P.282/2001 of 3 April 2002, 20 ASA Bull 358 (2002): 'While failure to comply with the obligation to report procedural defects in good time is generally punishable by waiver, an exception must be made for particularly serious defects which must be remedied ex officio and which can be invoked right up to the end of the case (cf. Jean-François Egli, La protection de la bonne foi dans le procès, in Juridiction constitutionnelle et juridiction administrative, Zurich 1992, pp. 225 ff, 239 let. B). Lack of capacity to be a party and to sue clearly falls into this category of defects.' (Informal English translation of the French original).

> difetto di personalità giuridica e della capacità di essere parte in un procedimento giudiziario, perché altrimenti ci si troverebbe nella situazione di dover riconoscere la qualità di parte a un'entità giuridicamente inesistente (DTF 128 III 191 consid. 8 non pubblicato). [25]

Subsequently, the Swiss Federal Tribunal clarified the notion of very serious irregularity by characterizing it as 'an irregularity that cannot be fixed' (in French, 'vice irréparable' ou 'vice particulièrement grave'):

> Aux termes de l'art. 20 CIA, la récusation doit être demandée d'entrée de cause, ou dès que la partie requérante a connaissance des motifs de récusation. Bien que cette disposition ne prévoie pas une durée ferme du délai, elle oblige les parties à faire preuve de diligence. Il leur appartient donc de faire valoir leurs moyens de récusation sans tarder. Si elles s'en abstiennent, elles sont déchues de la possibilité d'invoquer ultérieurement la cause de récusation (cf. TF in SJ 1980, p. 75 et 1983 p. 541 ss), *sauf si celle-ci se rapporte à un vice irréparable* (cf. par ex. ATF 107 Ia 161 /162); en effet, l'un des buts de l'arbitrage est de permettre une solution rapide des litiges, de sorte que les parties sont tenues par les règles de la bonne foi d'éviter tout ce qui pourrait retarder sans nécessité absolue le déroulement normal de la procédure arbitrale (ATF 109 Ia 83 consid. 2a, ATF 108 Ia 201).[26]
>
> En tout état de cause, s'il est vrai que le principe de la bonne foi, applicable également dans le domaine de la procédure (ATF 123 III 220 consid. 4d p. 228), commande au plaideur de se prévaloir de ses moyens sans tarder (arrêt 4C. 347/2000 du 6 avril 2001, consid. 2a), et si l'on admet par hypothèse que l'intimée n'a pas respecté cette injonction - ce qu'elle conteste et qui reste à démontrer - il ne s'ensuit pas pour autant que le Tribunal arbitral aurait dû écarter le moyen de défense soulevé par elle, sous peine de violer l'ordre public. C'est le lieu de rappeler que si l'inobservation de l'obligation de signaler à temps les vices de procédure est sanctionnée, en général, par la péremption, *une exception doit être faite pour les vices particulièrement graves qui doivent être redressés d'office et qui peuvent être invoqués jusqu'en fin de cause* (cf. Jean-François Egli, La protection de la bonne foi dans le procès, in Juridiction constitutionnelle et juridiction administrative, Zurich 1992, p. 225 ss, 239 let. B). Or, le défaut de capacité d'être partie et d'ester en justice entre de toute évidence dans cette catégorie de vices. On ne voit donc pas que le juge puisse y remédier, même par le recours à l'interdiction de

25. DSFT 4P.146/2005 of 10 October 2005: 'Since this is a procedural issue, it must be asserted immediately (see above in consid. 4.2). However, the Federal Supreme Court has already admitted the possibility of making an exception in the case of particularly serious defects, which need to be remedied ex officio and at any stage of the case. These include the lack of legal personality and of the capacity to be a party to a court proceeding, because otherwise one would find oneself in the situation of having to recognize the status of party to a legally nonexistent entity (BGE 128 III 191 consid. 8 unpublished).' (Informal English translation of the Italian original).
26. DSFT 111 Ia 259 of 8 November 1985: 'Under art. 20 CIA, challenge must be requested from the outset, or as soon as the requesting party is aware of the grounds for challenge. Although this provision does not stipulate a fixed time limit, it does oblige the parties to act with diligence. It is therefore incumbent on them to put forward their grounds for challenge without delay. If they fail to do so, they are deprived of the possibility of subsequently invoking the ground for recusal (cf. TF in SJ 1980, p. 75 and 1983 pp. 541 ff), unless it relates to an irreparable defect (cf. eg. ATF 107 Ia 161/162); in fact, one of the aims of arbitration is to enable disputes to be settled rapidly, so that the parties are bound by the rules of good faith to avoid anything that could delay the normal course of the arbitration proceedings without absolute necessity (ATF 109 Ia 83 consid. 2a, ATF 108 Ia 201).' (Informal English translation of the French original).

l'abus de droit, en donnant vie à une entité juridiquement inexistante. Le Tribunal arbitral s'en est abstenu à juste titre, qui a néanmoins tenu compte du comportement procédural de l'intimée dans la répartition des frais. La recourante ne saurait lui en faire grief.[27]

The Swiss exception is, in fact, arguably narrower than it may seem at first sight. The notion of very serious irregularities appears to be confined to those situations where, regardless of the argument of the parties and their behaviour, it was simply impossible to settle the matter by arbitration due to an objective impossibility that is not susceptible of being affected by the intention of the parties and their behaviour.

As one can see, if good faith is a real gatekeeper of any action to set aside an award, it plays a comparatively limited role, if at all, when it comes to deciding the merits of any action to set aside.

§11.02 THE LIMITED RELEVANCE OF GOOD FAITH AS A GROUND FOR ANNULMENT

The starting point of the analysis regarding the role of good faith in actions to set aside is the uncontroversial finding that good faith is not a ground to set aside an award (§11.02[A]). These grounds do contain the violation of international public policy, and good faith is from time to time mentioned as belonging to international public policy, but no annulment decision was ever rendered on that basis (§11.02[B]). In fact, good faith may have a role to play if the ground for annulment is based on the lack of an arbitration agreement (§11.02[C]), but it does not seem to have any relevance in an annulment based on the prohibition of corruption as part of international public policy (§11.02[D]).

[A] Annulment Grounds Are Exhaustive, and Good Faith Is Not One of Them

Both in France and in Switzerland, annulment grounds are exhaustively set out in legislation. They are, in fact, very close as the French CPC adopted the Swiss

27. DSFT 4P.282/2001 of 3 April 2002, 20 ASA Bull 358 (2002): 'In any case, while it is true that the principle of good faith, which is also applicable in procedural matters (ATF 123 III 220 consid. 4d p. 228), requires the litigant to put forward his case without delay (decision 4C. 347/2000 of April 6, 2001, consid. 2a), and if we accept that the respondent did not comply with this injunction – which it disputes and which remains to be proven – it does not follow that the Arbitral Tribunal should have set aside the defence raised by it, on pain of violating public policy. It should be remembered that, while failure to comply with the obligation to report procedural defects in good time is generally punishable by lapse of time, an exception must be made for particularly serious defects which must be remedied ex officio and which can be invoked right up to the end of the case (cf. Jean-François Egli, La protection de la bonne foi dans le procès, in Juridiction constitutionnelle et juridiction administrative, Zurich 1992, pp. 225 ff, 239 let. B). Lack of capacity to be a party and to sue clearly falls into this category of defects. It is therefore hard to see how the judge can remedy it, even by resorting to the prohibition of abuse of rights, by giving life to a legally non-existent entity. The Arbitral Tribunal rightly refrained from doing so, and nevertheless took account of the respondent's procedural conduct in apportioning costs. The appellant cannot complain about this.' (Informal English translation of the French original).

formulation for the annulment ground based on the lack of jurisdiction when France enacted its new arbitration decree in 2011.

As a result, Article 1520 of the French CPC provides:

> Le recours en annulation n'est ouvert que si:
> 1° Le tribunal arbitral s'est déclaré à tort compétent ou incompétent; ou
> 2° Le tribunal arbitral a été irrégulièrement constitué; ou
> 3° Le tribunal arbitral a statué sans se conformer à la mission qui lui avait été confiée; ou
> 4° Le principe de la contradiction n'a pas été respecté; ou
> 5° La reconnaissance ou l'exécution de la sentence est contraire à l'ordre public international.
>
> An action for annulment is only available if:
> 1° the arbitral tribunal has wrongly declared itself competent or incompetent; or
> 2° the arbitral tribunal was improperly constituted; or
> 3° The arbitral tribunal has ruled without complying with its terms of reference; or
> 4° The principle of adversarial proceedings was not respected; or
> 5° Recognition or enforcement of the award is contrary to international public policy.

This mirrors very closely Article 190 of the SPILA, which provides, for its part, as follows:

> 1 La sentence est définitive dès sa communication.
> 2 Elle ne peut être attaquée que:
> a. lorsque l'arbitre unique a été irrégulièrement désigné ou le tribunal arbitral irrégulièrement composé;
> b. lorsque le tribunal arbitral s'est déclaré à tort compétent ou incompétent;
> c. lorsque le tribunal arbitral a statué au-delà des demandes dont il était saisi ou lorsqu'il a omis de se prononcer sur un des chefs de la demande;
> d. lorsque l'égalité des parties ou leur droit d'être entendues en procédure contradictoire n'a pas été respecté;
> e. lorsque la sentence est incompatible avec l'ordre public.
> 1 The award is final as soon as it is communicated.
> 2 It may only be challenged:
> a. when the sole arbitrator has been improperly appointed or the arbitral tribunal improperly composed;
> b. when the arbitral tribunal has wrongly declared itself competent or incompetent;
> c. when the arbitral tribunal has ruled beyond the scope of the claims submitted to it or when it has omitted to rule on one of the heads of claim;
> d. when the equality of the parties or their right to be heard in adversarial proceedings has not been respected;
> e. when the award is incompatible with public policy.

As is obvious, good faith is not mentioned on any of these grounds. It is not even alluded to. It follows that if good faith has any role to play, that role can only be one of a qualifier of an existing annulment ground. Lack of good faith is not an annulment ground per se. It has to fit, or perhaps be moulded, into one of the existing grounds.

[B] Good Faith Has Been Referred to as a Substantive Principle of International Public Policy, but No Annulment Was Ever Decided on That Ground

Both in France and in Switzerland, good faith has been referred to as belonging to substantive public policy. These references to good faith are generally made in the context of the duty to perform contracts in good faith, namely the principle of *pacta sunt servanda.*

This is quite clear in France:

> Considérant que l'exécution de bonne foi des conventions est un principe général de droit public international, dont l'existence même n'est d'ailleurs pas mise en cause par les auteurs du recours en annulation (qui contestent seulement son application en l'espèce) et dont l'arbitre a notamment pour mission d'assurer le respect.[28]
>
> L'arbitre international, dont la mission consiste aussi à assurer le respect de l'ordre public international, a le pouvoir de sanctionner les comportements contraires à la bonne foi qui doit présider aux relations entre partenaires du commerce international.[29]

However, no award was even annulled on this ground in France. The cases which referred to good faith in the context of annulment proceedings are now quite old, and at the time, good faith was used primarily in order to rescue awards that were criticized and not to set them aside. As will be seen below, recent case law tends to confirm that good faith is not directly relevant to breaches of international public policy.

In Switzerland, it is arguably clearer given that the Swiss Federal Tribunal held that the respect of good faith is part of substantive public policy:

> Selon la jurisprudence, une sentence est contraire à l'ordre public lorsqu'elle viole des principes juridiques fondamentaux au point de ne plus être conciliable avec l'ordre juridique et le système de valeurs déterminants. Au nombre de ces principes figurent, notamment, la fidélité contractuelle ("*pacta sunt servanda*"), *le respect des règles de la bonne foi,* l'interdiction de l'abus de droit, la prohibition des mesures discriminatoires ou spoliatrices, ainsi que la protection des personnes civilement incapables ...
>
> Il n'est, en effet, pas contraire à des principes fondamentaux de l'ordre juridique international d'admettre que des liens contractuels puissent se créer, sans que cela corresponde à la volonté interne d'une partie, lorsque celle-ci adopte une attitude qui autorise l'autre partie à conclure de bonne foi à l'existence d'une telle volonté (cf. ATF 69 II 319, 322). Or, c'est précisément sur une considération

28. C.A. Paris, 12 janv. 1993, *République de Côte d'Ivoire et autres v. société Norbert Beyrard*: 'Considering that the performance of agreements in good faith is a general principle of international public law, the very existence of which is not called into question by the authors of the action for annulment (who are only contesting its application in the present case) and one of the arbitrator's duties is to ensure compliance with it.' (Informal English translation of the French original).
29. C.A. Paris, 29 mars 1991, *Ganz v. SCFT*: 'The international arbitrator, whose mission is also to ensure compliance with international public policy, has the power to sanction conduct contrary to the good faith that must govern relations between partners in international trade.' (Informal English translation of the French original).

> de ce genre que le Tribunal arbitral a fondé, pour l'essentiel, sa sentence. Savoir s'il l'a fait à juste titre, c'est-à-dire en conformité avec le droit matériel applicable, importe peu du point de vue de l'ordre public négatif, au sens où on l'entend ici, dans la mesure où le contenu du droit applicable ne constitue pas un critère en la matière, étant donné la fonction purement protectrice de la réserve de l'ordre public.[30]

But again, there is no example of an award having been set aside for breach of good faith.

The reality is that good faith is not directly relevant to breaches of international public policy in the context of an action to set aside.

[C] Good Faith May Have Relevance When It Comes to the Existence of an Arbitration Agreement

Good faith does appear to have relevance when a party is denying the existence of an arbitration agreement that it has otherwise performed. In this example, good faith acts as a shield and not a sword.

In France, this was clearly established in the *Soerni* matter:

> Considérant que le principe de capacité, selon lequel il est impossible de refuser l'accord d'arbitrer auquel on a consenti repose sur la bonne foi, singulièrement absente de l'attitude de la société Soerni et de ses dirigeants, et s'inscrit dans le contexte du principe de validité de la clause d'arbitrage qui a pour fondement la commune volonté des parties;
>
> Que précisément en la cause, la volonté d'arbitrer de la société Soerni résulte de sa connaissance de l'existence d'une référence claire à la convention d'arbitrage dans la lettre d'exonération de responsabilité dont les mentions ont été rappelées plus haut, connaissance qui fait à son tour présumer de son acceptation, la présence d'une clause d'arbitrage dans un connaissement étant par ailleurs un usage largement répandu pour ce type de contrat qui n'est pas étranger aux activités de la société Soerni.[31]

30. DSFT 120 II 55 of 19 April 1994: 'According to case law, an award is contrary to public policy when it violates fundamental legal principles to such an extent that it can no longer be reconciled with the prevailing legal order and system of values. These principles include, in particular, contractual fidelity ("*pacta sunt servanda*"), respect for the rules of good faith, the prohibition of an abuse of rights, the prohibition of discriminatory or spoliatory measures, and the protection of civilly incompetent persons ... Indeed, it is not contrary to fundamental principles of the international legal order to admit that contractual links can be created, without corresponding to the internal will of a party, when that party adopts an attitude which authorizes the other party to conclude in good faith that such a will exists (cf. ATF 69 II 319, 322). The Arbitral Tribunal essentially based its award on just such a consideration. Whether it did so correctly, i.e., in accordance with the applicable substantive law, is of little importance from the point of view of negative public policy, in the sense in which it is understood here, insofar as the content of the applicable law is not a criterion in this matter, given the purely protective function of the public policy exception.' (Informal English translation of the French original).
31. C.A. Paris, 15 mai 2008, n° 06/22308: 'Considering that the principle of capacity, according to which it is impossible to refuse an agreement to arbitrate to which one has consented, is based on good faith, which is singularly absent from the attitude of the Soerni company and its directors, and falls within the context of the principle of validity of the arbitration clause, which

This ultimately led to the case law on the principle of validity of the arbitration agreement, which is now firmly established before French courts.[32]

By contrast, in Switzerland, good faith can also operate as a shield when one party denies the existence of an agreement:

> De fait, la péremption de l'exception d'incompétence est une chose, la péremption du droit de soulever cette exception en est une autre. Celui qui entre en matière sans réserve sur le fond dans une procédure arbitrale reconnaît, par cet acte concluant, la compétence du tribunal arbitral et perd, en conséquence, définitivement le droit d'exciper de l'incompétence dudit tribunal. Inversement, celui qui fait défaut n'encourt pas semblable déchéance, en règle générale, car son abstention ne saurait être assimilée à une reconnaissance tacite de la compétence du tribunal arbitral (Lalive/Poudret/Reymond, op.cit., n. 3 ad art. 8 CIA et n. 12 ad art. 186 LDIP); il lui est donc permis de se raviser et d'intervenir dans la procédure pendante pour contester la compétence du tribunal arbitral à son égard, tout ceci sous réserve du respect du principe de la bonne foi (Article 2 al. 1 CC).[33]

Even though the Swiss Federal Tribunal has consistently held that the existence of an arbitration agreement could not be presumed and that there was no *favor arbitrandum* when it came to establishing whether the parties had indeed entered into an arbitration agreement,[34] one fails to see why the general principle identified above would not apply to arbitration agreements, as opposed to underlying agreements, in appropriate circumstances.

[D] Good Faith Is Irrelevant for Corruption Allegations

Some decisions have expressly ruled out any role for good faith in actions to set aside.

For French courts, this is clearly the case if the annulment ground is based on the existence of corruption:

> La prohibition de la corruption d'agents publics étrangers est au nombre des principes dont l'ordre juridique français ne saurait souffrir la violation même dans

is based on the common will of the parties; In this particular case, Soerni's willingness to arbitrate stems from its knowledge of the existence of a clear reference to the arbitration agreement in the above-mentioned letter of exemption from liability, a knowledge which in turn presupposes its acceptance, the presence of an arbitration clause in a bill of lading being a widespread practice for this type of contract, which is not foreign to Soerni's activities.' (Informal English translation of the French original).

32. Civ. 1ère, 8 juillet 2009, n° 08-16.025.
33. DSFT 120 II 155 of 19 April 1994: 'In fact, it is one thing for a plea of lack of jurisdiction to be waived, but quite another for the right to raise such a plea to be waived. Anyone who enters into an arbitration without reservation on the merits recognizes, by this conclusive action, the jurisdiction of the arbitral tribunal and consequently definitively waives the right to plead lack of jurisdiction of the said tribunal. Conversely, a party who fails to do so does not, as a general rule, waive such right, since his abstention cannot be assimilated to a tacit recognition of the arbitral tribunal's jurisdiction (LALIVE/POUDRET/REYMOND, op.cit, n. 3 ad art. 8 CIA and n. 12 ad art. 186 LDIP); he is therefore entitled to change his mind and intervene in the pending proceedings to contest the arbitral tribunal's jurisdiction over him, subject to observance of the principle of good faith (art. 2 al. 1 CC).' (Informal English translation of the French original).
34. DSFT 4P.176/2001 of 16 October 2001; DSFT 4A_150/2017 of 4 October 2017.

> un contexte international. Elle relève par conséquent de l'ordre public international. ... A cet égard, l'éventuelle mauvaise foi de la partie débitrice est indifférente, dès lors qu'est seulement en cause le refus de l'ordre juridique français de prêter le secours des voies de droit au paiement de sommes pour une cause illicite.[35]

This solution seems to be of general application insofar as the ground to set aside is based on a prohibition which is internationally recognized and internationally given effect because it is ultimately based on an international convention.

35. C.A. Paris, 28 mai 2019, n° 16/11182: 'The prohibition of bribery of foreign public officials is one of the principles whose violation cannot be tolerated under French law, even in an international context. It is therefore a matter of international public policy. ... In this respect, any bad faith on the part of the debtor is irrelevant, since what is at issue is only the refusal of the French legal system to lend the assistance of legal remedies to the payment of sums for an illicit cause ...' (Informal English translation of the French original).

ASA SPECIAL SERIES*

1. *Le nouveau droit suisse de l'arbitrage international*, 1989.
2. *The New Swiss Law on International Arbitration*, 1990.
3. Michael E. Schneider (ed.), *Verträge und Schiedsverfahren im europäischen Umbruch*, 1990.
4. *Dispute Resolution on International Markets*, 1993.
5. *Investing in Eastern-European Countries – And Arbitration*, 1993.
6. Marc Blessing (ed.), *Objective Arbitrability – Antitrust Disputes – Intellectual Property Disputes*, 1994.
7. *Profiles of ASA Members (1994)*, 1994.
8. Marc Blessing (ed.), *The Arbitration Agreement: Its Multifold Critical Aspects*, 1994.
9. Marc Blessing (ed.), *The New York Convention of 1958*, 1996.
10. *Profiles of ASA Members (1998)*, 1998.
11. *Arbitration of Sports-Related Disputes*, 1998.
12. Pierre Karrer (ed.), *International Arbitration Do's and Don'ts*, Second Edition, 1998.
13. Pierre Karrer (ed.), *The Claims Resolution Process on Dormant Accounts in Switzerland*, 2000.
14. *Profiles of ASA Members (2000)*, 2000.
15. Pierre Karrer (ed.), *Arbitral Tribunals or State Courts: Who Must Defer to Whom?*, 2001.
16. Pierre Karrer (ed.), *Glossary of Arbitration and ADR Terms and Abbreviations*, First Edition, 2001.
17. Pierre Karrer (ed.), *International Arbitration Do's and Don'ts*, Third Edition, 2001.
18. Pierre Karrer (ed.), *Conflicts of Interest in International Commercial Arbitration*, 2001.
19. *Profiles of ASA Members (2002)*, 2002.
20. Gabrielle Kaufmann-Kohler & Viviane Frossard (eds), *Arbitration in Banking and Financial Matters*, 2003.
21. Pierre Karrer (ed.), *International Arbitration Do's and Don'ts*, Forth Edition, 2004.
22. Gabrielle Kaufmann-Kohler & Blaise Stucki (eds), *The Swiss Rules of International Arbitration*, 2004.
23. *Profiles of ASA Members (2005)*, 2005.
24. Gabrielle Kaufmann-Kohler & Alexandra Johnson (eds), *Arbitration of Merger and Acquisition Disputes*, 2005.
25. Pierre Karrer (ed.), *International Arbitration Do's and Don'ts*, Fifth Edition, 2005.
26. Markus Wirth (ed.), Best Practices in International Arbitration, 2006.

* Volumes 47 and onward are published by Wolters Kluwer.

27. Pierre Karrer (ed.), Glossary of Arbitration and ADR Terms and Abbreviations, Second Edition, 2006.
28. Pierre Karrer (ed.), Glossary of Arbitration and ADR Terms and Abbreviations, Third Edition, 2008.
29. Markus Wirth (ed.), *The Resolution of the Dispute, from the Hearing to the Award*, 2007.
30. Michael E. Schneider & Joachim Knoll (eds), *Performance as a Remedy: Non-Monetary Relief in International Arbitration*, 2011.
31. Pierre Karrer (ed.), *International Arbitration Do's and Don'ts*, Sixth Edition, 2009.
32. Pierre Karrer (ed.), *Glossary of Arbitration and ADR Terms and Abbreviations*, Fourth Edition, 2009.
33. *Profiles of ASA Members (2009)*, 2009.
34. Anne K. Hoffmann (ed.), *Protection of Foreign Investments through Modern Treaty Arbitration: Diversity and Harmonisation*, 2010.
35. Markus Wirth, Christina Rouvinez & Joachim Knoll (eds), *Search for "Truth" in Arbitration: Is Finding the Truth What Dispute Resolution Is About?*, 2011.
36. Elliott Geisinger & Guillaume Tattevin (eds), *Advocacy in International Commercial Arbitration*, 2013.
37. Daniele Favalli (ed.), *Sense and Non-sense of Guidelines, Rules and Other Para-regulatory Texts in International Arbitration*, 2015.
38. Pierre Tercier (ed.), *Post Award Issues*, 2012.
39. **Not published**.
40. Philipp Habegger, Daniel Hochstrasser, Gabrielle Nater-Bass & Urs Weber-Stecher (eds), Arbitral Institutions under Scrutiny, 2013.
41. Elliott Geisinger & Elena Trabaldo de Mestral (eds), *Sports Arbitration: A Coach for Other Players*, 2014.
42. Bernhard Berger & Michael E. Schneider (eds), *Inside the Black Box: How Arbitral Tribunals Operate and Reach Their Decisions*, 2013.
43. Elliott Geisinger (ed.), *Confidential and Restricted Access Information in International Arbitration*, 2016.
44. Nathalie Voser (ed.), *10 Years of Swiss Rules of International Arbitration*, 2014.
45. Domitille Baizeau & Frank Spoorenberg (eds), *Arbitrators' Initiative: When, Why and How Should It Be Used?*, 2016.
46. Sebastien Besson & Harold Frey (eds), *Expert Evidence: Conflicting Assumptions and How to Handle Them in Arbitration*, 2020.
47. Andrea Meier & Christian Oetiker (eds), *Arbitration and Corruption*, 2021.
48. Felix Dasser (ed.), *Clear Path or Jungle in Commercial Arbitrators' Conflict of Interest?*, 2021.
49. Elliott E. Geisinger, Christoph Müller, Andrea Menaker & Sabrina Pearson-Wenger (eds), *Good Faith in International Arbitration: Myth, Reality, Label … or All of the Above?*, 2024.